# THE TRUTH WAR

# THE
# TRUTH
## WAR

FIGHTING *for* CERTAINTY *in an* AGE *of* DECEPTION

# JOHN
# MACARTHUR

*Published by*
THOMAS NELSON™
*Since 1798*

www.thomasnelson.com

Copyright © 2007 by John MacArthur

Published by Nelson Books, a division of Thomas Nelson, Inc., P.O. Box 141000, Nashville, Tennessee 37214.

Published in association with the literary agency of Wolgemuth & Associates, Inc.

Thomas Nelson, Inc. titles may be purchased in bulk for educational, business, fund-raising, or sales promotional use. For information, please e-mail SpecialMarkets@ThomasNelson.com.

All Scripture quotations, unless otherwise indicated, are from The New King James Version, copyright 1979, 1980, 1982, Thomas Nelson, Inc., Publishers.

Scriptures marked KJV are from the King James Version of the Bible.

Scriptures marked NASB are from the New American Standard Bible®. Copyright © 1960, 1962, 1963, 1968, 1971, 1972, 1973, 1975, 1977, 1995 by the Lockman Foundation. Used by permission.

Scriptures marked NIV are from The Holy Bible, New International Version. Copyright © 1973, 1978, 1984, International Bible Society. Used by permission of Zondervan.

Library of Congress Cataloging-in-Publication Data

MacArthur, John, 1939-
  The truth war : fighting for certainty in an age of deception / John MacArthur.
    p. cm.
  ISBN-13: 978-0-7852-6263-3 (hardcover)
  ISBN-10: 0-7852-6263-6 (hardcover)
  1. Truth--Religious aspects--Christianity. 2. Evangelicalism. 3. Christian life. I. Title.
  BV4509.5.M253 2007
  239--dc22

                        2006032323

Printed in the United States of America

07 08 09 10 11 12 (QW) 9 8 7 6 5 4 3 2

Through the years my partnership with Phil Johnson
has proven to be divinely ordained. The contribution of his
theological knowledge, clear thinking, and strong conviction
has been essential to the success of our collaboration
in projects like these. I owe Phil a deep debt of gratitude
for his considerable editorial efforts in this book.

THE Church of Christ is continually represented under the figure of an army; yet its Captain is the Prince of Peace; its object is the establishment of peace, and its soldiers are men of a peaceful disposition. The spirit of war is at the extremely opposite point to the spirit of the gospel.

Yet nevertheless, the church on earth has, and until the second advent must be, the church militant, the church armed, the church warring, the church conquering. And how is this?

It is in the very order of things that so it must be. Truth could not be truth in this world if it were not a warring thing, and we should at once suspect that it were not true if error were friends with it. The spotless purity of truth must always be at war with the blackness of heresy and lies.

—C. H. SPURGEON[1]

# CONTENTS

# INTRODUCTION

## WHY TRUTH IS WORTH FIGHTING FOR

*W*ho would have thought that people claiming to be Christians—even pastors—would attack the very notion of truth? But they are.

A recent issue of *Christianity Today* featured a cover article about the "Emerging Church." That is the popular name for an informal affiliation of Christian communities worldwide who want to revamp the church, change the way Christians interact with their culture, and remodel the way we think about truth itself. The article included a profile of Rob and Kristen Bell, the husband and wife team who founded Mars Hill—a very large and steadily growing Emerging community in Grand Rapids, Michigan. According to the article, the Bells

> found themselves increasingly uncomfortable with church. "Life in the church had become so small," Kristen says. "It had worked for me for a long time. Then it stopped working." The Bells started questioning their assumptions about the Bible itself—"discovering the Bible as a human product," as Rob puts it, rather than the product of divine fiat. "The Bible is still in the center for us," Rob says, "but it's a different kind of center. We want to embrace mystery, rather than conquer it." "I

grew up thinking that we've figured out the Bible," Kristen says, "that we knew what it means. *Now I have no idea what most of it means.* And yet I feel like life is big again—like life used to be black and white, and now it's in color."[1]

One dominant theme pervades the whole article: in the Emerging Church movement, *truth* (to whatever degree such a concept is even recognized) is assumed to be inherently hazy, indistinct, and uncertain—perhaps even ultimately unknowable.

> THE IDEA THAT THE CHRISTIAN MESSAGE SHOULD BE KEPT PLIABLE AND AMBIGUOUS SEEMS ESPECIALLY ATTRACTIVE TO YOUNG PEOPLE WHO ARE IN TUNE WITH THE CULTURE AND IN LOVE WITH THE SPIRIT OF THE AGE.

Each of the Emerging Church leaders profiled in the article expressed a high level of discomfort with any hint of certainty about what the Bible means, even on something as basic as the gospel. Brian McLaren, for instance, is a popular author and former pastor who is the best-known figure and one of the most influential voices in the Emerging Church movement. McLaren is quoted in the *Christianity Today* article, saying at one point: "I don't think we've got the gospel right yet. . . . I don't think the liberals have it right. But I don't think we have it right either. None of us has arrived at orthodoxy."[2]

Elsewhere, McLaren likens the conventional notion of *orthodoxy* to a claim that we "have the truth captured, stuffed, and mounted on the wall."[3] He likewise caricatures systematic theology as an unconscious attempt to "have final orthodoxy nailed down, freeze-dried, and shrink-wrapped forever."[4]

That is very popular stuff these days. McLaren alone has

written or coauthored about a dozen books, and his utter contempt for certainty is a motif he returns to again and again. In 2003 Zondervan and Youth Specialties teamed up to start a line of products called Emergent/YS. They publish books, DVDs, and audio products at a prolific rate, with titles ranging from Rob Bell's *Velvet Elvis: Repainting the Christian Faith* to *Adventures in Missing the Point*, an aptly titled collaboration of Brian McLaren and Tony Campolo.

The idea that the Christian message should be kept pliable and ambiguous seems especially attractive to young people who are in tune with the culture and in love with the spirit of the age and can't stand to have authoritative biblical truth applied with precision as a corrective to worldly lifestyles, unholy minds, and ungodly behavior. And the poison of this perspective is being increasingly injected into the evangelical church body.

But that is not authentic Christianity. Not knowing what you believe (especially on a matter as essential to Christianity as the gospel) is by definition a kind of unbelief. Refusing to acknowledge and defend the revealed truth of God is a particularly stubborn and pernicious kind of unbelief. Advocating ambiguity, exalting uncertainty, or otherwise deliberately clouding the truth is a sinful way of nurturing unbelief.

Every true Christian should know and love the truth. Scripture says one of the key characteristics of "those who perish" (people who are damned by their unbelief) is that "they did not receive the love of the truth, that they might be saved" (2 Thessalonians 2:10). The clear implication is that a genuine love for the truth is built into saving faith. It is therefore one of the distinguishing qualities of every true believer. In Jesus' words, they have known the truth, and the truth has set them free (John 8:32).

In an age when the very idea of truth is being scorned and attacked (even within the church, where people *ought* to revere the truth most highly), Solomon's wise advice has never been more timely: "Buy the truth, and do not sell it" (Proverbs 23:23).

## The Eternal Value of the Truth

Nothing in all the world is more important or more valuable than the truth. And the church is supposed to be "the pillar and ground of the truth" (1 Timothy 3:15).

History is filled with accounts of people who chose to accept torture or death rather than deny the truth. In previous generations it was generally considered heroic to give your life for what you believed in. That is not necessarily the case anymore.

Part of the problem, of course, is that terrorists and suicide bombers have co-opted the idea of "martyrdom" and turned it on its head. They call themselves "martyrs," but they are suicidal murderers who kill people for *not* believing. Their violent aggression is actually the polar opposite of martyrdom, and the ruthless ideologies that drive them are the exact antitheses of truth. There is nothing heroic about what they do and nothing noble about what they stand for. But they are significant symbols of a deeply troubling trend that plagues this current generation worldwide. It seems there is no shortage of people nowadays willing to kill for a lie. Yet few seem to be willing to speak up for truth—much less die for it.

Consider the testimonies of the Christian martyrs throughout history. They were valiant warriors for the truth. They were not terrorists or violent people, of course. But they "fought" for the truth by proclaiming it in the face of fierce opposition, by living lives that gave testimony to the power and goodness of truth, and by refusing to renounce or forsake the truth no matter what threats were made against them.

The pattern starts in the first generation of church history with the apostles themselves. All of them, with the possible exception of John, died as martyrs. (Even John paid á dear price for standing in the truth, as he was tortured and exiled for his faith.) Truth was something they loved and fought and eventually died for, and they handed that same legacy to the next generation.

Ignatius and Polycarp, for example, were early Christian truth warriors. (Both were personal friends and disciples of the apostle John, so they lived and ministered when Christianity was still very new.) History records that both of them willingly gave their lives rather than renounce Christ and turn from the truth. Ignatius was personally interrogated by the emperor Trajan, who demanded that he make a public sacrifice to idols to prove his loyalty to Rome. Ignatius could have saved his life by yielding to that pressure. Some might try to excuse such an outward act under pressure, as long as he didn't deny Christ in his heart. But the truth was more important to Ignatius than his life. He refused to sacrifice to the idols, and Trajan ordered that he be thrown to wild beasts in the stadium for the amusement of pagan crowds.

Ignatius's friend Polycarp, wanted by authorities (because he also was known to be a leader among the Christians), gave himself up willingly, knowing full well that it would cost him his life. Brought to a stadium before a bloodthirsty mob, he was ordered to curse Christ. Polycarp refused, saying, "Eighty-six years have I served him, and he never once wronged me. How then shall I blaspheme my King who saved me?" He was burned alive on the spot.[5]

In every generation across the history of the church, countless martyrs have similarly died rather than deny the truth. Were such people just fools, making too much of their own convictions? Was their absolute confidence in what they believed actually misguided zeal? Did they die needlessly?

Many these days evidently think so—including some who

profess faith in Christ. Living in a culture where violent persecution is almost unknown, multitudes who call themselves Christians seem to have forgotten what faithfulness to the truth often costs.

Did I say "often"? As a matter of fact, faithfulness to the truth is *always* costly in some way or another (2 Timothy 3:12), and that is precisely why Jesus insisted that anyone who wants to be His disciple must be willing to take up a cross (Luke 9:23–26).[6]

> MUCH OF THE VISIBLE CHURCH NOWADAYS SEEMS TO THINK CHRISTIANS ARE SUPPOSED TO BE AT PLAY RATHER THAN AT WAR. THE IDEA OF ACTUALLY *FIGHTING* FOR DOCTRINAL TRUTH IS THE FURTHEST THING FROM MOST CHURCHGOERS' THOUGHTS.

The evangelical movement itself must take some of the blame for devaluing the truth by catering to people's itching ears (2 Timothy 4:1–4). Does anyone really imagine that many of the entertainment-hungry churchgoers who pack today's megachurches would be willing to give their lives for the truth? As a matter of fact, many of them are unwilling to take a bold stand for the truth even among other Christians in an environment where there is no serious threat against them and the worst effect of such a stand might be that someone's feelings get hurt.

Much of the visible church nowadays seems to think Christians are supposed to be at play rather than at war. The idea of actually *fighting* for doctrinal truth is the furthest thing from most churchgoers' thoughts. Contemporary Christians are determined to get the world to *like* them—and of course in the process they also want to have as much fun as possible. They are so obsessed with making the church seem "cool" to unbelievers that they can't be bothered with questions about whether another person's doctrine is sound or not. In a climate like that, the thought of even identifying someone else's teaching as false (much less "contending earnestly" for the faith) is a distasteful and dangerously countercultural suggestion. Christians have bought into the notion that almost nothing is more "uncool" in the world's eyes than when someone shows a sincere concern about the danger of heresy. After all, the world simply doesn't take spiritual truth that seriously, so they cannot fathom why anyone would.

But Christians, of all people, ought to be *most* willing to live and die for the truth. Remember, we know the truth, and the truth has set us free (John 8:32). We should not be ashamed to say so boldly (Psalm 107:2). And if called upon to sacrifice for the truth's sake, we need to be willing and prepared to give our lives. Again, that is exactly what Jesus was speaking about when He called His disciples to take up a cross (Matthew 16:24). Cowardice and authentic faith are antithetical.

## What Is Truth?

Of course, God and truth are inseparable. Every thought about the essence of truth—what it is, what makes it "true," and how we can possibly know anything for sure, quickly moves us back to God. That is why God incarnate—Jesus Christ—is called the truth (John 14:6).

That is also why it is not particularly surprising when someone who repudiates God rejects His truth as well. If a person can't tolerate the thought of God, there is simply no comfortable place for the concept of truth in that person's worldview, either. So the consistent atheist, agnostic, or idolater might as well hate the very idea of truth. After all, to reject God is to reject the Giver of all truth, the final Judge of what really is true, and the very essence and embodiment of truth itself.

As we will observe shortly, that is precisely the conclusion at which many in the academic and philosophical realms have now arrived. They no longer believe in truth as a sure and knowable reality. Make no mistake: unbelief is the seed of that opinion. The contemporary aversion to truth is simply a natural expression of fallen humanity's innate hostility toward God (Romans 8:7).

But these days a majority of Americans claim to believe in the God of the Bible, yet still they say they are comfortably uncertain about what is true. A suffocating apathy about the whole concept of truth dominates much of today's society—including an expanding segment of the evangelical movement.

Many self-styled evangelicals today are openly questioning whether such a thing as truth even exists.[7] Others suppose that even if truth *does* exist, we can't be sure what it is, so it can't really matter much. The twin problems of uncertainty and apathy about the truth are epidemic, even among some of the evangelical movement's most popular authors and spokespersons. Some flatly refuse to stand for anything because they have decided that even Scripture isn't really clear enough to argue about.

Except for the massive scale on which such thinking has attained popularity today, and the way it is seeping into the church, such ideas themselves are really nothing new or particularly shocking. It is exactly the same attitude with which Pilate summarily dismissed Christ: "What is truth?" (John 18:38).

Certain avant-garde evangelicals sometimes act as if the demise of certainty is a dramatic new intellectual development, rather than seeing it for what it actually is: an echo of the old unbelief. It is unbelief cloaked in a religious disguise and seeking legitimacy as if it were merely a humbler kind of faith. But it's not faith at all. In reality, the contemporary refusal to regard any truth as sure and certain is the worst kind of infidelity. The church's duty has always been to confront such skepticism and answer it by clearly proclaiming the truth God has revealed in His Word. We have been given a clear message for the purpose of confronting the world's unbelief. That is what we are called, commanded, and commissioned to do (1 Corinthians 1:17–31). Faithfulness to Christ demands it. The honor of God requires it. We cannot sit by and do nothing while worldly, revisionist, and skeptical attitudes about truth are infiltrating the church. We must not embrace such confusion in the name of charity, collegiality, or unity. We have to stand and fight for the truth— and be prepared to die for it—as faithful Christians always have.

> CHURCH LEADERS ARE OBSESSED WITH STYLE AND METHODOLOGY, LOSING INTEREST IN THE GLORY OF GOD AND BECOMING GROSSLY APATHETIC ABOUT TRUTH AND SOUND DOCTRINE. FOR THE MOMENT AT LEAST, THE BATTLE APPEARS TO BE TURNING IN THE ENEMY'S FAVOR.

According to Scripture, the ages-old conflict over the truth is spiritual *warfare*—a cosmic battle between God and the powers of darkness (Ephesians 6:12). And one of our enemies' favorite tactics is to disguise themselves as angels of light and infiltrate the community of believers (2 Corinthians 11:13–15). This is nothing new either, but I'm convinced it has become a very serious problem in the current generation. Unfortunately, precious few Christians seem willing to take the threat seriously. The church has grown lazy, worldly, and self-satisfied. Church leaders are obsessed with style and methodology, losing interest in the glory of God and becoming grossly apathetic about truth and sound doctrine. For the moment at least, the battle appears to be turning in the enemy's favor.

When God gave the second commandment, which forbade idolatry, He added this warning: "I, the Lord your God, am a jealous God, visiting the iniquity of the fathers upon the children to the third and fourth generations of those who hate Me" (Exodus 20:5). Scripture elsewhere makes it clear that children are never directly punished for the *guilt* of their fathers' sins (Deuteronomy 24:16; Ezekiel 18:19–32), but the natural consequences of those sins do indeed pass from generation to generation. Children learn from their fathers' examples and imitate what they see. One generation's teaching establishes a spiritual legacy that succeeding generations inherit. If today's "fathers" abandon the truth, it will take generations to recover.

Church leaders are especially responsible for setting the example. What we desperately need today are "shepherds according to [God's] heart, who will feed [believers] with knowledge and understanding" (Jeremiah 3:15; Acts 20:28–31). But it is every believer's solemn duty to resist every attack on the truth, to abhor the very thought of falsehood, and not to compromise in any way with the enemy, who is above all a liar and the father of lies (John 8:44).

The Truth War is, after all, *war*. Warfare is always serious, but this is the battle of the ages for the highest of prizes, and therefore it requires of us the utmost diligence.

## Why Truth Is Inextricably Bound to God

We'll begin chapter 1 by defining truth in biblical terms. We'll also notice that every attempt to define truth in *non*biblical terms has ultimately failed. That is because God is the source of all that exists (Romans 11:36). He alone defines and delimits what is true. He is also the ultimate revealer of all truth. Every truth revealed in nature was authored by Him (Psalm 19:1–6); and some of it is His own self-revelation (Romans 1:20). He gave us minds and consciences to perceive the truth and comprehend right from wrong, and He even wired us with a fundamental understanding of His law written on our hearts (Romans 2:14–15). On top of all that, He gave us the perfect, infallible truth of Scripture (Psalm 19:7–11), which is a sufficient revelation of everything that pertains to life and godliness (2 Timothy 3:15–17; 2 Peter 1:3), in order to lead us to Him as Savior and Lord. Finally, He sent Christ, the very embodiment of truth itself, as the culmination of divine revelation (Hebrews 1:1–3). The ultimate reason for *all* of this was for God to reveal Himself to His creatures (Ezekiel 38:23).

All truth therefore starts with what is true of God: who He is, what His mind knows, what His holiness entails, what His will approves, and so on. In other words, all truth is determined and properly explained by the being of God. Therefore, every notion of His nonexistence is by definition untrue. That is precisely what the Bible teaches: "The fool has said in his heart, 'There is no God'" (Psalm 14:1; 53:1).

The ramifications of all truth starting with God are profound. Returning to a point we touched on earlier: here is the reason why once someone denies God, logical consistency will ultimately force that person to deny all truth. A denial that God exists instantly removes the whole justification for any kind of knowledge. As Scripture says, "The fear of the LORD is the beginning of knowledge" (Proverbs 1:7).

So the necessary starting point for gaining authentic understanding of the fundamental concept of truth itself is an acknowledgment of the one true God. As Augustine said, we believe in order to understand, and our faith in turn is fed and strengthened as we gain better understanding. Both faith in God as He has revealed Himself and the understanding wrought by faith are therefore essential if we hope to apprehend truth in any serious and meaningful sense.

Scripture describes all authentic Christians as those who *know* the truth and have been liberated by it (John 8:32). They *believe* it with a whole heart (2 Thessalonians 2:13). They *obey* the truth through the Spirit of God (1 Peter 1:22). And they have received a fervent *love* for the truth through the gracious work of God in their hearts (2 Thessalonians 2:10). According to the Bible, then, you haven't really grasped the truth at all if there is no sense in which you know it, believe it, submit to it, and love it.

Clearly, the existence of absolute truth and its inseparable relationship to the person of God is the most essential tenet of all truly biblical Christianity. Speaking plainly: if you are one of those who questions whether truth is really important, please don't call your belief system "Christianity," because that is not what it is.

> A BIBLICAL PERSPECTIVE OF TRUTH ALSO NECESSARILY ENTAILS THE RECOGNITION THAT ULTIMATE TRUTH IS AN OBJECTIVE REALITY. TRUTH EXISTS OUTSIDE OF US AND REMAINS THE SAME REGARDLESS OF HOW WE MAY PERCEIVE IT. TRUTH BY DEFINITION IS AS FIXED AND CONSTANT AS GOD IS IMMUTABLE.

A biblical perspective of truth also necessarily entails the recognition that ultimate truth is an objective reality. Truth exists outside of us and remains the same regardless of how we may perceive it. Truth by definition is as fixed and constant as God is immutable. That is because real truth (what Francis Schaeffer called "true truth") is the unchanged and unchanging expression of who God is; it is not our own personal and arbitrary interpretation of reality.

Amazingly, Christians in our generation need to be reminded of these things. Truth is never determined by looking at God's Word and asking, "What does this mean to me?" Whenever I hear someone talk like that, I'm inclined to ask, "What did the Bible mean before you existed? What does *God* mean by what He says?" Those are the proper questions to be asking. Truth and meaning are not determined by our intuition, experience, or desire. The true meaning of Scripture—or anything else, for that matter—has already been determined and fixed by the mind of God. The task of an interpreter is to discern *that* meaning. And proper interpretation must precede application.

The meaning of God's Word is neither as obscure nor as difficult to grasp as people today often pretend. Admittedly, some things in the Bible *are* hard to understand (2 Peter 3:16), but its central, essential truth is plain enough that no one need be confused by it. "Whoever walks the road, although a fool, shall not go astray" (Isaiah 35:8).

Moreover, our individual perception of truth certainly can and does change. Of course we gain better understanding as we grow. We all begin by being nourished on the milk of the Word. As we gain the ability to chew and digest harder truths, we are supposed to be strengthened by the meat of the Word (1 Corinthians 3:2; Hebrews 5:12). That is, we move from a merely childlike knowledge to a more mature grasp of truth in all its richness and relationship to other truth.

But truth itself does not change just because our point of view does. As we mature in our ability to perceive truth, truth itself remains fixed. Our duty is to conform all our thoughts to the truth (Psalm 19:14); we are not entitled to redefine "truth" to fit our own personal viewpoints, preferences, or desires. We must not ignore or discard selected truths just because we might find them hard to receive or difficult to fathom. Above all, we can't get apathetic or lazy about the truth when the price of understanding or defending the truth turns out to be demanding or costly. Such a self-willed approach to the truth is tantamount to usurping God (Psalm 12:4). People who take that route guarantee their own destruction (Romans 2:8–9).

Moreover, God *has* revealed Himself and His truth with

sufficient clarity. Even apart from the explicit, special revelation of the Bible, God has made some of the principle elements of spiritual truth clear enough for everyone. Scripture says, for example, that the cardinal truths concerning God, His power, His glory, and His righteousness are naturally known to all people through creation and conscience (Romans 1:19–20; 2:14–16). That truth is adequately clear and sufficient to leave the entire human race "without excuse" (Romans 1:20). All those who are condemned in the final judgment will be held responsible for rejecting whatever truth was available to them. The fact that a just and righteous God holds both unbelievers and believers alike responsible for obedience to His revelation is irrefutable proof that He has made the truth sufficiently clear for us. To claim that the Bible is not sufficiently clear is to assault God's own wisdom and integrity.

## How Truth Is Under Assault in the Church Today

The clarity and sufficiency of Scripture, the lostness of unredeemed humanity, and the justice of God in condemning sinners are all long-standing convictions in every major strain of historic Christianity. Christians have differed among themselves about peripheral questions or lesser points of doctrine. But historically and collectively, Christians have always been in full agreement that whatever is true—whatever is objectively and ontologically true—is true *whether any given individual understands it, likes it, or receives it as truth*. In other words, because reality is created and truth is defined by God, what is really true is true for everyone, regardless of anyone's personal perspective or individual preferences.

These days, however, people are experimenting with subjective, relativistic ideas of truth and labeling them "Christian." This trend signals a significant departure from biblical and historic Christianity. Carried to its necessary conclusion, it will lead inevitably to the abandonment or compromise of every essential element of the true Christian faith. It is, I am convinced, another major onslaught in an ages-old battle against truth by the powers of darkness. The fact that this error is being taught and defended and promoted by people who profess to know and love Christ does not alter the fact that it is error. And the fact that relativism is often propagated in books found on the best-seller racks in evangelical bookstores does not alter the seriousness of the error. The remodeling of our ideas about truth and certainty poses a severe danger to the heart and core of the Christian gospel.

> PEOPLE ARE EXPERIMENTING WITH SUBJECTIVE, RELATIVISTIC IDEAS OF TRUTH AND LABELING THEM "CHRISTIAN." THIS TREND SIGNALS A SIGNIFICANT DEPARTURE FROM BIBLICAL AND HISTORIC CHRISTIANITY.

As always, a war is being waged against the truth. We are on one side or the other. There is no middle ground—no safe zone for the uncommitted. Lately the question of truth itself—what it is and whether we can truly know it at all—has become one of the major points of contention.

We also happen to be living in a generation when many so-called Christians have no taste for conflict and contention. Multitudes of biblically and doctrinally malnourished Christians have come to think of controversy as something that should always be avoided, whatever the cost. Sadly, that is what many weak pastors have modeled for them.

Controversy and conflict in the church are never to be relished or engaged in without sufficient cause. But in every generation, the battle for the truth has proved ultimately unavoidable, because the enemies of truth are relentless. Truth is *always* under assault. And it is actually a sin *not* to fight when vital truths are under attack.

That is true even though fighting sometimes results in conflict within the visible community of professing Christians. In fact, whenever the enemies of gospel truth succeed in infiltrating the church, faithful believers are obliged to take the battle to them even there. That is certainly the case today, as it has been since apostolic times.

# How Faithful Christians *Must* Respond

As the Holy Spirit drew New Testament revelation to its completion, the importance of fighting for the truth emerged as one of the dominant themes. Tucked into the end of the New Testament, in the shadow of Revelation (which describes the final battle and ultimate triumph of truth), we find three very short epistles whose common theme is devotion to the truth in the midst of conflict. The apostle John wrote two of them. Second John contains the word *truth* five times in the first four verses alone. It ends with this sobering message (vv. 7–11):

> Many deceivers have gone out into the world who do not confess Jesus
> Christ as coming in the flesh. This is a deceiver and an antichrist. Look
> to yourselves, that we do not lose those things we worked for, but that
> we may receive a full reward. Whoever transgresses and does not abide
> in the doctrine of Christ does not have God. He who abides in the doc-
> trine of Christ has both the Father and the Son. If anyone comes to you
> and does not bring this doctrine, do not receive him into your house nor
> greet him; for he who greets him shares in his evil deeds.

Third John likewise has truth as a major theme. The word *truth* appears six times in the epistle's fourteen verses. The apostle John was writing to defend the truth against Diotrephes, who loved having preeminence in the church more than he loved the truth. By contrast, he commends Demetrius, saying he "has a good testimony from all, and from the truth itself" (v. 12).

Jude wrote the third in the trio of "postcard" epistles. His whole point in writing was to remind believers of their duty to fight for the truth. It wasn't what he intended to write about. When he took up his pen to write, his plan was "to write . . . concerning our common salvation." But he was compelled by the Holy Spirit instead to exhort us with all passion "to contend earnestly for the faith which was once for all delivered to the saints" (Jude 3).

Jude was talking specifically about battling the influence of false teachers who had secretly infiltrated the Christian community. These men were apparently turning Christian pulpits into platforms from which they broadcast lies that undermined the heart of Christian doctrine: "For certain men have crept in unnoticed, who long ago were marked out for this condemnation, ungodly men, who turn the grace of our God into lewdness and deny the only Lord God and our Lord Jesus Christ" (v. 4).

That inspired warning from Jude 3–4 is what has prompted me to write this book. I have already written a complete commentary on Jude,[8] and there is no need to cover the same ground again. So in this book, I want to focus very closely on those two verses (vv. 3–4) in particular. We will look at Jude's warning from several different angles. We will examine why defending the faith inevitably requires warfare, rather than the gullibly sanguine stance many Christians today seem to favor. We will see why indifference, timidity, compromise, and nonresistance are all ruled out as options for Christians when the gospel is under attack. We will examine some of the major engagements in the Truth War throughout church history. And above all, we will discuss why Jude's warning is particularly applicable for the times in which we live.

My heart resonates with Jude's concern for the church, his love for the gospel, and his passion for the truth. I too would prefer to write about something positive—concerning such things as the riches of salvation and all the joy and blessings that belong to all who are truly in Christ; our love for the Lord; and especially His grace and glory. In fact, this book is ultimately about all those things and how to safeguard them, because they are precisely the points of truth that are ultimately at stake in the Truth War.

Yet rather than deal with those things in a completely positive and nonpolemical way, I find myself compelled to echo the inspired words of Jude and exhort my readers who truly love Christ: *you need to contend earnestly for the faith*. Truth is under heavy attack, and there are too few courageous warriors who are willing to fight. When we stand before the judgment seat of Christ, believers from this generation will not be able to justify their apathy by complaining that the strife of conflict over truth just seemed "too negative" for the kind of culture we lived in—or that the issues were "merely doctrinal" and therefore not worth the effort.

Remember, Christ rebuked the churches in Revelation 2–3 who had tolerated false teachers in their midst (2:14–16; 20–23). He expressly *commended* the Ephesian church for examining the claims of certain false apostles and exposing them as liars (2:2). Churches have a clear duty to guard the faith against false teachers who infiltrate. Christ Himself demands it.

At the same time, we need to notice carefully that a polemical defense of the faith by no means guarantees a healthy church, much less a healthy individual Christian. Christ also *rebuked* the doctrinally sound Ephesians for departing from their first love (Revelation 2:4). As vital as it is for us to enlist in the Truth War and do battle for our faith, it is even more important to remember why we are fighting—not merely for the thrill of vanquishing some foe or winning some argument, but out of a genuine love for Christ, who is the living, breathing embodiment of all that we hold true and worth fighting for.

# 1

## CAN TRUTH SURVIVE IN A POSTMODERN SOCIETY?

*Jesus answered, "You say rightly that I am a king. For
this cause I was born, and for this cause I have come into
the world, that I should bear witness to the truth.
Everyone who is of the truth hears My voice."
Pilate said to Him, "What is truth?"*

—John 18:37–38

Considering who stood before him and the gravity of the
issues he was being asked to decide, Pilate's attitude was astonishingly dismissive. But he did raise a vital question: *What is truth?*

Where, after all, does this concept come from, and why is it so
basic to all human thought? Every idea we have, every relationship
we cultivate, every belief we cherish, every fact we know, every
argument we make, every conversation we engage in, and every
thought we think presupposes that there is such a thing as "truth."
The idea is an essential concept, without which the human mind
could not function.

Even if you are one of those trendy thinkers who claims to be
skeptical about whether "truth" is really a useful category anymore,
to express that opinion you must presume that truth is meaningful on
some fundamental level. One of the most basic, universal, and undeniable axioms of all human thought is the absolute necessity of truth.

1

(And we might add that the necessity of absolute truth is its close corollary.)

## A BIBLICAL DEFINITION

So what is truth?

Here is a simple definition drawn from what the Bible teaches: *truth is that which is consistent with the mind, will, character, glory, and being of God.* Even more to the point: *truth is the self-expression of God.* That is the biblical meaning of truth, and it is the definition I employ throughout this book. Because the definition of truth flows from God, truth is *theological.*

> TRUTH IS THAT WHICH IS CONSISTENT WITH THE MIND, WILL, CHARACTER, GLORY, AND BEING OF GOD. EVEN MORE TO THE POINT: TRUTH IS THE SELF-EXPRESSION OF GOD.

Truth is also *ontological*—which is a fancy way of saying it is the way things really are. Reality is what it is because God declared it so and made it so. Therefore God is the author, source, determiner, governor, arbiter, ultimate standard, and final judge of all truth.

The Old Testament refers to the Almighty as the "God of truth" (Deuteronomy 32:4; Psalm 31:5; Isaiah 65:16). When Jesus said of Himself, "I am . . . the truth (John 14:6, emphasis added), He was thereby making a profound claim about His own deity. He was also making it clear that *all* truth must ultimately be defined in terms of God and His eternal glory. After all, Jesus is "the brightness of [God's] glory and the express image of His person" (Hebrews 1:3). *He is truth incarnate*—the perfect expression of God and therefore the absolute embodiment of all that is true.

Jesus also said that the written Word of God is truth. It does not merely contain nuggets of truth; it *is* pure, unchangeable, and inviolable truth that (according to Jesus) "cannot be broken" (John 10:35). Praying to His heavenly Father on behalf of His disciples, He said this: "Sanctify them by Your truth. Your word is truth" (John 17:17). Moreover, the Word of God is eternal truth "which lives and abides forever" (1 Peter 1:23).

Of course there cannot be any discord or difference of opinion between the *written* Word of God (Scripture) and the *incarnate* Word of God (Jesus). In the first place, truth by definition cannot contradict itself. Second, Scripture is called "the word of Christ" (Colossians 3:16). It is *His* message, *His* self-expression. In other words, the truth of Christ and the truth of the Bible are of the very same character. They are in perfect agreement in every respect. Both are equally true. God has revealed Himself to humanity through Scripture and through His Son. Both perfectly embody the essence of what truth is.

Remember, Scripture also says God reveals basic truth about Himself in nature. The heavens declare His glory (Psalm 19:1). His other invisible attributes (such as His wisdom, power, and beauty) are on constant display in what He has created (Romans 1:20). Knowledge of Him is inborn in the human heart (Romans 1:19), and a sense of the moral character and loftiness of His law is implicit in every human conscience (Romans 2:15). Those things are universally self-evident truths. According to Romans 1:20, denial of the spiritual truths we know innately always involves a deliberate and culpable unbelief. And for those who wonder whether basic truths about God and His moral standards really are stamped on the human heart, ample proof can be found in the long history of human law and religion. To suppress this truth is to dishonor God, displace His glory, and incur His wrath (vv. 19–20).

3

Still, the only infallible interpreter of what we see in nature or know innately in our own consciences is the explicit revelation of Scripture. Since Scripture is also the one place where we are given the way of salvation, entrance into the kingdom of God, and an infallible account of Christ, the Bible is the touchstone to which all truth claims should be brought and by which all other truth must finally be measured.

## THE INADEQUACY OF ALL OTHER DEFINITIONS

An obvious corollary of what I am saying is that truth means nothing apart from God. Truth cannot be adequately explained, recognized, understood, or defined without God as the source. Since He alone is eternal and self-existent and He alone is the Creator of all else, He is the fountain of all truth.

If you don't believe that, try defining truth without reference to God, and see how quickly all such definitions fail. The moment you begin to ponder the essence of truth, you are brought face-to-face with the requirement of a universal absolute—the eternal reality of God. Conversely, the whole concept of truth instantly becomes nonsense (and every imagination of the human heart therefore turns to sheer foolishness) as soon as people attempt to remove the thought of God from their minds.

That, of course, is precisely how the apostle Paul traced the relentless decline of human ideas in Romans 1:21–22: "Although they knew God, they did not glorify Him as God, nor were thankful, but became futile in their thoughts, and their foolish hearts were darkened. Professing to be wise, they became fools."

There are serious *moral* implications, too, whenever someone tries to dissociate truth from the knowledge of God. Paul went on to write, "Even as they did not like to retain God in their knowledge, God gave them over to a debased mind, to do those things which are not fitting" (Roman 1:28). Abandon a biblical definition of truth, and unrighteousness is the inescapable result. We see it happening before our eyes in every corner of contemporary society. In fact, the widespread acceptance of homosexuality, rebellion, and all forms of iniquity that we see in our society today is a verbatim fulfillment of what Romans 1 says always happens when a society denies and suppresses the essential connection between God and truth.

> THE MOMENT YOU BEGIN TO PONDER THE ESSENCE OF TRUTH, YOU ARE BROUGHT FACE-TO-FACE WITH THE REQUIREMENT OF A UNIVERSAL ABSOLUTE—THE ETERNAL REALITY OF GOD.

If you reflect on the subject with any degree of sobriety, you will soon see that even the most fundamental moral distinctions— good and evil, right and wrong, beauty and ugliness, or honor and dishonor—cannot possibly have any true or constant meaning apart from God. That is because truth and knowledge themselves simply have no coherent significance apart from a fixed source, namely, God. How could they? God embodies the very definition of truth. Every truth claim apart from Him is preposterous.

In fact, human philosophers have sought for thousands of years to explain truth and account for human knowledge apart from God—and all who have tried have ultimately been unsuccessful. That has led to an ominous shift in the world of secular thought in recent years. Here's a thumbnail sketch of how the change came about: Ancient Greek philosophers simply assumed the validity of truth and human knowledge without attempting to account for how we know what we know. But about five hundred years before the time of Christ, Socrates, Plato, and Aristotle began to consider the problems of how to define knowledge, how to discover whether a belief is true, and how to determine whether we're actually justified in believing anything. For some two thousand years, nearly all philosophers more or less presupposed that knowledge is conveyed somehow through nature, and they set forth a number of naturalistic explanations attempting to describe how truth and knowledge can be communicated to the human mind.

Then in the middle of the seventeenth century, at the dawn of the so-called Enlightenment, philosophers such as Rene DesCartes and John Locke began to grapple very seriously with the question of how we gain knowledge. That branch of philosophy became known as epistemology—the study of knowledge and how human minds apprehend truth.

THE ONE MOST VALUABLE LESSON HUMANITY OUGHT TO HAVE LEARNED FROM PHILOSOPHY IS THAT IT IS IMPOSSIBLE TO MAKE SENSE OF TRUTH WITHOUT ACKNOWLEDGING GOD AS THE NECESSARY STARTING POINT.

DesCartes was a rationalist, believing that truth is known by reason, starting with a few foundational, self-evident truths and using logical deductions to build more sophisticated structures of knowledge on that foundation. Locke argued, instead, that the human mind begins as a blank slate and acquires knowledge purely through the senses. (Locke's view is known as empiricism.) Immanuel Kant demonstrated that neither logic alone nor experience alone (hence neither rationalism nor empiricism) could account for all human knowledge, and he devised a view that combined elements of rationalism and empiricism. G. W. F. Hegel argued in turn that even Kant's view was inadequate, and he proposed a more fluid view of truth, denying that reality is a constant. Instead, he said, what is true evolves and changes with the advancement of time. Hegel's views opened the door to various kinds of irrationalism, represented by "modern" systems of thought ranging from the philosophies of Kierkegaard, Nietzsche, and Marx to the pragmatism of Henry James.

Elaborate epistemologies have thus been proposed and methodically debunked one after another—like a long chain in which every previous link is broken. After thousands of years, the very best of human philosophers have all utterly failed to account for truth and the origin of human knowledge apart from God.

In fact, the one most valuable lesson humanity ought to have learned from philosophy is that it is impossible to make sense of truth without acknowledging God as the necessary starting point.

## The Great "Paradigm Shift"

Lately, many unbelieving intellectuals have admitted the chain is broken and have decided the culprit is the absurdity of any quest for truth. In effect, they have given up that pursuit as something wholly futile. The world of human ideas is therefore currently in a serious state of flux. On almost every level of society, we are witnessing a profoundly radical paradigm shift—a wholesale overhaul in the way people think about truth itself.

Unfortunately, instead of acknowledging what truth demands and yielding to the necessity of belief in the God of truth, contemporary Western thought has devised ways to rid human philosophy of any coherent notion of truth altogether. The concept of truth is therefore under heavy attack in the philosophical community, the academic world, and the realm of worldly religion. The way people think about truth is being totally revamped and the vocabulary of human knowledge completely redefined. The goal, clearly, is to usher every notion of truth off into oblivion.

The goal of human philosophy used to be truth without God. Today's philosophies are open to the notion of God without truth— or to be more accurate, personal "spirituality" in which everyone is free to create his or her own god. Personal gods pose no threat to sinful self-will, because they suit each sinner's personal preferences anyway, and they make no demands on anyone else.

That fact underscores the true reason for every denial of truth: "Men loved darkness rather than light, because their deeds were evil" (John 3:19). Here the Lord Jesus says people reject truth (light) for reasons that are fundamentally moral, not intellectual. Truth is clear—too clear. It reveals and condemns sin. Therefore, "everyone practicing evil hates the light and does not come to the light, lest his deeds should be exposed" (v. 20). Sinners love their sin, so they flee from the light, denying that it even exists.

The war against truth is nothing new, of course. It began in the garden when the serpent said to the woman, "Has God indeed said . . . ?" (Genesis 3:1). A relentless battle has raged ever since—between truth and falsehood, good and evil, light and darkness, assurance and doubt, belief and skepticism, righteousness and sin. It is a savage spiritual conflict that literally spans all of human history. But the ferocity and irrationality of this present onslaught seems quite unprecedented.

The far-reaching ramifications of the recent paradigm shift are obvious already. Over the past generation—and especially the past two decades—we have seen convulsive changes in society's moral values, philosophy, religion, and the arts. The upheaval has been so profound that our grandparents' generation (and practically every prior generation of human history) scarcely would have thought the landscape could possibly change so quickly. Almost no aspect of human discourse has been left unaffected. The traditional, nominal devotion to ideals and moral standards derived from Scripture is dying with the senior generation.

Many believe the paradigm shift has already brought us beyond the age of modernity to the next great epoch in the development of human thought: the *postmodern* era.

# MODERNITY

*Modernity*, in simple terms, was characterized by the belief that truth exists and that the scientific method is the only reliable way to determine that truth. In the so-called "modern" era, most academic disciplines (philosophy, science, literature, and education) were driven primarily by rationalistic presuppositions. In other words, modern thought treated human reason as the final arbiter of what is true. The modern mind discounted the idea of the supernatural and looked for scientific and rationalistic explanations for everything. But modern thinkers retained their belief that knowledge of the truth is possible. They were still seeking universal and absolute truths that applied to everyone. Scientific methodologies became the chief means by which modern people sought to gain that knowledge.

Those presuppositions gave birth to Darwinism, which in turn spawned a string of humanistic ideas and worldviews. Most prominent among them were several atheistic, rationalistic, utopian philosophies—including Marxism, fascism, socialism, communism, and theological liberalism.

Modernism's devastating repercussions were soon felt worldwide. Various struggles between those ideologies (and others like them) dominated the twentieth century. All failed. After two world wars, nonstop social revolutions, civil unrest, and a long ideological cold war, modernity was declared dead by most in the academic world. The symbolic death of the modern era was marked by the fall of the Berlin Wall, one of the more apt and imposing monuments to modern ideology. Because the wall was a concrete expression of modernity's misguided utopian worldview, its sudden demolition was also a perfect symbol for the collapse of modernity.

> MODERNITY, IN SIMPLE TERMS, WAS CHARACTERIZED BY THE BELIEF THAT TRUTH EXISTS AND THAT THE SCIENTIFIC METHOD IS THE ONLY RELIABLE WAY TO DETERMINE THAT TRUTH.

Most, if not all, of the major dogmas and worldviews from the modern era are now deemed completely outmoded and hopelessly discredited in virtually every corner of the intellectual and academic world. Even modernist religion's fascination with higher criticism has given way to abstract spirituality.

The overconfident rationalism and human conceit that characterized the modern era has finally—and fittingly—had most of the wind taken out of its sails.

## POSTMODERNISM

Accordingly, the new ways of thinking have been collectively nicknamed postmodern.

If you have been paying attention to the world around us, you have probably heard that expression a lot recently. The term *postmodernism* has been used increasingly since the 1980s to describe several popular trends in architecture, art, literature, history, culture, and religion. It is not an easy term to explain, because it describes a way of thinking that defies (and even rejects) any clear definition.

Postmodernism in general is marked by *a tendency to dismiss the possibility of any sure and settled knowledge of the truth*. Postmodernism suggests that if objective truth exists, it cannot be known objectively or with any degree of certainty. That is because (according to postmodernists), the subjectivity of the human mind makes knowledge of objective truth impossible. So it is useless to think of truth in objective terms. Objectivity is an illusion. Nothing is certain, and the thoughtful person will never speak with too much conviction about anything. Strong convictions about any point of truth are judged supremely arrogant and hopelessly naive. Everyone is entitled to his own truth.

Postmodernism therefore has no positive agenda to assert anything as true or good. Perhaps you have noticed that only the most heinous crimes are still seen as evil. (Actually, there are many today who are prepared to dispute whether *anything* is "evil," so such language is fast disappearing from public discourse.) That is because the notion of evil itself does not fit in the postmodern scheme of things. If we can't really know anything for certain, how can we judge anything evil?

Therefore postmodernism's one goal and singular activity is the systematic deconstruction of every other truth claim. The chief tools being employed to accomplish this are relativism, subjectivism, the denial of every dogma, the dissection and annihilation of every clear definition, the relentless questioning of every axiom, the undue exaltation of mystery and paradox, the deliberate

> POSTMODERNISM SUGGESTS THAT IF OBJECTIVE TRUTH EXISTS, IT CANNOT BE KNOWN OBJECTIVELY OR WITH ANY DEGREE OF CERTAINTY. THAT IS BECAUSE (ACCORDING TO POSTMODERNISTS), THE SUBJECTIVITY OF THE HUMAN MIND MAKES KNOWLEDGE OF OBJECTIVE TRUTH IMPOSSIBLE.

exaggeration of every ambiguity, and above all the cultivation of uncertainty about *everything*.

If you were to challenge me to boil down postmodern thought into its pure essence and identify the gist of it in one single, simple, central characteristic, I would say it is *the rejection of every expression of certainty*. In the postmodern perspective, certainty is regarded as inherently arrogant, elitist, intolerant, oppressive—and therefore always wrong.

> THE POSTMODERNIST RECOILS FROM ABSOLUTES AND DOES NOT WANT TO CONCEDE ANY TRUTHS THAT MIGHT SEEM AXIOMATIC OR SELF-EVIDENT. INSTEAD, TRUTH, IF ACKNOWLEDGED AT ALL, BECOMES SOMETHING INFINITELY PLIABLE AND ULTIMATELY UNKNOWABLE IN ANY OBJECTIVE SENSE.

The demise of modernity and the resulting blow to rationalistic human arrogance is certainly something to celebrate. From a spiritual perspective, however, the rise of postmodernism has been anything but a positive development.

Postmodernism has resulted in a widespread rejection of truth and the enshrinement of skepticism. Postmodernists despise truth claims. They also spurn every attempt to construct a coherent worldview, labeling all comprehensive ideologies and belief systems "metanarratives," or grand stories. Such "stories," they say, can't possibly do justice to everyone's individual perspective, and therefore they are always inadequate.

Postmodernism's preference for subjectivity over objectivity makes it inherently relativistic. Naturally, the postmodernist recoils from absolutes and does not want to concede any truths that might seem axiomatic or self-evident. Instead, truth, if acknowledged at all, becomes something infinitely pliable and ultimately unknowable in any objective sense.

Postmodernism therefore signals a major triumph for relativism—the view that truth is not fixed and objective, but something individually determined by each person's unique, subjective perception. All this is ultimately a vain attempt to try to eliminate morality and guilt from human life.

# GETTING PROPOSITIONS OFF THE PREMISES

One other extremely important point has to be mentioned with regard to postmodern notions of truth: *Postmodernists are generally suspicious of rational and logical forms. They especially do not like to discuss truth in plain propositional terms.*

As we are seeing, postmodernism is largely a reaction against the unbridled rationalism of modernity. But many postmodernists' response to rationalism is a serious overreaction. Lots of postmodernists seem to entertain the notion that *ir*rationality is superior to rationalism.

Actually, both ways of thinking are dead wrong and equally hostile to authentic truth and biblical Christianity. One extreme is as deadly as the other. *Rationalism* needs to be rejected without abandoning *rationality*.

Rationality (the right use of sanctified reason through sound logic) is never condemned in Scripture. Faith is not irrational. Authentic biblical truth demands that we employ logic and clear, sensible thinking. Truth can always be analyzed and examined and compared under the bright light of other truth, and it does not melt into absurdity. Truth by definition is never self-contradictory or nonsensical. And contrary to popular thinking, it is not rationalism to insist that coherence is a necessary quality of all truth. Christ is truth incarnate, and He cannot deny himself (2 Timothy 2:13). Self-denying truth is an absolute contradiction in terms. "No lie is of the truth" (1 John 2:21).

Nor is logic a uniquely "Greek" category that is somehow hostile to the Hebrew context of Scripture. (That is a common myth and a gross oversimplification that is often set forth in support of postmodernism's flirtation with irrationality.) Scripture frequently employs logical devices, such as antithesis, if-then arguments, syllogisms, and propositions. These are all standard logical forms, and Scripture is full of them. (See, e.g., Paul's long string of deductive arguments about the importance of the resurrection in 1 Corinthians 15:12–19.)

Yet we often encounter people enthralled with postmodern ideas who argue vehemently that truth cannot be expressed in bare propositions like mathematical formulae. Even some professing Christians nowadays argue along these lines: "If truth is personal, it cannot be propositional. If truth is embodied in the person of Christ, then the form of a proposition can't possibly express authentic truth. That is why most of Scripture is told to us in narrative form—as a story—not as a set of propositions."

The reason behind postmodernism's contempt for propositional truth is not difficult to understand. A proposition *is an idea framed as a logical statement that affirms or denies something, and it is expressed in such a way that it must be either true or false*. There is no third option between true and false. (This is the "excluded middle" in logic.) The whole point of a proposition is to boil a truth-statement down to such pristine clarity that it must be either affirmed or denied. In other words, propositions are the simplest expressions of truth value used to express the substance of what we believe. Postmodernism, frankly, cannot endure that kind of stark clarity.

In reality, however, postmodernism's rejection of the propositional form turns out to be totally untenable. It is impossible to discuss truth at all—or even tell a story—without resorting to the use of propositions. Until fairly recently, the validity and necessity of expressing truth in propositional form was considered self-evident by virtually everyone who ever studied logic, semantics, philosophy, or theology. Ironically, to make any cogent argument *against* the use of propositions, a person would have to employ propositional statements! So every argument against propositions is instantly self-defeating.

Let's be clear: truth certainly does entail more than bare propositions. There is without question a *personal* element to the truth. Jesus Himself made that point when He declared Himself truth incarnate. Scripture also teaches that faith means receiving Christ for all that He is—knowing Him in a real and personal sense and being indwelt by Him—not merely assenting to a short list of disembodied truths *about* Him (Matthew 7:21–23).

So it is quite true that faith cannot be reduced to mere assent to a finite set of propositions (James 2:19). I have made that point repeatedly in previous books. Saving faith is more than a merely intellectual nod of approval to the bare facts of a minimalist gospel outline. Authentic faith in Christ involves love for His person and willingness to surrender to His authority. The human heart, will, and intellect all consent in the act of faith. In that sense, it is certainly correct, even *necessary*, to acknowledge that mere propositions can't do full justice to all the dimensions of truth.

On the other hand, truth simply cannot survive if stripped of propositional content. While it is quite true that believing the truth entails more than the assent of the human intellect to certain propositions, it is equally true that authentic faith never involves anything less. To reject the propositional content of the gospel is to forfeit saving faith, period.

Postmodernists are uncomfortable with propositions for an obvious reason: they don't like the clarity and inflexibility required to deal with truth in propositional form. A proposition is the simplest form of any truth claim, and postmodernism's fundamental starting point is its contempt for all truth claims. The "fuzzy logic" of ideas told in "story" form sounds so much more elastic—even though it really is not. Propositions are necessary building blocks for every means of conveying truth—including stories.

But the attack on propositional expressions of truth is the natural and necessary outworking of postmodernism's general distrust of logic, distaste for certainty, and dislike for clarity. To maintain the ambiguity and pliability of "truth" necessary for the postmodern perspective, clear and definitive propositions must be discounted as a means of expressing truth. Propositions force us to face facts and either affirm or deny them, and that kind of clarity simply does not play well in a postmodern culture.

## UNCERTAINTY IS THE NEW TRUTH

Of course, postmodernism is considerably more complex than those few descriptive paragraphs can possibly relate, but that is a sufficient thumbnail sketch of what the expression signifies. We will delve into some of the major characteristics of the postmodern paradigm shift throughout the book. But to get us started, let's consider this notion that certainty about *anything* is inherently arrogant.

That view is wildly popular today. The belief that no one can really know anything for certain is emerging as virtually the one dogma postmodernists will tolerate. Uncertainty is the new truth. Doubt and skepticism have been canonized as a form of humility. Right and wrong have been redefined in terms of subjective feelings and personal perspectives.

Those views are infiltrating the church too. In some circles within the visible church, cynicism is now virtually regarded as the most splendid of all virtues. I began this book with a prime example of that cynicism, as seen in the so-called Emerging Church movement.

A relentless tone of postmodern angst about *too much certainty* pervades that whole movement. No wonder: the Emerging Church began as a self-conscious effort to make Christianity more suitable to a postmodern culture. Emerging Christians are determined to adapt the Christian faith, the structure of the church, the language of faith, and even the gospel message itself to the ideas and rhetoric of postmodernism.

Postmodernity is a major theme in the literature of the Emerging Church movement. Several leading voices in the movement have suggested that postmodernism is something the church should embrace and adopt. Others might be more tentative about endorsing postmodernism entirely, but they insist that Christians at least need to start speaking the postmodern dialect if we want to reach a postmodern generation. That, they say, will require a retooling of the message we bring to the world, not to mention a revamping of the means by which we deliver it. Some in the movement have openly questioned whether there is even any legitimate role for preaching in a postmodern culture. "Dialogue" is the preferred method of communication. Accordingly, some Emerging-style congregations have done away with pastors altogether and replaced them with "narrators." Others have replaced the sermon with a free-ranging dialogue in which no one takes any leading role. For obvious reasons, an authoritative "thus saith the Lord" is not welcome in such a setting.

> UNCERTAINTY IS THE NEW TRUTH. DOUBT AND SKEPTICISM HAVE BEEN CANONIZED AS A FORM OF HUMILITY. RIGHT AND WRONG HAVE BEEN REDEFINED IN TERMS OF SUBJECTIVE FEELINGS AND PERSONAL PERSPECTIVES.

Of course, the first casualty of that way of thinking is every kind of *certainty*. The central propositions and bedrock convictions of biblical Christianity—such as firm belief in the inspiration and authority of Scripture, a sound understanding of the true gospel, full assurance of salvation, settled confidence in the lordship of Christ, and the narrow exclusivity of Christ as the only way of salvation—do not reconcile well with postmodernism's contempt for clear, authoritative truth claims. The *medium* of postmodern dialogue thereby instantly and automatically changes the *message*. And the rhetoric of the Emerging Church movement itself reflects that.

Listen, for example, to how Brian McLaren sums up his views on orthodoxy, certainty, and the question of whether the truths of Christianity are sound and reliable in the first place:

> How ironic that I am writing about orthodoxy, which implies to many a final capturing of the truth about God, which is the glory of God. Sit down here next to me in this little restaurant and ask me if Christianity (my version of it, yours, the Pope's, whoever's) is orthodox, meaning true, and here's my honest answer: a little, but not yet. Assuming by Christianity you mean the Christian understanding of the world and God, Christian opinions on soul, text, and culture . . . I'd have to say that we probably have a couple of things right, but a lot of things wrong.[1]

McLaren suggests that clarity itself is of dubious value. He clearly prefers ambiguity and equivocation, and his books are therefore full of deliberate doublespeak. In his introduction to *A Generous Orthodoxy,* he admits, "I have gone out of my way to be provocative, mischievous, and unclear, reflecting my belief that clarity is sometimes overrated, and that shock, obscurity, playfulness, and intrigue (carefully articulated) often stimulate more thought than clarity."[2] A common theme that runs throughout most of McLaren's writings is the idea that "there is great danger in the quest to be right."[3]

Postmodern influences have come into the evangelical movement through other avenues as well. *Beyond Foundationalism: Shaping Theology in a Postmodern Context*, by Stanley Grenz and John Franke, was published in 2001 and has made a significant impact in the evangelical academic community, garnering lots of positive reviews and stimulating numerous papers and lectures from evangelical leaders who evidently find much to agree with in the book.

But as the subtitle suggests, the book pleads for a whole new approach to theology, with the goal of "contextualizing" Christianity for a postmodern culture. "The categories and paradigms of the modern world" are in collapse, the authors note in the book's opening sentence.[4] They go on to assert that Christian theology therefore needs to be rethought, revised, and adapted in order to keep in step and remain relevant in these changing times.

Grenz and Franke argue that the Spirit of God speaks through Scripture, tradition, and culture, and theologians must seek to hear the voice of the Spirit in each one. Moreover, since culture is constantly in flux, they say, it is right and fitting for Christian theology to be in a perpetual state of transition and ferment too. No issue should ever be regarded as finally settled.

The obvious casualty of all this is any sure and certain knowledge of biblical truth. That is okay with Grenz and Franke. They are convinced that every desire to gain a fixed and positive knowledge of any truth actually belongs to the collapsing categories of enlightenment rationalism. That is precisely what they mean by the reference to "foundationalism" in the book's title. They define *Classical foundationalism* as a "quest for complete epistemological certitude."[5]

Certitude naturally comes under repeated attack in the book.

This culminates in the incredible claim that certainty is ultimately incompatible with hope.[6] Of course, there are some things we don't yet see clearly and still hope for (Romans 8:24–25). But it seems rather far-fetched to conclude that there is nothing we can know with a true and settled certainty.

Some readers have nevertheless found the Grenz-Franke argument persuasive, including John Armstrong. Armstrong is a writer, conference speaker, and former pastor who at one time was a defender of Reformation theology and a student of revival. The name of his ministry, Reformation and Revival, reflected that.

But after reading *Beyond Foundationalism*, Armstrong wrote a series of articles in his ministry newsletter declaring that he has changed his mind about several vital points of doctrine—including faith and understanding, the sacraments, the doctrine of revelation, and Christology—among other things. Crediting Grenz and Franke for helping him see the light, Armstrong writes, "I have been forced, upon deeper reflection about theological method, to give up what I call epistemological certitude."[7] He goes on to explain: "Reformed dogmaticians and teachers on the conservative side seek a steady, unshakable and certain knowledge. . . . John Franke suggests that the agenda employed by such theologians 'glorifies reason and deifies science.' I have changed my mind about the way to do theology, and I confess I now agree with Franke's conclusion."[8]

Armstrong reveals how far he has moved from his starting point with this statement: "If there is a foundation in Christian theology, and I believe that there must be, then it is not found in the Church, Scripture, tradition or culture." Scripture is not the foundation for Christian doctrine? Then what is? Armstrong's answer echoes the central thesis of *Beyond Foundationalism*: "If we must speak of 'foundations' for Christian faith and its theological enterprise, then we must speak only of the triune God as disclosed in polyphonic fashion through Scripture, the church, and even the world."[9]

Armstrong tries awkwardly to give lip service to the authority of Scripture by suggesting (in language Karl Barth might have applauded) that our doctrine must "always [be] in accordance with the normative witness to divine self-disclosure contained in Scripture."[10] Cutting through the jargon and reading that statement in its best light, Armstrong seems to be acknowledging (for a moment, at least) that God's self-revelation in Scripture ought to be the ultimate yardstick for measuring all our thoughts, beliefs, and teachings about God. But even that morsel is instantly snatched away with the other hand and quickly replaced with a wholly subjective, irrational, postmodern antihermeneutic: "Theology must be a humble human attempt to 'hear him'—never about rational approaches to texts."[11]

Armstrong identifies the illusion of many under the sway of this error by boasting that his radical turnaround is the epitome of "humility" and "the very essence of servant-leadership."[12] (In accordance with his shifting views, Armstrong has changed the name of his ministry from Reformation and Revival to Act 3—stressing his goal of being "missional" in the third millennium.)

Meanwhile, Armstrong employs caricature and exaggeration to attack the views he himself once held. He claims he has "routinely" heard "prominent Christians say: 'I have never changed my mind—never.'"[13] He cites Wayne Grudem's *Systematic Theology* as an example of the "'concordance' view of theology. You gather all the verses on a given subject, sort them all out, put them in their proper place in your system, and then develop (or write) a theology, formal or otherwise. This theology is then transferred as if the system itself contains, or is, the truth of God."[14]

Armstrong, Grenz, Franke, and the Emerging postmodernists have blurred the line between certainty and omniscience. They seem to presume that if we cannot know everything perfectly, we really cannot know anything with any degree of certainty. That is an appealing argument to the postmodern mind, but it is entirely at odds with what Scripture teaches: "We have the mind of Christ" (1 Corinthians 2:16).

> THE EMERGING POSTMODERNISTS HAVE BLURRED THE LINE BETWEEN CERTAINTY AND OMNISCIENCE. THEY SEEM TO PRESUME THAT IF WE CANNOT KNOW EVERYTHING PERFECTLY, WE REALLY CANNOT KNOW *ANYTHING* WITH ANY DEGREE OF CERTAINTY.

That is not to suggest, of course, that we have exhaustive knowledge. But we do have infallible knowledge of what Scripture reveals, as the Spirit of God teaches us through the Word of God: "We have received, not the spirit of the world, but the Spirit who is from God, that we might know the things that have been freely given to us by God" (1 Corinthians 2:12). The fact that our knowledge grows fuller and deeper—and we all therefore change our minds about *some* things as we gain more and more light—doesn't mean that everything we know is uncertain, outdated, or in need of an overhaul every few years. The words of 1 John 2:20–21 apply in their true sense to every believer: "You have an anointing from the Holy One, and you know all things. I have not written to you because you do not know the truth, but because you know it, and that no lie is of the truth."

The message coming from postmodernized evangelicals is exactly the opposite: Certainty is overrated. Assurance is arrogant. Better to keep changing your mind and keep your theology in a constant state of flux.

By such means, the ages-old war against truth has moved right into the Christian community, and the church itself has already become a battleground—and ominously, precious few in the church today are prepared for the fight.

## WAR IN THE CHURCH

This is by no means the first time the Truth War has intruded into the church. It has happened in every major era of church history. Battles over the truth were raging inside the Christian community even in apostolic times, when the church was just beginning. In fact, the record of Scripture indicates that false teachers in the church immediately became a significant and widespread problem wherever the gospel went. Virtually all the major epistles in the New Testament address the problem in one way or another. The apostle Paul was constantly engaged in battle against the lies of "false apostles [and] deceitful workers [who transformed] themselves into apostles of Christ" (2 Corinthians 11:13). Paul said that was to be expected. It is, after all, one of the favorite strategies of the evil one: "No wonder! For Satan himself transforms himself into an angel of light. Therefore it is no great thing if his ministers also transform themselves into ministers of righteousness"(vv. 14–15).

It takes a willful naïveté to deny that such a thing could happen in our time. As a matter of fact, it is happening on a massive scale. Now is not a good time for Christians to flirt with the spirit of the age. We cannot afford to be apathetic about the truth God has put in our trust. It is our duty to guard, proclaim, and pass that truth on to the next generation (1 Timothy 6:20–21). We who love Christ and believe the truth embodied in His teaching must awaken to the reality of the battle that is raging all around us. We must do our part in the ages-old Truth War. We are under a sacred obligation to join the battle and contend for the faith.

> THE CURRENT CLIMATE OF POSTMODERNISM *DOES* REPRESENT A WONDERFUL WINDOW OF OPPORTUNITY FOR THE CHURCH OF JESUS CHRIST. THE ARROGANT RATIONALISM THAT DOMINATED THE MODERN ERA IS ALREADY IN ITS DEATH THROES. MOST OF THE WORLD IS CAUGHT UP IN DISILLUSIONMENT AND CONFUSION. PEOPLE ARE UNSURE ABOUT VIRTUALLY EVERYTHING AND DO NOT KNOW WHERE TO TURN FOR TRUTH.

In one narrow respect, the driving idea behind the Emerging Church movement is correct: The current climate of postmodernism *does* represent a wonderful window of opportunity for the church of Jesus Christ. The arrogant rationalism that dominated the modern era is already in its death throes. Most of the world is caught up in disillusionment and confusion. People are unsure about virtually everything and do not know where to turn for truth.

However, the absolute *worst* strategy for ministering the gospel in a climate like this is for Christians to imitate the uncertainty or echo the cynicism of the postmodern perspective—and in effect drag the Bible and the gospel into it. Instead, we need to affirm *against* the spirit of the age that God has spoken with the utmost clarity, authority, and finality through His Son (Hebrews 1:1–2). And we have the infallible record of that message in Scripture (2 Peter 1:19–21).

Postmodernism is simply the latest expression of worldly unbelief. Its core value—a dubious ambivalence toward truth—is merely skepticism distilled to its pure essence. There is nothing virtuous or genuinely humble about it. It is proud rebellion against divine revelation.

In fact, postmodernism's hesitancy about truth is exactly antithetical to the bold confidence Scripture says is the birthright of every believer (Ephesians 3:12). Such assurance is wrought by the Spirit of God Himself in those who believe (1 Thessalonians 1:5). We need to make the most of that assurance and not fear to confront the world with it.

The gospel message in all its component facts is a clear, definitive, confident, authoritative proclamation that Jesus is Lord, and that He gives eternal and abundant life to all who *believe*. We who truly know Christ and have received that gift of eternal life have also received from Him a clear, definitive commission to deliver the gospel message boldly as His ambassadors. If we are likewise not clear and distinct in our proclamation of the message, we are not being good ambassadors.

But we are not merely ambassadors. We are simultaneously soldiers, commissioned to wage war for the defense and dissemination of the truth in the face of countless onslaughts against it. We are *ambassadors*—with a message of good news for people who walk in a land of darkness and dwell in the land of the shadow of death (Isaiah 9:2). And we are *soldiers*—charged with pulling down ideological strongholds and casting down the lies and deception spawned by the forces of evil (2 Corinthians 10:3–5; 2 Timothy 2:3–4).

Notice carefully: our task as ambassadors is to bring good news to people. Our mission as soldiers is to overthrow false *ideas*. We must keep those objectives straight; we are not entitled to wage warfare against people or to enter into diplomatic relations with anti-Christian ideas. Our warfare is not against flesh and blood (Ephesians 6:12); and our duty as ambassadors does not permit us to compromise or align ourselves with any kind of human philosophies, religious deceit, or any other kind of falsehood (Colossians 2:8).

If those sound like difficult assignments to keep in balance and maintain in proper perspective, it is because they are indeed.

Jude certainly understood this. The Holy Spirit inspired him to write his short epistle to people who were struggling with some of these very same issues. He nevertheless urged them to contend earnestly for the faith against all falsehood, while doing everything possible to deliver souls from destruction: "pulling them out of the fire, hating even the garment defiled by the flesh" (Jude 23).

So we are ambassador-soldiers, reaching out to sinners with the truth even as we make every effort to destroy the lies and other forms of evil that hold them in deadly bondage. That is a perfect summary of every Christian's duty in the Truth War.

Martin Luther, that noble gospel soldier, threw down the gauntlet at the feet of every Christian in every generation after him, when he said:

> If I profess with the loudest voice and clearest exposition every portion of the truth of God except precisely that little point which the world and the devil are at that moment attacking, I am not confessing Christ, however boldly I may be professing Christ. Where the battle rages, there the loyalty of the soldier is proved; and to be steady on all the battlefield besides, is mere flight and disgrace if he flinches at that point.[15]

# 2

## SPIRITUAL WARFARE: DUTY, DANGER, AND GUARANTEED TRIUMPH

*To those who are called, sanctified by God the Father,*
*and preserved in Jesus Christ: mercy, peace,*
*and love be multiplied to you.*

—Jude 1–2

"War is hell."

So said General William Tecumseh Sherman. By the time Sherman retired from active duty, that famous aphorism had already become virtually synonymous with his name. There were several conflicting accounts about when and how he said it. Near the end of his life, Sherman himself said he couldn't remember exactly where he first said it, but he still agreed with the opinion.

In fact, Sherman's contempt for war was well-known throughout most of his career as a soldier. A month after the American Civil War ended, while Sherman was at the height of his fame and the pinnacle of his success as a soldier, he wrote to a friend, "I am sick and tired of fighting."[1]

He was not yet finished fighting, however. His next major duty was a fourteen-year-long stint as commanding general of the U.S.

Army. Those years saw some of the most difficult battles in the horrible Indian wars that marred the settling of the American West. As much as Sherman despised warfare, he couldn't seem to get away from fighting.

General Sherman has been described by various historians as a brilliant strategist, an uncompromising combatant, and a ruthless fighting man. His career was highly controversial, and history's judgment has been mixed regarding his personal character and the conduct of the armies he commanded. As a soldier, he was by no means an ideal model in every sense. But one exemplary fact about him is clear from all the accounts of his life: although he really did despise warfare, few soldiers in all of history have been more determined or more tenacious warriors.

Whatever we might think of General Sherman as a man, there is something commendable and courageous about his soldier's perspective of battle. We ought to despise warfare with every fiber of our souls. War is one of the most calamitous consequences of evil. It is catastrophic. It is always ugly. It should never be glamorized, and no sane person should ever desire the conflict or savor the strife of war. There are times, however, when evil makes warfare absolutely necessary. And when we have a moral obligation to fight, we should never shirk that duty, compromise with the enemy, or enter the battle halfheartedly.

As detestable as warfare of any kind might be, there are causes for which *not* fighting is a far greater evil.

## WHY THE WARFARE IS NOT CARNAL

We need to be perfectly clear about what kind of fighting Christians are supposed to be doing. The spiritual warfare described in the New Testament is not a literal flesh-and-blood battle waged with earthly weapons and physical violence. There was a time not long ago when that practically went without saying. No more.

We live in an era when religious fanatics routinely blow themselves up, fly planes into buildings, or commit unthinkably evil acts of barbaric terrorism in the name of religion. The biblical strategy for spiritual warfare has nothing whatsoever in common with the tactics of Islamic jihad.

Scripture is clear that physical force is not a legitimate tool for the advancement of the kingdom of God. The church has no authority from their Lord to wield a sword for any reason—certainly not for the expansion of their influence, and not even to fend off their enemies. Those things have been perfectly clear and almost universally affirmed by godly, Bible-believing Christians since the night of Jesus' betrayal, when Jesus commanded Peter, "Put your sword in its place, for all who take the sword will perish by the sword" (Matthew 26:52).

> WAR IS ONE OF THE MOST CALAMITOUS CONSEQUENCES OF EVIL. IT IS CATASTROPHIC. IT IS ALWAYS UGLY. IT SHOULD NEVER BE GLAMORIZED, AND NO SANE PERSON SHOULD EVER DESIRE THE CONFLICT OR SAVOR THE STRIFE OF WAR. THERE ARE TIMES, HOWEVER, WHEN EVIL MAKES WARFARE ABSOLUTELY NECESSARY.

By the way, this is not to suggest that the use of force is forbidden for individual Christians acting lawfully in self-defense or in defending their families against criminal or military aggression. Physical resistance in such cases is nowhere forbidden in the Bible. (The turn-the-other-cheek principle of Matthew 5:39–40 pertains to personal insults and acts of persecution for Christ's sake, not all types of criminal assault. In normal cases where a person is resisting unlawful threats to property or life and limb, the use of force in proper measure is perfectly lawful by biblical principles—Nehemiah 4:14.) Of course, believers who are policemen, soldiers, or otherwise agents duly authorized by the government must be willing to use deadly force when necessary as part of their duty to the civil government. Scripture nowhere endorses any kind of absolute pacifism.

The point is that *the church as a body*, and *Christians acting in the name of Christ*, are never entitled to employ force for any purpose related to the work of advancing Christ's kingdom on earth. The Truth War has nothing to do with carnal warfare or physical violence. In the words of Charles Spurgeon, "For the church of God ever to avail itself of force would be clean contrary to the spirit of Christianity: for the Christian bishop to become a soldier, or employ the secular arm [of military force], would seem the very climax of contradiction."[2]

Of course tragic episodes of wars, crusades, and inquisitions have been carried out in Christ's name, sometimes even under the direct authority of ecclesiastical institutions. All of them have been unjust and unjustifiable on any biblical grounds. They have also been unmitigated disasters as far as the true ministry of the church is concerned. Sometimes such wars and violence occur when the church is utterly corrupted by the culture. (That is especially true of the religious militarism occasionally seen in Byzantine and medieval times.) In other instances, confusion about the relationship between church and state has empowered a few overzealous political leaders or misguided military commanders who thought they could wage holy war in the name of Christ. (That was a serious problem, for example, during the English Revolution. The conduct of Cromwell's military campaigns no doubt seriously undermined the true piety and influence of the Puritan movement.

And in the name of preserving religious freedom in Scotland, the Covenanters retaliated against English brutality by killing a number of Englishmen.)

The Bible says categorically that the Truth War is a completely different kind of war, fought with entirely different weaponry and with totally different objectives in view. "We do not wrestle against flesh and blood" (Ephesians 6:12). "We do not war according to the flesh. For the weapons of our warfare arc not carnal" (2 Corinthians 10:3–4). Every mention of spiritual weaponry in the New Testament makes this point perfectly clear. The tools of our warfare are not the kind that could be forged on any earthly anvil. Our only offensive weapons are "the word of truth [and] the power of God"; and our only defensive armor is "the armor of righteousness" (2 Corinthians 6:7).

> THE TRUTH WAR IS NOT A CARNAL WAR. IT IS NOT ABOUT TERRITORY AND NATIONS. IT IS NOT A BATTLE FOR LANDS AND CITIES. IT IS NOT A CLAN WAR OR A PERSONALITY CONFLICT BETWEEN INDIVIDUALS. IT IS NOT A FIGHT FOR CLOUT BETWEEN RELIGIOUS DENOMINATIONS. IT IS NOT A SKIRMISH OVER MATERIAL POSSESSIONS. IT IS A BATTLE FOR THE TRUTH.

In John 18:36, Jesus Himself said to Pilate, "My kingdom is not of this world. If My kingdom were of this world, My servants would fight." Notice carefully once more: our Lord was plainly not advocating total pacifism. If His kingdom were an earthly entity, He says, His servants would indeed fight. Those who teach that violence per se is unjustifiable in any and every circumstance have misunderstood the teaching of Scripture. In fact, Romans 13:1–4 expressly grants *governments* the authority to wield the sword in order to punish evildoers, defend their national security, and maintain civil peace.

What I am stressing here is that permission to use physical force is never granted to the *church*. That is because the people of God corporately have a different—and far more important—kind of warfare to wage. The Truth War is not a carnal war. It is not about territory and nations. It is not a battle for lands and cities. It is not a clan war or a personality conflict between individuals. It is not a fight for clout between religious denominations. It is not a skirmish over material possessions. It is a battle for the truth. It is about ideas. It is a fight for the mind. It is a battle against false doctrines, evil ideologies, and wrong beliefs. It is a war for *truth*.

Paul makes this clear in 2 Corinthians 10:5, where he spells out the ultimate objective of the Truth War: "casting down arguments and every high thing that exalts itself against the knowledge of God, bringing every thought into captivity to the obedience of Christ." The battlefield is the mind; the goal is the absolute triumph of truth; the priceless spoils of conquest are souls won out of the bondage of sin; the outcome is our willing submission to Christ; the highest prize is the honor given to Him as Lord; and the ultimate victory is completely His.

## WHY TRUTH IS SO VITAL

With increasing frequency nowadays, I hear people say things like, "Come, now, let's not bicker about what we believe. It's only doctrine. Let's focus instead on how we live. The way of Jesus is surely more important than our arguments over the words of Jesus. Let's set aside our disagreements over creeds and dogmas and devote ourselves instead to showing the love of Christ by the way we conduct our lives."

Many people these days evidently find that suggestion appealing. On the surface, it may sound generous, kindhearted, modest, and altruistic. But the view itself is a serious violation of "the *way* of Jesus," who taught that salvation hinges on hearing and believing His *Word* (John 5:24). He said, "The words that I speak to you are spirit, and they are life" (John 6:63). To those who doubted His truth claims, He said, "If you do not believe that I am He, you will die in your sins" (John 8:24). He never left any room for someone to imagine that the propositional content of His teaching is optional as long as we mimic His behavior.

In fact, the New Testament consistently stresses otherwise. One vital principle about our redemption from sin destroys the whole argument: faith, not works, is the sole instrument of justification (Galatians 2:16; Ephesians 2:8–9). In other words, *what we believe* rather than *what we do* is what secures us a righteous standing before God—because we lay hold of justifying righteousness by faith alone, and not by our works (Romans 4:5).

Paul says in Romans 9:31–32 that "Israel, pursuing the law of righteousness, has not attained to the law of righteousness. Why? Because they did not seek it by faith, but as it were, by the works of the law." In other words, regardless of how meticulous they may have been in their external observance of God's law, their *unbelief* was sufficient to exclude them from the kingdom. "They being ignorant of God's righteousness, and seeking to establish their own righteousness, have not submitted to the righteousness of God. For Christ is the end of the law for righteousness to everyone who believes" (Romans 10:3–4). They doubted the truth of Christ, and that proved spiritually fatal in spite of how well they had perfected an external display of piety.

Notice: Paul expressly says they were pursuing righteousness. But they were looking for it in all the wrong places. Because they clung to wrong *beliefs* about the righteousness God requires and rejected the righteousness Christ would have provided for them, they were eternally condemned. Their failure was first of all an error about a vital article of faith, not merely a flaw in their practice. Their whole belief system (not merely their behavior) was wrong. Unbelief was enough to condemn them, regardless of how they acted.

It is not kindness at all, but the worst form of cruelty, to suggest that what people believe doesn't really matter much if they feel spiritual and do good. In fact, on the face of it, that claim is a blatant contradiction of the gospel message.

Besides, *real* righteousness simply cannot exist in isolation from belief in the truth. To make the case for any concept of "practical good" that subsists apart from sound doctrine, one quickly has to remove just about everything that is *truly* righteous from the definition of *good*. Naturally, it doesn't take very long for that kind of thinking to undermine the foundations of Christianity itself.

Brian McLaren, for example, goes so far as to suggest that followers of other religions can also be followers of Christ in practical terms without leaving other religions or identifying with Christianity. "I don't believe making disciples must equal making adherents to the Christian religion," he says. "It may be advisable in many (not all!) circumstances to help people become followers of Jesus *and* remain within their Buddhist, Hindu, or Jewish contexts."[3]

McLaren is leading the parade for those who do not seem to think wrong beliefs, superstition, false religion, and false gods are evils that people need to be delivered from. Instead, he suggests that even the false religions themselves may ultimately be redeemable:

> Although I don't hope all Buddhists will become (cultural) Christians, I do hope all who feel so called will become Buddhist followers of Jesus; I believe they should be given that opportunity and invitation. I don't hope all Jews or Hindus will become members of the Christian

religion. But I do hope all who feel so called will become Jewish or Hindu followers of Jesus.

Ultimately, I hope that Jesus will save Buddhism, Islam and every other religion, including the Christian religion, which often seems to need saving about as much as any other religion does. (In this context, I do wish all Christians would become followers of Jesus, but perhaps this is too much to ask. After all, I'm not doing such a hot job of it myself.)[4]

The logical starting point of McLaren's book A Generous Orthodoxy is his belief that doctrinal distinctives are of "marginal" value.[5] A predictably postmodern dubiousness seems to color McLaren's treatment of practically all objective truth claims—and it's a skepticism that extends even to the authority of Scripture itself. He seems deeply suspicious of any truth-based definition of orthodoxy. He writes as if orthopraxy (practical righteousness) were what really matters most. In fact, one gets the impression from the book that he thinks right behavior automatically trumps right belief. When McLaren finally gives a description of what he means by orthodoxy, even that turns out to be about "how we search for a kind of truth . . ."[6] rather than about the truth itself.

Despite his well-known preference for ambiguity, McLaren is surprisingly frank about his perspective on this. He believes both the church's methodology and the Christian message itself need to be constantly in flux: "Our message and methodology have changed, do change, and must change if we are faithful to the ongoing and unchanging mission of Jesus Christ."[7] He says the message changes "not because we've got it wrong and we're closer to finally 'getting it right,'" but because the "context" of the culture in which we live is dynamic. We must, after all, keep up with these postmodern times.

Notice: McLaren acknowledges that an ever-changing message does not bring anyone any closer to "getting it right," and he is not the least bit troubled by that. In the final analysis, he says, "'getting it right' is beside the point: the point is 'being and doing good' as followers of Jesus in our unique time and place, fitting in with the ongoing story of God's saving love for planet Earth."[8] All of that is an exemplary statement of the typical postmodern perspective.

But the thing to notice here is that in McLaren's system, orthodoxy is really all about practice, not about true beliefs. While acknowledging that this idea is "scandalous," he nonetheless affirms it as the central message of his book.[9] It is frankly hard to see such a perspective as anything other than plain, old-fashioned unbelief, rooted in a rejection of the clear teaching of Scripture. McLaren has elevated the sinner's own good works above the importance of faith grounded in the truth of the gospel. No wonder he feels such an affinity with Buddhists and Hindus—at the end of the day, many of his ideas about the role of righteousness and good works in religion are not fundamentally different from theirs.

And bear in mind that in McLaren's own moral hierarchy, one of the highest values (if not the supreme virtue by which all others are measured) is a particular notion of "humility"—namely, the standard postmodern species of humility, which starts with the assumption that certainty, assurance, and bold convictions are arrogant and therefore wrong. So the ramifications of McLaren's continual stress on right *practice* apart from an equal stress on right *belief* turn out to be profound. "Right practice" by his definition virtually begins with the relinquishment of all certainty about "right belief." One gets the distinct impression that objective, propositional truth means so little to McLaren that he would consider a broad-minded Hindu who always tries to speak positively and tolerantly about others' beliefs a better "Christian" than the preacher who openly curses someone else for teaching a wrong view of the law and gospel.

That, of course, would make the apostle Paul a bad Christian (Galatians 1:8–9)—not to mention Jesus (Matthew 23).

No one except the grossest hypocrite would ever suggest that how we act is utterly immaterial as long as we subscribe to the right creeds and confessions. McLaren nevertheless begins his book with precisely that kind of caricature. He claims that "many orthodoxies have always and everywhere assumed that ortho*doxy* (right thinking and opinion about the gospel) and ortho*praxy* (right practice of the gospel) could and should be separated, so that one could at least be proud of getting an A in orthodoxy even when one earned a D in orthopraxy, which is only an elective class anyway."[10]

In reality, no true Christian anywhere has ever deliberately advocated such a twisted view of orthodoxy. Scripture is clear: "As the body without the spirit is dead, so faith without works is dead also" (James 2:26). A high view of orthodoxy cannot nullify or undermine the importance of orthopraxy. That might *seem* to be the case if you start with the presupposition that certainty and strong convictions are always wrong and arguments about the truth value of propositions are always arrogant. But surely from a biblical perspective we can recognize the truth of James 2 without automatically discounting sound doctrine and settled assurance altogether.

> BIBLICAL ORTHODOXY ENCOMPASSES ORTHOPRAXY. BOTH RIGHT DOCTRINE AND RIGHT LIVING ARE ABSOLUTELY ESSENTIAL AND TOTALLY INSEPARABLE FOR THE TRUE CHILD OF GOD. THAT IS THE CONSISTENT TEACHING OF CHRIST HIMSELF.

Biblical orthodoxy encompasses orthopraxy. Both right doctrine and right living are absolutely essential and totally inseparable for the true child of God. That is the consistent teaching of Christ Himself. "If you abide in My word, you are My disciples indeed. And you shall know the truth, and the truth shall make you free" (John 8:31–32).

Furthermore, Scripture does clearly and consistently teach the primacy of right belief as the foundation of right behavior. In other words, righteous living is properly seen as a fruit of authentic faith, and never the other way around. Pious actions devoid of any real love for the truth do not even constitute genuine orthopraxy by any measure. On the contrary, that is the worst kind of self-righteousness hypocrisy.

So truth is worth fighting over. As we have seen, it is the one thing in this world the church is supposed to fight for. Lose that fight and all else is lost.

It is obvious to most sensible people that not every point of truth is of *equal* importance, and therefore every trifling disagreement does not need to be pursued with equal fervor. In fact, one of the most important points in the whole issue of spiritual warfare is the question of what is insignificant and what is really worth fighting for. (I addressed that question in some detail more than a decade ago in a book titled *Reckless Faith*.[11] It is a question that deserves more careful consideration than most Christians evidently care to give it.)

But Brian McLaren leapfrogs over that part of the discussion, because one of his fundamental presuppositions is that there is really not much in the realm of propositional truth that *is* worth fighting over. He gives a somewhat qualified affirmation of the Apostles' Creed and the Nicene Creed. He then repeatedly insinuates that once you get past those two ancient creeds, the only issues at stake are mere "denominational distinctives" and doctrinal trivia that should all be relegated to the "marginal" category.[12]

That is simply not an honest assessment of what is happening in the Truth War today. The main battlegrounds—the ideas McLaren himself spends most of his book attacking—are the objectivity and knowability of truth as it is revealed in God's Word. So what is *really* at stake are the very same truths the serpent sought to subvert when he asked Eve, "Has God indeed said . . . ?" (Genesis 3:1). They are the same truths that have *always* been at the heart of the Truth War—the inspiration, authority, inerrancy, sufficiency, and perspicuity (clarity) of Scripture—not to mention several essential aspects of the gospel message. Surely *those* are issues that cannot be swept aside or discounted as marginal in the name of a twisted notion of charity or false humility. When you reflect on how much of the Christian message is undermined by postmodernist notions about truth, it turns out the current controversies are infinitely more serious than McLaren wants to pretend.

Furthermore, when you realize that *not one* of those issues is mentioned in the two creeds McLaren names (because those doctrines weren't even seriously challenged by the early heretics the creeds were written to answer)—it should be instantly obvious that there are several very crucial doctrines worth fighting for beyond the few that are catalogued in a couple of Christendom's most ancient creeds. The vast majority of Christians throughout history have also understood that the truth of the gospel is even worth *dying* for. It is frankly difficult to see how anyone viewing truth from a post-modernist perspective could ever begin to understand why.

Truth—including historical facts, assurance, and objective, distinct, knowable, authoritative propositions that demand to be embraced as true—is an essential concept in authentic Christianity. All the other aspects of religious experience flow from the truth we believe and simply give expression to it. Take away the ground of truth, and all you have is fluctuating religious sentiment.

Remember, the apostle Paul called the church "the pillar and ground of the truth" (1 Timothy 3:15). We have a duty to uphold the truth and to wield the sword of God's Word against every human speculation and every worldly hypothesis raised up against the knowledge of God. The struggle will continue until every thought is brought into captivity to the obedience of Christ (2 Corinthians 10:5). The church *must* pursue that fight, and if church leaders are not setting the example, they are not being faithful to their calling.

## WHY APOSTASY IS SUCH A THREAT

Ever since that day in the garden when the serpent tempted Eve, he has relentlessly attacked the truth with lies, using the same strategies over and over to sow doubt and disbelief in the human mind. "We are not ignorant of his devices" (2 Corinthians 2:11).

The form of his evil dialectic rarely changes. He *questions* the truth God has revealed ("Has God indeed said, 'You shall not eat of every tree of the garden'?" [Genesis 3:1]). Then he *contradicts* what God has said ("You will not surely die" [v. 4]). Finally, he *concocts an alternative version of "truth"* ("God knows that in the day you eat of it your eyes will be opened, and you will be like God, knowing good and evil" [v. 5]). The devil's alternative credo often has a few carefully chosen elements of truth in the mix—but always diluted and thoroughly blended with falsehoods, contradictions, misrepresentations, distortions, and every other imaginable perversion of reality. Add it all up and the bottom line is a big lie.

Furthermore, in the promotion of his dishonesty, Satan employs every agent he can dupe into being a shill for him—demons, unbelievers, and (most effectively) people who are in some way actually associated with the truth, or (even worse) who merely *pretend* to be agents of the truth and angels of light. That, as we noted in chapter 1, is one of Satan's favorite and time-tested strategies (2 Corinthians 11:13–15).

It was happening already, on a wide scale, while the church was still in its infancy. After three years founding and diligently teaching the church at Ephesus, Paul warned the elders in that young congregation about what he knew would happen as soon as he moved on: "For I know this, that after my departure savage wolves will come in among you, not sparing the flock. Also from among yourselves men will rise up, speaking perverse things, to draw away the disciples after themselves. Therefore watch, and remember that for three years I did not cease to warn everyone night and day with tears" (Acts 20:29–31).

> THE DEVIL'S ALTERNATIVE CREDO OFTEN HAS A FEW CAREFULLY CHOSEN ELEMENTS OF TRUTH IN THE MIX—BUT ALWAYS DILUTED AND THOROUGHLY BLENDED WITH FALSEHOODS, CONTRADICTIONS, MISREPRESENTATIONS, DISTORTIONS, AND EVERY OTHER IMAGINABLE PERVERSION OF REALITY. ADD IT ALL UP AND THE BOTTOM LINE IS A BIG LIE.

The primary threat Paul was concerned about would come from within the church itself—*even from among the elders of the church.* He was speaking prophetically; thus the tone of absolute certainty: "I *know* this." God had revealed to Paul that a challenge to the truth would arise from within the church's own leadership, and people would be drawn away.

It happened just that way too. By the end of the first century, when the apostle John wrote Revelation, Christ's message to the church at Ephesus included a commendation to that church for having "tested those who say they are apostles and are not, and have found them liars" (Revelation 2:2). In the same context, Christ condemned "the deeds of the Nicolaitans" (v. 6).

The Nicolaitans were a dangerous sect, and they may well have been the very "wolves" Paul cautioned against in the famous prophetic warning of Acts 20. If so, the group's teachings might even have originated with one or more of the earliest elders in the Ephesian church. (Some early sources, including Irenaeus in the mid-second century, identified the sect with "Nicolas, a proselyte from Antioch," who was appointed to leadership in the Jerusalem church in Acts 6:5. There is no clear proof of that, but there is a considerable amount of evidence that Nicolaitanism was indeed bred and incubated by men who had achieved stature as leaders in the church.)

Apparently, when the Nicolaitans were rejected in Ephesus, they went to a nearby church plant at Pergamos, where they gained a following in that church. Christ's message to Pergamos in Revelation 2:12–17 is almost entirely given to rebuke, because the church had embraced "those who hold the doctrine of the Nicolaitans" (v. 15).

What was that doctrine? It is described in verse 14 as a kind of radical licentiousness: "You have there those who hold the doctrine of Balaam, who taught Balak to put a stumbling block before the children of Israel, to eat things sacrificed to idols, and to commit sexual immorality." They were using Christian liberty as a cloak for vice and an opportunity for the flesh (Galatians 5:13; 1 Peter 2:16).

This was evidently the very same kind of error the epistle of Jude was written to address, because Jude refers to the false teachers he opposed as "ungodly men, who turn the grace of our God into lewdness" (Jude 4), and he says they "run greedily in the error of Balaam for profit" (v. 11).

Licentious behavior and greed were key characteristics of all forms of *gnosticism*. That was a deadly brand of false religion that flourished in the second century and often infiltrated the church, masquerading as Christianity. Nicolaitanism has many of the hallmarks of later forms of gnosticism. It seems to be one of the earliest expressions of the gnostic tendency in the ancient church. Clearly, similar doctrines had already intruded into the church and begun to take root when Jude wrote.

We will examine the gnostic error in more detail in chapter 4, but simply notice for now that the whole point of Jude's epistle is to confront this type of error and encourage believers to *fight* for the true faith. Notice also that Jude does not waste any subtlety or employ any understatements in his evaluation of the apostates of his day. Friendly dialogue with them was not part of his plan for dealing with their error (see also 2 John 7–11).

*Apostasy* is the technical name for serious, soul-destroying error that arises from within the church. It comes from the Greek word *apostasia*, which occurs in 2 Thessalonians 2:3 and is translated "falling away." The word is closely related to the Greek word for "divorce." It speaks of abandonment, a separation, a defection—the abdication of truth altogether.

Can a genuine Christian fall away from the faith and become an apostate? No. Scripture is quite clear about that. Those who do depart from the faith, like Judas, simply demonstrate that they never had true faith to begin with. "They went out from us, but they were not of us; for if they had been of us, *they would have continued with us;* but they went out that they might be made manifest, that none of them were of us" (1 John 2:19, emphasis added). Jesus said of his true sheep, "I give them eternal life, and they shall never perish; neither shall anyone snatch them out of My hand. My Father, who has given them to Me, is greater than all; and no one is able to snatch them out of My Father's hand" (John 10:28–29).

Nonetheless, there are lots of apostate people. Ever since the time of Judas, there have been people who profess faith in Christ and identify themselves as disciples but who never genuinely embrace the truth. They may *understand* the truth. They may even seem to follow it enthusiastically for a while. They might identify with a church and therefore become an active and integral part of the earthly Christian community. Sometimes they even become leaders in a church. But they never really *believe* the truth with an undivided heart. Like tares among wheat, they have an appearance of authenticity for a while, but they are incapable of producing any useful fruit (Matthew 13:24–30).

An *apostate* is therefore a defector from the truth—someone who has known the truth, given some show of affirmation to it, perhaps even proclaimed it for a while—but then rejected it in the end. The typical apostate may still purport to believe the truth and proclaim the truth; but in reality he opposes the truth and undermines it. He is a traitor to the faith and secretly an enemy in the Truth War. But he wants everyone to think otherwise. Most apostates seek to remain within the church and actively seek acceptance among the people of God. Because everything they do undermines faith and corrupts the truth, such people pose a grave danger to the health of the flock—even though they usually bend over backward to appear friendly, likable, and pious. That is why Jesus compares them to ravenous wolves in sheep's clothing (Matthew 7:15).

A few apostates are outspoken and aggressive in their opposition to the truth, but most are subtler. Regardless of how friendly, benign, or self-effacing they may appear, these wolves in sheep's clothing are invariably driven by evil and self-aggrandizing motives—such as pride, rebellion, greed, lust, or whatever (2 Peter 2:10–19). That is not to suggest they always know full well that they *are* apostates. Many of them are so blinded by their evil desires that they really imagine they are serving Christ when in fact they are opposing Him (John 16:2).

Others may start out actually meaning well, but they never get past being double-minded. They are like seeds sprouting in shallow or weedy soil. They often show prodigious signs of life for a time. But ultimately their own shallowness or worldliness make it impossible for God's Word to take root (Matthew 13:20–22). Despite whatever temporary appearance of spiritual life they might display, they are incapable of producing real fruit, and they eventually fall away. Don't let the temporary appearance of spiritual health and vigor at the start fool you. When such a person abandons the faith, it proves he or she was always unregenerate and unbelieving—still dead in trespasses and sins.

Apostasy can have far-reaching and disastrous effects on an entire congregation's spiritual health. When false teaching goes unchallenged, it breeds more confusion and draws still more shallow and insincere people into the fold. If not vigorously resisted, apostasy will spread like leaven through seminaries, denominations, missions agencies, and other Christian institutions. False teaching thus attacks the church like a parasite, affecting our corporate testimony, inoculating people against the real truth of the gospel, proliferating false and halfhearted "disciples," and filling the church with people who are actually unbelievers. By such means, entire churches and denominations have been taken over by apostasy.

> WHEN FALSE TEACHING GOES UNCHALLENGED, IT BREEDS MORE CONFUSION AND DRAWS STILL MORE SHALLOW AND INSINCERE PEOPLE INTO THE FOLD.

In fact, that has happened countless times throughout church history. It has especially happened on a wide scale over the past century and a half, wherever modernism, theological liberalism, neoorthodoxy, "process theology," and a host of similar ideas have spread. Whole denominations (even many where the gospel was once proclaimed clearly) have been left spiritually bankrupt because error and unbelief were tolerated rather than being opposed.

Obviously, the cause of truth is hurt when this happens. People who embrace apostasy are destroyed by it. Churches wither and die because of it. Consider the fact that by the end of the first century, when the apostle John wrote Revelation 2–3, five out of the seven churches in Asia Minor were either beginning to defect from the faith or were already apostate bodies. (Sardis was already apostate; Laodicea was teetering on the precipice of final rejection.) Christ's central message to all but two of the churches included a mandate to deal with apostates in their midst. The battle for truth in the church has always been a very, very difficult but necessary conflict.

## WHY THE EVANGELICAL MOVEMENT IS IN TROUBLE TODAY

Apostasy poses real and present dangers today as always. Actually, the threat may be more imminent and more dangerous than ever, because most Christians nowadays simply don't care about the prevalence of false doctrine, nor do they take seriously their duty to fight against apostasy. Instead, they want a friendly atmosphere of open acceptance for everyone, tolerance of opposing ideas, and charitable dialogue with the apostates.

Evangelicalism as a movement has historically stood against handling important Bible doctrine in such an indifferent way—as if truth itself were pliable. Evangelicals' primary distinctive used to be their commitment to the purity of the gospel. That commitment is reflected in the word *evangelical* itself (which is derived from the Greek word for "gospel"). William Tyndale was one of the first to use the expression, speaking of "evangelical truth" as a synonym for the gospel. And the evangelical movement has always treated the gospel as the core and foundation of all truth.

Since the Protestant Reformation, the term has historically been used to signify a particular strain of conservative Protestantism in which a handful of key gospel doctrines are regarded as absolutely essential to authentic Christianity. These nonnegotiable evangelical distinctives include the doctrine of justification by faith, the principle of substitutionary atonement, and the absolute authority and perfect sufficiency of Scripture. (Of course, necessarily implied and included in that short list are a number of other vital doctrines, including Christ's deity, His virgin birth, and His bodily resurrection.)

Evangelicalism has furthermore always expressly denied that any good works or sacraments have any merit before God or any instrumental efficacy for justification. So the stress in historic evangelicalism is properly placed on the primacy of faith over works. Evangelicals have always resisted the pressure to elevate good works over sound doctrine, insisting that truly good works are the fruit of faith, never a valid substitute for it.

> THE EVANGELICAL MOVEMENT ISN'T REALLY VERY EVANGELICAL ANYMORE. THE TYPICAL EVANGELICAL LEADER TODAY IS FAR MORE LIKELY TO EXPRESS INDIGNATION AT SOMEONE WHO CALLS FOR DOCTRINAL CLARITY AND ACCURACY THAN TO FIRMLY OPPOSE ANOTHER SELF-STYLED EVANGELICAL WHO IS ACTIVELY ATTACKING SOME VITAL BIBLICAL TRUTH.

But the evangelical movement isn't really very evangelical anymore. The typical evangelical leader today is far more likely to express indignation at someone who calls for doctrinal clarity and accuracy than to firmly oppose another self-styled evangelical who is actively attacking some vital biblical truth.

Meanwhile, much of the evangelical movement has been acting for a long time as if our *main* duty is just to keep in step with the fads of worldly culture in order to gain the approval of each succeeding generation. That strategy will never fail to find enthusiastic support among those who are immature, weak, ignorant, or cowardly, but it can never be truly effective. Without the truth, no spiritual transformation is possible (1 Peter 1:22–25; John 17:17).

Evangelicals who are so desperate to follow the culture invariably lag several years behind anyway, somehow managing to look awkward and clumsy by always failing to keep in step, no matter how hard they try. But, then, the church is not supposed to ape the world's fads or court the world's favor anyway. Jesus said, "If the world hates you, you know that it hated Me before it hated you. If you were of the world, the world would love its own. Yet because you are not of the world, but I chose you out of the world, therefore the world hates you" (John 15:18–19).

The campaign to make Christianity seem "contemporary" and sophisticated in the world's eyes is proving especially disastrous right now. As postmodern culture becomes more and more hostile to authority, clarity, and authoritative proclamations of truth, evangelicalism is blithely drifting more and more into postmodern ways of thinking about truth, imagining that this is the way to "reach" the culture. Consequently, Christians are less and less willing to fight for the truth.

## HOW CHRISTIANS ARE KEPT SECURE

Something similar was apparently happening in the apostolic church. That is why the central point of Jude's brief but powerful epistle was a challenge designed to motivate Christians to become soldiers in the Truth War.

But Jude's *starting* point, interestingly enough, was to stress the security of the true believer. He addresses his epistle "To those who are called, sanctified by God the Father, and preserved in

Jesus Christ" (v. 1). All the urgings, warnings, and encouragements in the verses to come do not apply to anyone who is half-hearted or double-minded. He is addressing those with true faith.

Jude recognizes that all war is ugly, dangerous, distasteful, and something every sane person would prefer to avoid altogether. Warfare in the spiritual realm is no different in that respect from carnal warfare; if anything, it is even *more* menacing. If conventional warfare is (as General Sherman said) the closest thing to hell on earth, spiritual warfare is actually more horrifying still—because it is literally a hostile engagement with the forces of hell in the spiritual realm, where the enemy is never even fully visible.

Remember: our real enemies are not mere flesh and blood. This is cosmic warfare, engaging the armies of hell, which are arrayed against Christ. Their weapons consist of lies of all kinds—elaborate lies, massive philosophical lies, evil lies that appeal to humanity's fallen sinfulness, lies that inflate human pride, and lies that closely resemble the truth. Our one weapon is the simple truth of Christ as revealed in His Word.

It is a frightening scenario, especially when we fully realize our own utter frailty, our own tendency to self-deception, and our own proclivity to sin. Very little would seem to qualify us to be soldiers in the Truth War. But for one thing: we follow a Commander who has been given all authority—absolute lordship—in heaven and on earth (Matthew 28:18). As Paul said, Christ is "far above all principality and power and might and dominion, and every name that is named, not only in this age but also in that which is to come. And [God] put all things under His feet, and gave Him to be head over all things to the church" (Ephesians 1:21–22). He is truth incarnate. And if you are a true believer, you are called, sanctified, and preserved in Him.

In the ultimate and eternal sense, no true Christian has ever been or ever will be a casualty in the Truth War. We are loved, called, blessed, made holy, and kept secure—even in the midst of escalating apostasy. Despite all the dangers posed by hellish lies and cosmic warfare, we are preserved in Christ and guaranteed to triumph in the end.

That is the starting point of Jude's epistle. That is also precisely where Jude *ends* his epistle, commending his readers to "Him who is able to keep you from stumbling, and to present you faultless before the presence of His glory with exceeding joy" (v. 24).

So this is the context in which Scripture calls us to wage war on behalf of the truth: The task is intimidating. The enemy is fearsome. The dangers are daunting. The spectacle of such a battle is appalling. And the price of involvement is total self-sacrifice—which is just what every true Christian renders to Christ at salvation (Luke 9:23–25). But we are promised that such a sacrifice will always be worthwhile, and our final triumph is likewise guaranteed—because we are "preserved in Jesus Christ."

That is surely something to keep in mind as you think about your part in the Truth War. It is perfectly natural to feel inadequate. We *are* completely inadequate in and of ourselves (2 Corinthians 3:5-6). But Christ is perfectly sufficient, and we are united with Him by faith. There is no reason for dread or apprehension. Our triumph is certain in the end, because Christ has already won the ultimate victory on our behalf. True believers are always ultimately secure in the faith, "kept by the power of God through faith for salvation ready to be revealed in the last time" (1 Peter 1:5). Remember Jesus' own words: "My sheep hear My voice, and I know them, and they follow Me. And I give them eternal life, and they shall never perish; neither shall anyone snatch them out of My hand. My Father, who has given them to Me, is greater than all; and no one is able to snatch them out of My Father's hand" (John 10:27–29). And damning lies collapse under the power of the truth

(2 Corinthians 10:4–5).

So if you are a believer, get into the battle. Fight for the truth. Contend earnestly for the faith. Apostasy is present in the church, and it is probably going to get worse. But we who believe in Jesus Christ have nothing to fear. We are called and loved and kept secure in Him, so we can be supremely confident, even in this era of doubt and uncertainty. Because the One who *is* truth incarnate—the One whose honor and glory are therefore on the line—is both our Commander and our Protector. And His Word is a formidable weapon.

# 3

## CONSTRAINED INTO CONFLICT:
## WHY WE MUST FIGHT FOR THE FAITH

*Beloved, while I was very diligent to write to you concerning our common salvation, I found it necessary to write to you exhorting you to contend earnestly for the faith which was once for all delivered to the saints.*

—Jude 3

Since the catalyst for this book is Jude's challenge to people under his pastoral care, I want you to meet him.

Jude was the younger half brother of Christ.

How do we know that? Well, first of all, Scripture says that after the birth of Jesus, Joseph and Mary had at least four other sons. (Mark 6:3 indicates that they had daughters too—although the girls' names are not given and we don't even know how many there were.) The household in which Jesus grew up seems to have been a fairly large family by today's standards. In Matthew 13:55, Jesus' four half brothers are expressly mentioned by name.

In that context, Matthew is describing how people in Jesus' hometown of Nazareth responded to his authoritative teaching by questioning His credentials. They expressed disbelief and amazement that a teacher like Jesus could come from the family of a lowly carpenter in their own unremarkable village. In the process, they mentioned Jesus' parents and His siblings. As Matthew records the names of the four younger sons in the family, notice the last person on the list: "Is this not the carpenter's son? Is not His mother called Mary? And His brothers James, Joses, Simon, and *Judas*?" (emphasis added).

"Judas" is a simple transliteration of Jude's Greek name. In the original biblical manuscripts, it is exactly the same name used to signify Judas Iscariot. But to distinguish Jesus' brother from the traitor, the author of the epistle is always known in English as Jude. Incidentally, the only place in the English Bible where Jude's name actually appears in that familiar shortened form is the first word of the first verse of his short epistle. Even there, the name given in the Greek manuscripts is *Ioudas*.

*Judas* (meaning "praise YHWH") is an Anglicized Greek variant of *Judah*, one of the twelve tribes of Israel. This was quite a common name in first-century Israel. The New Testament introduces us to at least seven different men named Judas, including two of the original twelve disciples.

There was, of course, the notorious false disciple named Iscariot. But there was also a faithful member of the Twelve named Judas. John 14:22 has parentheses with the note "not Iscariot" following his name. Acts 1:13 refers to that lesser-known disciple named Judas as "Judas the son of James." He is normally called Lebbaeus and Thaddaeus rather than Judas (Matthew 10:3). That disciple is not the author of the epistle. (Although such a connection has sometimes erroneously been made, we shall shortly see why it is a mistake.)

Other Judases in the New Testament include an insurgent named Judas of Galilee (Acts 5:37); Judas Barsabas, a church leader who delivered news about the Jerusalem Council's ruling to believers in Antioch (Acts 15:22); and a man named Judas who lived in Damascus on Straight Street, in whose home the apostle Paul stayed immediately after his conversion (Acts 9:11).

Our Jude stands out from all the others. A considerable amount of biblical evidence suggests that the "Judas" named as a younger son of Joseph and Mary in Matthew 13:55 is none other than the human author of the epistle—Jude. Although Jude himself gives scant details about his identity, what few facts he reveals correlate perfectly with what we know of the younger half brother of Christ.

## BONDSERVANT OF CHRIST, BROTHER OF JAMES

As a matter of fact, the best clues we have about Jude's true identity come from the epistle itself. What Jude *doesn't* say about himself is almost as interesting as what he *does* say.

Notice, first of all, what he *does* say. In the very opening words of the epistle, he describes himself as "Jude, a bondservant of Jesus Christ, and brother of James" (v. 1).

Who is this "James"? As we have seen, James is the lead name in both of the biblical lists of Joseph and Mary's natural sons. The apostle Paul (in Galatians 1:19) likewise mentions "James, the Lord's brother" as a key leader in the early Jerusalem church. In 1 Corinthians 9:5, Paul includes a general reference to "the brothers of the Lord" without naming any of them. There he speaks of them as distinct from the apostles, but he clearly accords them a similar importance in the work of the early church.

The James and Judas who were Jesus' half brothers are the only brothers with those names explicitly mentioned anywhere in Scripture. The father of the apostle Judas Lebbaeus Thaddaeus was a different man named James,[1] and the similarity of the names has unfortunately caused many people—including some fine commentators—to confuse the apostle Thaddaeus with Jude, author of our epistle. But they are not the same.

By the way, the "James" mentioned in Jude 1 was no apostle, either. The only *apostle* named James (son of Salome and Zebedee, and brother of John the beloved apostle) was martyred very early by Herod, according to Acts 12:1–2. He was long dead by the time Jude wrote. So the best-known James in the church when Jude introduced himself this way is the one whom Paul calls "James, the Lord's brother" (Galatians 1:19). He is the same James who wrote the New Testament epistle bearing his name. He also appears as the main spokesman for the Jerusalem church in Acts 15:13.

Now notice what Jude *doesn't* say about himself. He nowhere claims the title of an apostle. That fact would be odd indeed if our author were truly one of the original Twelve. Moreover, Jude seems to remove all doubt about whether he was one of the apostles in verses 17–18, where he specifically distinguishes himself from the apostles, referring to them in the third person ("*they* told you" [emphasis added]).

Second, notice that Jude likewise does not explicitly identify himself as Jesus' younger brother. That might seem strange at first glance, but it is understandable given the complexities of such a relationship and the history of Jude's own journey to faith.

Remember that Jesus' own brothers did not originally believe in Him. Mark 6:1–6 describes the same events as Matthew 13:54–58. The people of Nazareth "were astonished, saying, 'Where did this Man get these things? And what wisdom is this which is given to Him, that such mighty works are performed by His hands! Is this not the carpenter, the Son of Mary, and brother of *James, Joses, Judas,* and *Simon*? And are not His sisters here with us?' So they were offended at Him" (vv. 2–3, emphasis added).

The list in Mark 6:3 includes the very same names as Matthew 13:55, but Mark reverses the final two, putting Judas third and Simon last. James is first on both lists. The order suggests that James was the eldest of the four and "Judas" (as he is called in both lists) was one of the younger sons in the family of Joseph and Mary—perhaps the youngest of five boys (including Jesus, who of course was older than all His half brothers and sisters). Their ages in relationship to one another are never given, but Jude was at least four or five years behind his eldest brother. At this point in his life, he was apparently still living in his parents' home. Mark 6:3 seems to imply that the whole family was present when the village of Nazareth turned against Jesus, so Jude would have been an eyewitness to these events.

As a young man, Jude appears to have been confused by the fierce opposition to Jesus, and at first he himself was swept up in skepticism. John 7:5 says that during Jesus' earthly ministry, "even His brothers did not believe in Him." Later, of course, Jude *did* believe. But at first, he seems to have followed the crowd in their rejection of Jesus' authority.

So understanding Jude's true identity and his familial relationship to Christ gives us an interesting insight into the character of this man and what fueled his passion for defending the truth. His own experience—nearly being led astray by giving too much credence to popular opinion—certainly explains the intensity of his own zeal as a mature warrior for the truth.

A final reason for identifying Jude as Jesus' half brother is found in the sheer paucity of information Jude finds it necessary to give about himself. He and his family were apparently quite well-known in the early church, because even though he claims no title and cites no personal credentials, he requires little introduction. It was sufficient to identify himself in verse 1 simply as "a bondservant of Jesus Christ, and brother of James." Since there was no better-known James in the early church, and since no other brothers named "James" and "Jude" (or "Judas") are ever mentioned anywhere else in the Bible, the conclusion seems inescapable that "Jude . . . brother of James" is the same "Judas" named twice in the Gospels as a half brother of Christ.

How amazing that two of Jesus' own earthly brothers were used by the Spirit of God to write New Testament books. Neither was an apostle, but their work was recognized by the apostles and the early church as divinely inspired. And these epistles were both inspired and preserved by the Spirit of God and handed down to us as part of the New Testament canon.

Jude's humble identification of himself as "a bondservant of Jesus Christ" tells us a lot about this man. In Jude's own mind, whatever earthly connection he had with Jesus as a half brother by blood, and whatever personal relationship he had with Jesus as a close family member and younger brother, everything earthly gave way to a much more profound spiritual and heavenly relationship, in which Jude regarded Jesus as sovereign Lord and divine Master over his life.

> AS A YOUNG MAN, JUDE APPEARS TO HAVE BEEN CONFUSED BY THE FIERCE OPPOSITION TO JESUS, AND AT FIRST HE HIMSELF WAS SWEPT UP IN SKEPTICISM. JOHN 7:5 SAYS THAT DURING JESUS' EARTHLY MINISTRY, "EVEN HIS BROTHERS DID NOT BELIEVE IN HIM." LATER, OF COURSE, JUDE *DID* BELIEVE. BUT AT FIRST, HE SEEMS TO HAVE FOLLOWED THE CROWD IN THEIR REJECTION OF JESUS' AUTHORITY

That is particularly fascinating when we reflect on the earlier unbelief of Jude and his brothers (John 7:5). Apparently, *all* Jesus' unbelieving siblings became believers after the Resurrection. These two, James and Jude, clearly became influential church leaders. And although Jesus' other siblings are not mentioned by name outside the Gospels, they likewise must have been eyewitnesses to the

Resurrection. Acts 1:14 strongly implies that they all became believers, because it says, "Mary the mother of Jesus, *and* . . . *His brothers*" (emphasis added) were together with the apostles, all praying in one accord in the Upper Room just prior to Pentecost.

Since a mere forty days elapsed between Jesus' crucifixion (on Passover) and the descent of the Holy Spirit at Pentecost, it appears Jesus' earthly siblings came to saving faith after He died for them.

Jude must have been deeply humbled by his earlier unbelief, and he certainly would have been in awe of the reality that his eldest half brother was actually the incarnate Son of God, who died for Jude's sin and unbelief and then rose triumphantly from the dead. That event evidently changed Jude's whole perception of Jesus and who He was. He no longer thought of Him as a mere brother. Thus Jude simply refers to himself as "a bondservant of Jesus Christ"—and mentions that he is brother to James.

## A Sudden Change of Agenda

Although we are nowhere given the details of Jude's conversion or experience as a believer, by the time he penned his famous epistle, it was clear that he had become a respected voice of authority among the saints and an effective warrior for the truth. He doesn't identify his original audience. It could be a single church or a group of churches. He seems to have had Jewish believers predominantly in mind, as the epistle is full of Old Testament imagery. But there are no other solid clues about the original recipients of this epistle. Moreover, Jude wastes no time in the introduction establishing or defending his own credentials. It is plain to see that he was already well-known and highly regarded by the people to whom he wrote.

And Jude likewise knew them well. He was certain of their calling (v. 1). He gave them a warm but very brief blessing of

"Mercy, peace, and love" (v. 2). He called them "Beloved" (v. 3). He wrote as a familiar friend and spiritual mentor.

But Jude also wrote with a tone that is as urgent as the epistle is brief. Verses 3–4 explain the gravity of the issues that compelled Jude to write. He had initially intended to write an edifying message of comfort and encouragement about the salvation all believers enjoy. But he was dissuaded from that goal before he even began to write: "Beloved, while I was very diligent to write to you concerning our common salvation, I found it necessary to write to you exhorting you to contend earnestly for the faith which was once for all delivered to the saints. For certain men have crept in unnoticed, who long ago were marked out for this condemnation, ungodly men, who turn the grace of our God into lewdness and deny the only Lord God and our Lord Jesus Christ" (vv. 3–4).

The apostle Paul began his epistle to the Galatians with a similar note of urgency and solemnity, foregoing the gracious words of commendation that were an essential part of Paul's normal pattern. Even when he wrote to the problem-filled church at Corinth, Paul had words of approval and appreciation for them (see, for example, 1 Corinthians 1:4–9 and 2 Corinthians 1:7). But the great apostle completely omitted any note of encouragement when he wrote to the Galatians. Hardly a word of endorsement or praise for them can be found anywhere in the entire epistle. Instead, he pronounced a somber double curse against false teachers in their midst (Galatians 1:8–9). The opening nine verses of Galatians seem designed to leave readers shaken and breathless, and thereby to jolt them away from the false teachers' seductive influence.

Jude is driven by similar concerns, and he likewise hurries to the point. In some ways, the opening verses of Jude are even more abrupt than Galatians 1. Verses 3–4 constitute one of the most compelling and sobering introductions to any epistle in the New Testament. Think of it: Jude is saying that he sat down to write a positive,

WE SOMETIMES TEND TO THINK OF THE EARLY CHURCH AS PRISTINE, PURE, AND UNTROUBLED BY SERIOUS ERROR. THE TRUTH IS, IT WASN'T THAT WAY AT ALL. FROM THE VERY BEGINNING, THE ENEMIES OF TRUTH LAUNCHED AN EFFORT TO INFILTRATE AND CONFUSE THE PEOPLE OF GOD BY MANGLING THE TRUTH AND BY BLENDING LIES WITH CHRISTIAN DOCTRINE. ATTACKS AGAINST THE TRUTH REGULARLY CAME NOT ONLY FROM PERSECUTORS ON THE OUTSIDE BUT ALSO FROM FALSE TEACHERS AND PROFESSING BELIEVERS WITHIN THE VISIBLE COMMUNITY OF THE CHURCH.

encouraging epistle celebrating the joys of salvation, but—grasping the current urgency and willingly following the Holy Spirit's sovereign control and inspiration—he was compelled to write something other than he had intended. His letter thus became a short, strongly worded warning urging them to fight for the faith.

What do you suppose happened to make Jude change the tone and substance of what he wrote? Jude doesn't say. Perhaps before he got started writing, he received information from somewhere—a report, a letter, or an eyewitness account telling him of a threat to the spiritual well-being of this flock. Or it could simply be that the Lord supernaturally revealed something to him that prompted this change in the message.

Whatever the case, the Holy Spirit compelled Jude to take up an issue he had not planned to address. The glorious salvation about which Jude had planned to write was in danger of being severely compromised unless the church rose to the occasion of fighting for the gospel.

So what evidently started out as a warm, friendly attempt to offer comfort and encouragement turned out instead to be a shrill call to arms. The whole epistle is a war cry that applies to all believers in all ages. Jude urges us to join the Truth War and side with the Lord.

Does it amaze you to think this was necessary even in the days of the apostles? We sometimes tend to think of the early church as pristine, pure, and untroubled by serious error. The truth is, it wasn't that way at all. From the very beginning, the enemies of truth launched an effort to infiltrate and confuse the people of God by mangling the truth and by blending lies with Christian doctrine. Attacks against the truth regularly came not only from persecutors on the outside but also from false teachers and professing believers within the visible community of the church. Satan's strategy of placing his ministers within the church to sow bad doctrine was proving dangerously effective even while the New Testament was still being written (2 Corinthians 11:14–15).

Incidentally, Jude's epistle contains a nearly exact repetition of the words of the apostle Peter in 2 Peter 2:1–3:4, which had almost certainly already been written and circulated. In fact, we're drawn to the conclusion that 2 Peter was written before Jude because Jude 18 quotes 2 Peter 3:3, and in verse 17, Jude expressly acknowledges that it was from an apostle. Also, 2 Peter 2:1–2 and 3:3 anticipate the coming of false teachers; Jude expressly states that "certain men *have* crept in unnoticed" (v. 4, emphasis added; cf. 11–12, 17–18).

So false teachers had already infiltrated the church. They were at that moment safely ensconced in the community of believers. They were being accepted as fellow believers, and their poisonous false teaching was spreading in the church. Jude urged believers to oppose them rather than embrace them. The life of the church depended on it.

## STEALTH APOSTASY

False teaching by deceptive spiritual terrorists infiltrating the church has always plagued the church. Whether they are conscious of it or not, false teachers are satanic missionaries sent to produce more apostates. Satan's design is to lead people who have been exposed to the gospel away from it into damning error. There are always people in and around the church who have heard the truth and understood it but who have not yet embraced it and committed to it savingly. They can be led to reject it, and that is exactly what the evil one hopes to accomplish.

This problem was not unique to the congregation Jude was addressing. Apostasy is a familiar theme in Scripture. Jude is the only book of the Bible solely devoted to the subject (thus highlighting the urgency of Jude's message). But many of the New Testament epistles have quite a lot to say about the dangers of apostasy and false doctrine. This was clearly a major, widespread problem from the very earliest days of church history. Several of the Epistles—in particular Hebrews, 1 and 2 Corinthians, Galatians, Colossians, 1 and 2 Thessalonians, 2 and 3 John—were prompted in part or in whole by the need to address the errors of various false teachers who were leading people astray.

This was not unexpected, of course. Jesus Himself told a familiar parable illustrating how easily some people fall away from truth into apostasy. The parable of the soils is found in Matthew 13 and Luke 8, and it pictures God's Word as seed being sown in four types of soils: hard soil, shallow soil, weedy soil, and good soil. The soils represent human hearts in various stages of receptivity. Jesus explained the symbolism of the parable in Luke 8:11–15:

> "Now the parable is this: The seed is the word of God. Those by the wayside are the ones who hear; then the devil comes and takes away

the word out of their hearts, lest they should believe and be saved. But the ones on the rock are those who, when they hear, receive the word with joy; and these have no root, who believe for a while and in time of temptation fall away. Now the ones that fell among thorns are those who, when they have heard, go out and are choked with cares, riches, and pleasures of life, and bring no fruit to maturity. But the ones that fell on the good ground are those who, having heard the word with a noble and good heart, keep it and bear fruit with patience."

Notice: three of the four soils picture people who hear the Word and turn away. Some (the hard-soil hearers) turn away almost immediately because "the devil comes and takes away the word out of their hearts, lest they should believe and be saved." They are careless hearers—heedless, spiritually unresponsive people upon whom the Word of God has no lasting effect.

Others (the weedy-soil hearers) may show early signs of life but never bear any fruit because, before the Word of God can bear fruit in their lives, worldly desires choke the life out of any spiritual interests these people ever had. They may appear to grow and thrive for a time, but they never really experience conversion (which is the first and most essential "fruit" alluded to in this parable). And in the end, they fall away. As long as these worldly, superficial hearers identify with the people of God, they are a threat to the spiritual well-being of the church.

But the greatest threat of all comes from the shallow-soil hearers. They "receive the word with joy; [but they] have no root. [They] believe for a while [but] in time of temptation fall away." Their initial response to the gospel is all positive—even enthusiastically so. They give every appearance of genuine life and viability. But "these have no root," and therefore their "faith" cannot last. It will never bear any true spiritual fruit because it isn't even real faith. Such people "believe for a while" only in the most cursory sense:

they hear the truth, understand the truth, and superficially affirm the truth. But because they have no root, they will never produce authentic fruit.

Jude 12 actually borrows from the exact same imagery as the parable of the soils, describing apostates as "autumn trees without fruit, twice dead, pulled up by the roots." These superficial "saints" are actually rootless, fruitless, and dead. So they inevitably fall away.

That is the very essence of apostasy: hearing the truth, knowing what it is, professing to accept it, and then finally rejecting it. Because the final disavowal of the truth occurs with full knowledge and understanding, this is a fatal apostasy from which there is no hope of recovery. It is precisely the sin described in such chilling terms in Hebrews 6:4–6: "It is impossible for those who were once enlightened, and have tasted the heavenly gift, and have become partakers of the Holy Spirit, and have tasted the good word of God and the powers of the age to come, if they fall away, to renew them again to repentance, since they crucify again for themselves the Son of God, and put Him to an open shame."

Jesus' parable of the soils pictures what Hebrews 6 describes. It is also exactly what Jude is writing about: *apostasy.*

Apostasy is not merely a problem for peripheral or obviously half-hearted disciples. Christian leaders sometimes apostatize too. Because they love power and prestige—or because of other equally sinister motives, such as lust (Jude 4; 2 Peter 2:10) and greed (Jude 11; 1 Timothy 6:5)—even when they "fall away," apostate leaders don't necessarily leave the visible church. They frequently remain and continue to function as preachers, teachers, or authors. Certainly, they *pretend* to be Christians. They cover up their defection with subtlety. They profess faithfulness to the truth even as they try to undermine its foundations. Influential people who profess or pretend to believe the truth although they do not savingly believe it are probably the greatest internal danger the church faces.

Church history is filled with examples of this—from the Judaizers whose false gospel confused the Galatian churches, to the many corrupt televangelists of today whose avarice, moral failures, false prophecies, phony "miracles," and erroneous doctrine are a reproach to Christianity and a stumbling block to the undiscerning.

To some degree, apostasy is always a willful and deliberate sin. An apostate is not someone who is merely indifferent to God's Word or ignorant about what it teaches. Someone who has never even heard the truth is not an "apostate," even though he or she might be a teacher in a false religion. Apostasy is a far worse sin than that. An apostate is someone who has received the light but not the life, the seed but not the

> INFLUENTIAL PEOPLE WHO PROFESS OR PRETEND TO BELIEVE THE TRUTH ALTHOUGH THEY DO NOT SAVINGLY BELIEVE IT ARE PROBABLY THE GREATEST INTERNAL DANGER THE CHURCH FACES.

fruit, the written Word but not the living Word, the truth but not a love for the truth (2 Thessalonians 2:10).

That is not to suggest that apostates themselves are never deluded or confused. Usually these deceivers are themselves subject to blinding kinds of deception (2 Timothy 3:13). They may actually imagine that in some sense they are serving the cause of truth (cf. John 16:2). But at one point or another, they have willfully rejected the truth with sufficient knowledge and understanding to be fully responsible for it. That is what makes the sin of apostasy so evil: it begins with a deliberate rejection of the truth after the truth has been heard and understood.

Acts 8:9–25 gives a classic biblical example of how apostasy can occur. There we meet Simon, a magician who, according to Luke, had made his reputation by astonishing the people of Samaria with "sorcery" (most likely by sleight of hand), claiming he was someone great and powerful. In other words, Simon was a professional con artist. According to Luke, the people of Samaria believed Simon's tricks were wrought by "the great power of God" (v. 10).

But when the gospel came to Samaria, everything changed.

Verses 12–13 say, "When [the Samaritans] believed Philip as he preached the things concerning the kingdom of God and the name of Jesus Christ, both men and women were baptized. Then Simon himself also believed; and when he was baptized he continued with Philip, and was amazed, seeing the miracles and signs which were done."

We can be certain that Philip's message was a clear, complete, accurate, faithful presentation of the gospel of Jesus Christ. People—evidently lots of them—were being baptized. Philip was having a profound evangelistic impact among the Samaritans, and the gospel reverberated so deeply into the community that even Simon the magician "believed."

How authentic Simon's faith at first *appeared* is seen in the fact that he was baptized and "continued with Philip" and was amazed at what he saw. Signs and wonders (truly great miracles, not tricks) were taking place, and Simon was genuinely astonished. An expert in clever illusions and hocus-pocus, he saw plainly and understood immediately that Philip was no cheap grifter. He could see right away that Philip's message was truth, and Simon's initial response was all positive. At least on a superficial level, he "believed." That is, when he saw the truth and understood it, he didn't reject it outright.

But verses 18–19 tell us, "When Simon saw that through the laying on of the apostles' hands the Holy Spirit was given, he offered them money, saying, 'Give me this power also, that anyone on whom I lay hands may receive the Holy Spirit.'" Apparently, when the apostles laid hands on the new believers in Samaria, there was some visible manifestation of the Holy Spirit's coming to that person. In all likelihood, the Samaritan converts spoke in tongues miraculously (not with mere gibberish, but in known, recognizable languages) just as the first believers at Pentecost had. The outpouring of languages would have been a clear sign that the Samaritans were receiving the same Holy Spirit on the same terms as the original Jewish believers, lest there be a division in the church. When Simon witnessed such a wondrous sign, he desperately wanted the power to perform that miracle at will.

Remember, Simon had believed, been baptized, continued with Philip, observed all the signs, and was constantly and positively amazed. By all outward appearances, his faith seemed authentic. But Peter said to him, "Your money perish with you, because you thought that the gift of God could be purchased with money!" (v. 20). Peter clearly regarded Simon's request as evidence that the magician was not a real believer at all. "You have neither part nor portion in this matter, for your heart is not right in the sight of God" (v. 21).

That, by the way, is known as the *direct* method of confronting an apostate.

Notice that in Peter's subsequent call for Simon's repentance, the apostle speaks of forgiveness in almost hypothetical terms, suggesting that Simon's sin was so serious that it might not even be forgivable: "Repent therefore of this your wickedness, and pray God if perhaps the thought of your heart may be forgiven you. For I see that you are poisoned by bitterness and bound by iniquity" (vv. 22–23).

Simon pleaded for Philip to pray for him, "that none of the things which you have spoken may come upon me" (v. 24). He was obviously shaken and terrified by Philip's rebuke—for the moment, at least.

Simon's sense of dread at the prospect of his own apostasy does not seem to have lasted long. Apparently he fell away from Christ forever that very day. He is never again mentioned by Luke (or anywhere else in the biblical record). But Justin Martyr, an apologist in the early church who was himself a Samaritan and who lived barely a generation after Simon's time, recorded some details about Simon, and there is no reason to doubt Justin's account. He says Simon was from the Samaritan village of Gitta. Justin and Irenaeus (a close contemporary of Justin's and fellow apologist) both record that Simon began one of the very first quasi-Christian cults. According to Irenaeus, the magician borrowed biblical imagery and biblical terminology and adapted them to various myths that he invented about himself—including the blasphemous claim that Simon himself was the true God incarnate. Simon is regarded by many early church historians as the founder of the first full-fledged gnostic sect. He is known in church history as Simon Magus, and from his name is derived the term *simony*, the practice of selling ecclesiastical offices for money. No one is more dangerous to the Christian faith than an aggressive apostate. The career of Simon gave early proof of that.

> THOSE WHO HAVE SEEN THE TRUTH OF THE GOSPEL, PROFESSED TO BELIEVE IT, AND THEN TURNED AWAY FROM THE FAITH HAVE NO HOPE OF REDEMPTION. BOTH HEBREWS 6:4–6 AND 10:26–30 CONDEMN THAT KIND OF APOSTASY WITH A TONE OF UTTER FINALITY, SUGGESTING THAT THOSE WHO FALL AWAY WILLFULLY NEVER DO COME BACK TO THE FAITH.

Those who have seen the truth of the gospel, professed to believe it, and then turned away from the faith have no hope of redemption.

Both Hebrews 6:4–6 and 10:26–30 condemn that kind of apostasy with a tone of utter finality, suggesting that those who fall away willfully never do come back to the faith. Peter likewise said of apostates, "If, after they have escaped the pollutions of the world through the knowledge of the Lord and Savior Jesus Christ, they are again entangled in them and overcome, the latter end is worse for them than the beginning. For it would have been better for them not to have known the way of righteousness, than having known it, to turn from the holy commandment delivered to them" (2 Peter 2:20–21).

But people in that position often do devote their lives to attacking the truth they have rejected—and they normally use subtlety to do it. The rest of their lives, they say things like, "I've been there; done that—and it doesn't work. I used to believe that, but it's not true. I'm enlightened now. Let me enlighten you too." Or, as so many today are prone to say, "I used to be sure that I knew and understood what Scripture means; but I'm not so arrogant as to make that claim anymore."

Again, this is a classic echo of the serpent's message to Eve: "Has God indeed said . . . ? Well, listen to me instead, and your eyes will be opened, and you will be like God" (cf. Genesis 3:1, 5).

## THE LONG WAR FOR THE TRUTH

Like sin itself, apostasy is by no means a recent phenomenon, and it is not even something unique to the Christian era. From that moment in the garden when the serpent brought his war against truth into the world of humanity—through the close of the Old Testament canon and beyond, right down to the present day—the campaign against truth has been unrelenting and shockingly effective.

Again and again in the Old Testament, Israel was solemnly warned not to defect. Apostates nonetheless can be found in every period of Old Testament history. At times, it seemed as if the entire nation had apostatized at once. In Elijah's generation, for instance (at a time when the total population of Israel almost surely could be counted in the millions), the number of the faithful dwindled to some seven thousand (1 Kings 19:18). Elijah even imagined for a while that he was the last true believer alive!

During Jeremiah's lifetime, the size of the faithful remnant was probably smaller still. Almost everyone in Israel was utterly hostile to Jeremiah's ministry. After four decades of powerful preaching, the great prophet stood essentially alone. Scripture gives no indication that he ever saw a single convert.

Throughout Old Testament history, the problem of apostasy was pervasive, and times of widespread faithfulness in the nation, such as the sweeping revival described in Nehemiah 8, were exceptional and mostly short-lived. Nehemiah's revival quickly gave way to a watered-down and halfhearted form of religion (see Nehemiah 13). Spiritual lukewarmness dominated Israel's later history. The whole nation finally became so utterly apostate that when the promised Messiah was born, virtually everyone missed the true significance of the event. Within three years of the start of His public ministry, they were crying for Him to be murdered as a dangerous imposter and threat to their religion. From a human perspective, it might even seem as if the enemies of truth usually had the upper hand in the Old Testament era.

It is no surprise, then, that the word *apostasia* appears several times in the Septuagint (an ancient Greek translation of the Old Testament that predates Christ by a couple of hundred years). In Joshua 22:22, for example, apostasy is characterized as "rebellion [and] treachery" against "the LORD God of gods." Jeremiah 2:19 likewise employs the word *apostasia* to describe the backslidings of those who utterly forsook the Lord. That same verse defines the essence of all apostasy: "'The fear of Me is not in you,' says the Lord GOD of hosts."

So apostasy, appalling and dismal though it is, has been an ever-present reality throughout all of redemptive history. Many people who know the truth reject it anyway, and thus it has always been. In that respect, the times in which we live are by no means extraordinary.

Even Jesus' ministry provides a startling picture of real-life apostasy. John 6 records how large crowds showed up wherever He went while He was performing miracles. But they turned away en masse when He began to proclaim truth they did not want to hear. In most cases, it appears, their rejection of Christ was nothing less than final and irremediable apostasy. Near the end of that long, tragic chapter, verse 66 says this: "From that time many of His disciples went back and walked with Him no more."

Jesus' teaching made the truth starkly clear. These people, who evidently saw the truth plainly and understood Jesus' teaching perfectly well, turned away anyway. In fact, the utter clarity of the truth was the very thing that drove them away. When they saw the truth for what it was, they simply hated it. It was too demanding, too unpopular, too inconvenient, too much of a threat to their own agenda, and too much of a rebuke to their sin. Remember, "men loved darkness rather than light, because their deeds were evil" (John 3:19).

So that is how the New Testament era *began.* Scripture also teaches that apostasy will be widespread at the *end* of the age. In the Olivet Discourse, Jesus gave an extended description of the last days, including this: "Many false prophets will rise up and deceive many" (Matthew 24:11). Peter likewise prophesied that "scoffers will come in the last days, walking according to their own lusts, and saying, 'Where is the promise of His coming?'" (2 Peter 3:3–4). In 1 Timothy 4:1–2, the apostle Paul says, "The

Spirit expressly says that in latter times some will depart from the faith, giving heed to deceiving spirits and doctrines of demons, speaking lies in hypocrisy, having their own conscience seared with a hot iron." As a matter of fact, one of the major turning points at the end of this age will be a worldwide renunciation of the truth and a wholesale rejection of Christ, known as "the falling away" (apostasia), according to 2 Thessalonians 2:3.

So apostasy is a fact of all history, and there is never any kind of armistice in the Truth War. Our generation is certainly no exception to that rule. Some of the greatest threats to truth today come from within the visible church. Apostates are there in vast abundance—teaching lies, popularizing gross falsehoods, reinventing essential doctrines, and even redefining truth itself. They seem to be everywhere in the evangelical culture today, making merchandise of the gospel.

But false teachers aren't necessarily even that obvious. They don't wear badges identifying themselves as apostates. They usually try hard not to stand out as enemies of truth. They pretend devotion to Christ and demand tolerance from Christ's followers. They are often extremely likable, persuasive, and articulate people. According to Jude, that is what makes apostasy such an urgent matter of concern for the church. It produces people who can infiltrate the church by "[creeping] in *unnoticed*" (Jude 4, emphasis added).

Paradoxically, people sometimes imagine today that there are no such things as false teachers and apostates, since Christianity has become so broad and all-embracing. There is no need to engage in a battle for the truth—since truth itself is infinitely pliable and thus capable of making room for everyone's views. Some have even suggested that truth is broad enough to accommodate all well-intentioned ideas from non-Christian religions. The problem of apostasy, then, is especially acute in the radically tolerant climate of today's postmodern drift.

Many Christians today are weary of the long war over truth. They are uneasy about whether doctrinal disagreements and divisions are a blight on the spiritual unity of the church and therefore a poor testimony to the world. These and similar questions are constantly heard nowadays: "Isn't it time to set aside our differences and just love one another?" "Rather than battling people with whom we disagree over various points of doctrine, why not stage a cordial dialogue with them and listen to their ideas?" "Can't we have a friendly conversation rather than a bitter clash?" "Shouldn't we be congenial rather than contentious?" "Does the current generation really need to perpetuate the fight over beliefs and ideologies? Or can we at last declare peace and set aside all the debates over doctrine?"

> FALSE TEACHERS AREN'T NECESSARILY EVEN THAT OBVIOUS. THEY DON'T WEAR BADGES IDENTIFYING THEMSELVES AS APOSTATES. THEY USUALLY TRY HARD NOT TO STAND OUT AS ENEMIES OF TRUTH. THEY PRETEND DEVOTION TO CHRIST AND DEMAND TOLERANCE FROM CHRIST'S FOLLOWERS.

Of course, there is a legitimate concern in the tone of such questions. Scripture commands us: "If it is possible, as much as depends on you, live peaceably with all men" (Romans 12:18). "Pursue peace with all people" (Hebrews 12:14). "The fruit of the Spirit is love, joy, peace, longsuffering, kindness, goodness, faithfulness, gentleness, self-control" (Galatians 5:22–23). Taken together, these passages make it clear that what Scripture demands of us is the polar opposite of a cantankerous attitude. No one who exhibits the fruit of the Spirit can possibly take delight in conflict. So it should be plain that the call to contend for the faith is not a license for pugnacious spirits to promote strife deliberately over insignificant matters. Even when conflict proves unavoidable, we are not to adopt a mean spirit.

But conflict is not always avoidable. That is Jude's whole point in writing his epistle. To remain faithful to the truth, sometimes it is even necessary to wage "civil war" within the church—especially when enemies of truth posing as brethren and believers are smuggling dangerous heresy in by stealth.

## WHEN IT'S TIME TO GO TO WAR

Jude's words stress the pressing urgency and the absolute necessity of the Truth War: "I found it necessary to write to you exhorting you to contend earnestly for the faith" (v. 3). The expression "contend earnestly" is translated from a strong Greek verb *epagonizomai*, literally meaning "agonize against." The word describes an intensive, arduous, drawn-out fight. There is nothing passive, peaceful, or easy about it. Jude "exhorted" them—meaning he urged and commanded them—to wage a mighty battle on behalf of the true faith.

Jude himself says he felt the necessity to write this command. He employs a verb that speaks of pressure. In other words, he sensed a strong, God-given compulsion to write these things. He was not writing them because he took some kind of perverse glee in being militant. He was not responding to a momentary whimsy or personal anger. This was critical, and since the writers of Scripture never wrote by human self-will, but only as they were moved by the Spirit of God (2 Peter 1:21), the extreme urgency of Jude reflects the sovereign influence of the Holy Spirit, and therefore also the mind of Christ.

We thus have an urgent mandate from God Himself to do our part in the Truth War. The Holy Spirit, through the pen of Jude, is urging Christians to exercise caution, discernment, courage, and the will to contend earnestly for the truth.

Notice what we are supposed to be fighting for. It is not anything petty, personal, mundane, or ego related. This warfare has a very narrow objective. What we are called to defend is no less than "the faith which was once for all delivered to the saints."

Jude is speaking of apostolic doctrine (Acts 2:42)—objective Christian truth—*the* faith, as delivered from Jesus through the agency of the Holy Spirit by the apostles to the church. As he says in verse 17: "Remember the words which were spoken before by the apostles of our Lord Jesus Christ."

Notice: no one discovered or invented the Christian faith. It was delivered to us. It was not as if someone mystically ascended into the transcendental realm and drew down an understanding of the truth. We don't need an enlightened guru to open the mysteries of the faith for us (cf. 1 John 2:27). The truth was entrusted by God to the whole church—intact and "once for all." It came by revelation, through the teaching of the apostles as preserved for us in Scripture. Jude speaks of "the faith" as a complete body of truth already delivered—so there is no need to seek additional revelation or to embellish the substance of "the faith" in any way. Our task is simply to interpret, understand, publish, and defend the truth God has once and for all delivered to the church.

That is what the Truth War is ultimately all about. It is not mere wrangling between competing earthly ideologies. It is not simply a campaign to refine someone's religious creed or win a denominational spitting contest. It is not a battle of wits over arcane theological fine points. It is not an argument for sport. It is not like a school debate, staged to see who is more skilled or more clever in the art of argumentation. It is not merely academic in any sense. And it is

> WE MUST NOT TAKE OUR CUES FROM PEOPLE WHO ARE PERFECTLY HAPPY TO COMPROMISE THE TRUTH WHEREVER POSSIBLE "FOR HARMONY'S SAKE." FRIENDLY DIALOGUE MAY SOUND AFFABLE AND PLEASANT. BUT NEITHER CHRIST NOR THE APOSTLES EVER CONFRONTED SERIOUS, SOUL-DESTROYING ERROR BY BUILDING COLLEGIAL RELATIONSHIPS WITH FALSE TEACHERS.

certainly not a game. It is a very serious struggle to safeguard the heart and soul of truth itself and to unleash that truth against the powers of darkness—in hopes of rescuing the eternal souls of men and women who have been unwittingly ensnared by the trap of devilish deception.

This is a battle we cannot wage effectively if we always try to come across to the world as merely nice, nonchalant, docile, agreeable, and fun-loving people. We must not take our cues from people who are perfectly happy to compromise the truth wherever possible "for harmony's sake." Friendly dialogue may sound affable and pleasant. But neither Christ nor the apostles ever confronted serious, soul-destroying error by building collegial relationships with false teachers. In fact, we are expressly forbidden to do that (Romans 16:17; 2 Corinthians 6:14–15; 2 Thessalonians 3:6; 2 Timothy 3:5; 2 John 10–11). Scripture is clear about how we are to respond when the very foundations of the Christian faith are under attack, and Jude states it succinctly: it is our bounden duty to contend earnestly for the faith.

Notice carefully: Jude is not suggesting (nor am I) that Christians should contend among themselves over every petty disagreement or divide into factions over every personality conflict. In fact, that is the very thing the apostle Paul condemned in

1 Corinthians 3:3–7. Divisiveness and sectarianism are terrible sins that hurt the church when major divisions are manufactured out of petty differences over trivial, doubtful, indifferent, or less-than-vital matters (Romans 14:1).

Now, you might think that the difference between a picayune disagreement and a serious threat to some core truth of Christianity would always be obvious and clear-cut. Usually, it is. Most of the time, it is easy enough to see the distinction between a peripheral issue and a matter of urgent and fundamental importance. But not always. And here is where mature wisdom and careful discernment become absolutely crucial for every Christian: sometimes serious threats to our faith come in subtle disguise so that they are barely noticeable. And false teachers like to surround their deadly error with some truth. Therein lies the seduction. We must never assume that things like the teacher's reputation, the warmth of his personality, or majority opinion about him are perfectly safe barometers of whether his teaching is really dangerous or not. We also shouldn't imagine that common sense, intuition, or first impressions are reliable ways of determining whether this or that error poses a serious threat or not. Scripture, and Scripture alone, is the only safe guide in this area.

As we are about to see, that is one of the key lessons church history has to teach us.

# 4

## CREEPING APOSTASY: HOW FALSE TEACHERS SNEAK IN

*For certain men have crept in.*

—Jude 4

You can't necessarily tell a false teacher by the way he or she appears. Every false religious leader is, after all, "religious" by definition. Looking saintly is practically part of the job description. Jesus referred to purveyors of false religion as wolves in sheep's clothing (Matthew 7:15), and "whitewashed tombs . . . beautiful outwardly, but . . . full of dead men's bones and all uncleanness" (Matthew 23:27). In other words, their religion is an effort at clever camouflage.

Like the Pharisees whom Jesus targeted with those words, most false teachers are experts at feigned piety. Their masquerade can be quite convincing. They maintain a carefully polished veneer of charm and innocence—and at least the appearance of some kind of "spirituality." They usually come with permanent smiles, gentle words, likable personalities, and vocabularies full of biblical and spiritual words.

There are notable exceptions to this rule, of course. Grigory Rasputin, for example, was a licentious Russian Orthodox mystic, religious healer, and self-styled "holy man" whose influence corrupted the court of Tsar Nicholas II of Russia and helped bring about the downfall of the Romanov Dynasty in the early twentieth century. Rasputin looked and acted the way we might expect an overtly evil man to be. He rarely bathed, by all accounts he smelled bad, he was loud and rude, and his lascivious appetites were legendary. Yet he still managed to accumulate a large following of mostly female admirers, many of them coming from the highest ranks of regal St. Petersburg's society.

And who could forget Gene Scott, the eccentric televangelist from Southern California whose trademarks included a fat cigar, the lavish use of profanity and off-color remarks (even in his televised teaching), an extremely autocratic style, and a perpetually surly attitude, which he wore on his sleeve? His lifestyle was as flagrantly self-indulgent as his preaching style was crass. Donors to Scott's "church" signed pledges granting him sole authority to use their contributions any way he pleased. He was the polar opposite of what most people imagine a spiritual leader should be. He nonetheless attracted a significant following and amassed millions in personal assets.

If someone so plainly debauched and unspiritual can gain a large following of clueless disciples, imagine the dangers false teachers pose when they try to seem genuinely devout. Just picture what an enemy of the truth could do if he pretended to be a sincere believer and gained a reputation in the church as a respectable teacher.

As a matter of fact, most false teachers are not so conspicuously unspiritual as Rasputin or Gene Scott. They usually do a passable job of imitating the fruit of the Spirit. They disguise themselves as ministers of righteousness (2 Corinthians 11:14–15). They seem quite sincere. They look and sound and seem harmless enough. They know how to use spiritual-sounding language. They can even quote Scripture with some degree of skill. They know the truth well enough to use it for their own ends—sometimes taking cover behind one truth while they attack another. They know exactly how to gain trust and acceptance from the people of God.

Rarely are their assaults on the truth open and head-on attacks. Instead, they prefer to work underground, drilling little holes in the foundations of truth itself. They do this by suggesting subtle re-definitions, by making crafty modifications, or by suggesting that contemporary Christianity needs to reimagine, update, or simply jettison some supposedly obsolete doctrine. They usually try to sound as innocuous as possible while planting as many doubts as they can. Those doubts are like sticks of dynamite in the foundation holes they have drilled. They are actually working toward the wholesale demolition of the entire structure.

That is what Jude was speaking about when he warned about false teachers who "have crept in unnoticed" (v. 4). He was not describing an utter pagan who slipped in the side door under the cloak of disguise and covertly attended a single church service. He was talking about people who had already gained widespread acceptance and respect as members of the flock. In the worst cases, they had even attained some status as leaders and teachers in the church. They were now using their influence to undermine the Christian faith quietly and subtly for their own wicked ends.

Although at first glance these men might have *seemed* like valid and respectable leaders in the church, they were in fact the most dangerous kind of false teachers. They were spiritual para-sites, feeding on the church for their own selfish benefit. Despite whatever facade of spirituality they must have worn, their real motives were the same as the most wantonly licentious spiritual deviant. Under the mask they wore, they too were secret Rasputins—"ungodly men, who turn the grace of our God into lewdness and deny the only Lord God and our Lord Jesus Christ" (Jude 4).

Jude 12 in some English translations refers to these imposters as "spots in your love feasts" (v. 12). The Greek word translated "spots" is a very specific term often used to signify dangerous reefs in the sea, hidden just under the water's surface. In other words, these false teachers represented a deadly spiritual hazard. They deliberately lay in wait. They were hard to spot. But they were capable of causing disastrous spiritual shipwrecks (cf. 1 Timothy 1:19).

Yet Jude says, "In your love feasts . . . they feast with you without fear, serving only themselves" (v. 12). The term love feasts is a reference to the Lord's Table ordinance established by Christ for the church and the common meal that accompanied it. So Jude was speaking about people inside the church, familiar communicants at the table, who looked safe, seemed nice enough, and were well-known to people in the church. But in reality, they were counterfeit Christians with an evil agenda.

Can someone like that be even more dangerous than the hostile critic who stands outside the church and overtly opposes everything the Bible teaches? Absolutely. False teachers and doctrinal saboteurs inside the church have *always* confused more people and done more damage than open adversaries on the outside. Is an attacking enemy who promises his arrival in advance and wears a uniform for easy identification as dangerous as a terrorist who is hidden and acts with deadly surprise? The answer is obvious.

## AS IT WAS IN THE BEGINNING . . .

Since day one of church history, Christians have found it necessary to resist wave after wave of relentless assaults from countless enemies in the Truth War. But the most determined enemies and the most serious threats have always come from within the visible church herself. Someone who claims to be a Christian attacks some essential Christian truth, and the battle is on.

This pattern of attack from within became clear very early—even before the New Testament canon was complete. Jude was certainly not dealing with an isolated incident or a rare anomaly in some remote congregation. The enemy sows his tares everywhere the gospel goes, it seems. The New Testament indicates that false teachers rose up very early from almost every quarter of the primitive church. Don't forget that every writer in the New Testament at one point or another touches on this issue of false teaching inside the church. The theme also permeates Christ's messages to the churches in Revelation 2–3. The glorified Lord repeatedly commends those who have remained vigilant and who have purged false teachers from their midst (2:2, 6, 9); and He likewise rebukes those who seem oblivious to the problem—or even worse, who deliberately tolerate heretics in their congregations (2:14–16, 20).

> SPIRITUAL TERRORISTS AND SABOTEURS WITHIN THE CHURCH POSE A FAR MORE SERIOUS THREAT THAN MANIFESTLY HOSTILE FORCES ON THE OUTSIDE. FROM THE VERY START OF THE CHURCH AGE, ALL THE MOST SPIRITUALLY DEADLY ONSLAUGHTS AGAINST THE GOSPEL HAVE COME FROM PEOPLE WHO PRETENDED TO BE CHRISTIANS—NOT FROM ATHEISTS AND AGNOSTICS ON THE OUTSIDE.

It is also quite clear from the biblical record that spiritual terrorists and saboteurs within the church pose a far more serious threat than manifestly hostile forces on the outside. From the very start of the church age, all the most spiritually deadly onslaughts against the gospel have come from people who pretended to be Christians—not from atheists and agnostics on the outside. Moreover, the numerous occasions when false teaching showed up in the early church involved a surprising variety of errors.

An incident in Thessalonica, for example, reveals the extremes to which false teachers will sometimes go. Someone apparently orchestrated a scheme to make people in the Thessalonian church think the Lord had already returned to gather His people to Himself and the Thessalonians had been left behind. They received a phony letter, purporting to be from the apostle Paul, notifying them that the day of the Lord was already here (2 Thessalonians 2:1–2). A wave of fear swept through the church. "The day of the Lord" in Scripture always speaks of a time of cataclysmic judgment—a massive future outpouring of divine wrath that will ultimately usher in the final judgment and destruction of the whole sin-cursed universe (cf. 2 Peter 3:10). The Thessalonians no doubt began to wonder if their current sufferings might be only the beginning of many worse things to come. Had they for some reason been left to endure the Great Tribulation?

Evidently, the bogus letter had even been corroborated both "by spirit" (probably through a false prophecy) and "by word" (possibly by a lying witness who claimed to have heard the message from Paul's own mouth). But it was all just an elaborate ruse designed to discourage and confuse that church.

In another episode, referred to in 2 Timothy 2:17, Paul warned Timothy against the influence of Hymenaeus and Philetus, "who have strayed concerning the truth, saying that the resurrection is already past; and they overthrow the faith of some" (v. 18). That apparently wasn't an unusual case either, because Paul urged Timothy to be on guard against other heretics of the same sort and to shun them (v. 16).

The apostle John had a similar word of caution about the influence of a power-hungry leader in the church named Diotrephes, "who loves to have the preeminence"—and who had apparently made a career of opposing the apostle John (3 John 9).

So it is absolutely clear from Scripture that heretics, apostates, rebels, and false teachers infiltrated the church very early and in surprising abundance. And when Jude wrote this Spirit-inspired caution about the influence of false teachers who sneak in unnoticed—"ungodly men, who turn the grace of our God into lewdness and deny the only Lord God and our Lord Jesus Christ" (v. 4)—he wasn't speaking only to a single church facing an unusual peril. This is a message that applies to every true believer in every age.

What, specifically, might have prompted the urgency of Jude's message? He seems to have been addressing a significant and widespread error of a particular sort. Evidently, whatever threat he had in mind wasn't the teaching of a single individual, and it wasn't merely the vague possibility that some unknown person here or there might start teaching another lie. He was responding to a coordinated assault involving multiple false teachers whom Jude had in mind specifically—"certain men"—who posed a real and present danger.

Interestingly, Jude nowhere names these men or comments on the specific content of their false teaching. His main concern here is simply to underscore the absolute necessity for faithful Christians to be truth warriors. He is writing about the *principle* of contending for the faith, and he is highlighting the common characteristics of all false teachers. That is the big picture we need to keep in mind, and Jude didn't cloud the issue by being any more specific than he had to be.

But he does clearly seem to have a specific group of false teachers in mind. He may have been talking about the Judaizers (the same false, pharisaical cult Paul confronted repeatedly). Or he may have been dealing with some of the very early gnostics. Both sets of false teachers fit Jude's description perfectly. Those are the two waves of widespread heresy that stand out most clearly on the pages of the New Testament.

It is worth taking a closer look at what Jude and the apostles were up against.

# THE JUDAIZERS

The Judaizers mounted one of the earliest, most widespread, and most dangerous onslaughts against the gospel. They insisted that to be truly justified, Gentiles needed to observe certain Old Testament rituals (especially the rite of circumcision). The book of Galatians is Paul's answer to that heresy, and remember, he starts his reply to the Judaizers by summarily pronouncing a divine curse on them and their false gospel. The same false teaching is also addressed in Acts 15, in the book of Hebrews, and here and there throughout the New Testament Epistles, so this was quite a pervasive error and one of the very earliest examples of false doctrine that rose up from within the church.

Of course, the Judaizers claimed to be Christians, and they were accepted by almost everyone in the church as authentic believers. As a matter of fact, in Galatians 2:12, Paul refers to those who brought this error to Antioch as "certain men [who] came from James"—so the original Judaizers may have been men of some status in the Jerusalem church (where James, brother of Jude, was a leader). They may even have been sent by James on a legitimate mission to seek aid, to minister, or simply to establish ties of fellowship with the Gentile churches in the regions where Paul was ministering. But they seized the opportunity to undermine the clarity of the gospel and to confuse Gentile believers.

Because their teaching fatally corrupted the gospel, Paul instantly saw that the Judaizers' doctrine needed to be refuted and firmly opposed lest the gospel be lost to error within the church. Other key leaders in the early church, however, including the apostle Peter, were not as quick to see the danger. Galatians 2 is Paul's description of his obviously frustrating struggle to get the other apostles and key church leaders to take this heresy as seriously as he did. That is the same chapter where Paul recounts the famous incident in Antioch when he had to rebuke Peter publicly. He did so because Peter seemed to lend credibility and encouragement to the Judaizers.

The Judaizers' doctrine grew out of an extremely subtle error, which, at first glance, hardly seemed worth much of a fight. J. Gresham Machen (a famous theologian and author who took a bold stand against liberal theology at the start of the twentieth century) observed that from a purely rational point of view, the difference between Paul and the Judaizers might seem "very slight." The whole difference could be boiled down to a single point and stated in a simple proposition. In Machen's words:

> The difference [between Paul and the Judaizers] concerned only the logical—not even, perhaps, the temporal—order of three steps. Paul said that a man (1) first believes on Christ, (2) then is justified before God, (3) then immediately proceeds to keep God's law. The Judaizers said that a man (1) believes on Christ and (2) keeps the law of God the best he can, and then (3) is justified. The difference would seem to modern "practical" Christians to be a highly subtle and intangible matter, hardly worthy of consideration at all in view of the large measure of agreement in the practical realm.[1]

Machen then envisioned how a modern thinker might wish to deal with the kind of dispute Paul had with the Judaizers. Of course, in Machen's time, as in ours, the prevailing view was that for the sake of promoting moral reform in secular society, evangelicals should actively cooperate with anyone whose views on moral and spiritual issues so closely align with their own. Machen even envisioned what an ecumenical coalition might have meant in Paul's context. What if Paul regarded the Judaizers as "co-belligerents" and worked alongside them to try to sweep paganism out of the Galatian region? Machen wrote:

> What a splendid cleaning up of the Gentile cities it would have been if the Judaizers had succeeded in extending to those cities the observance of the Mosaic law, even including the unfortunate ceremonial observances! Surely Paul ought to have made common cause with teachers who were so nearly in agreement with him; surely he ought to have applied to them the great principle of Christian unity.[2]

Many Christians in Machen's generation wanted to declare a truce like that with modernism. Today there is the same pressure from evangelicals who want to accommodate *post*modernism. But, said Machen:

> Paul did nothing of the kind; and only because he (and others) did nothing of the kind does the Christian Church exist today. Paul saw very clearly that the difference between the Judaizers and himself was the difference between two entirely distinct types of religion; it was the difference between a religion of merit and a religion of grace. If Christ provides only a part of our salvation, leaving us to provide the rest, then we are still hopeless under the load of sin.[3]

In other words, the problem with the Judaizers was not merely that they disagreed with what Paul taught—but that their disagreement involved such a vital point. The whole gospel hinged on the very proposition that the Judaizers denied: *Sinners are justified solely on the basis of what Christ has already done on their behalf, and not in any way because of anything they do for Him.*

The way Paul dealt with the Judaizers is the only right way to respond to false teachers who corrupt or compromise essential elements of the gospel. They must be exposed for what they are, and their doctrines must be refuted with the clear proclamation of truth from Scripture. That is precisely what Jude is calling for when he commands us to contend earnestly for the faith.

As we have stressed already, Jude, Paul, and the apostle John all *commanded* Christians to fight for the truth (and even to cut off their fellowship with deliberate false teachers) whenever essential doctrines are at stake. The fact that certain serious errors may *appear* slight or insignificant at first glance does not diminish our duty to be discerning, cautious, and critical in our evaluations. In fact, the realization that even an apostle like Peter could be temporarily fooled by the subtlety of these false teachers ought to make us even *more* alert to the potential evils of seemingly "small" errors that can so easily undermine the heart of gospel truth.

This is serious business for every Christian in every era of church history, including ours. The Judaizers were by no means unique to that day and age. Similar threats to the gospel have arisen from within the church in every generation since apostolic times.

## THE GNOSTICS

Before the controversy with the Judaizers was completely quelled, another battle had already broken out on a whole new front in the Truth War. Primitive forms of gnosticism began to creep into the church. Most of the later New Testament Epistles argue against ideas that were fundamentally gnostic. The doctrinal arguments John makes in his first epistle, for example, make a fine catalogue of replies to some of the favorite false doctrines of gnosticism.

Gnosticism was not a single, unified cult. Gnostic thinking offered the possibility of "designer" religions, where each false teacher could basically invent his own unique sect. That is why gnosticism as a system wasn't easy to refute and isn't easy to describe. The ideas of one gnostic group weren't necessarily held by other gnostics. It took much labor and diligence to contend against this diverse set of false doctrines. And over several centuries' time, gnostics produced hundreds of varieties of counterfeit Christianity.

Every form of gnosticism starts with the notion that truth is a secret known only by a select few elevated, enlightened minds. (Hence the name, from *gnosis*, the Greek word for knowledge.)

> THE WAY PAUL DEALT WITH THE JUDAIZERS IS THE ONLY RIGHT WAY TO RESPOND TO FALSE TEACHERS WHO CORRUPT OR COMPROMISE ESSENTIAL ELEMENTS OF THE GOSPEL. THEY MUST BE EXPOSED FOR WHAT THEY ARE, AND THEIR DOCTRINES MUST BE REFUTED WITH THE CLEAR PROCLAMATION OF TRUTH FROM SCRIPTURE. THAT IS PRECISELY WHAT JUDE IS CALLING FOR WHEN HE COMMANDS US TO CONTEND EARNESTLY FOR THE FAITH.

Gnostics offered a sinister smorgasbord of ideas, myths, and superstitions, all borrowed from pagan mystery religions and human philosophy. Those beliefs were then blended with Christian imagery and terminology. When the gospel accounts of Jesus' teaching didn't fit gnostic doctrines, gnostics simply wrote their own fictional "gospels" and passed them off as more enlightened accounts of Christ's life and ministry.

Gnostic teachers accumulated both wealth and followers by promising their disciples the secret knowledge—for a price, of course. Naturally, most gnostic cults claimed to have a monopoly on the secrets of the universe. Because various groups of gnostics did not necessarily agree among themselves about what the secret knowledge was, gnosticism was a highly competitive brand of heresy, and most of its purveyors were therefore skilled polemicists.

Every major form of gnosticism was actually pagan to the core, but because gnostics had a peculiar tendency to synthesize Christian doctrine and symbolism with their worldly philosophies, they fooled many Christians. They borrowed biblical terminology and elements of Christian teaching. But they redefined all the terms and revamped all the teaching. Then they masqueraded as Christians and advertised their religion as a more enlightened version of Christianity. Gnostic leaders often aligned with established churches to gain credibility. They aggressively recruited followers from within the church itself. Because the gnostics employed familiar Christian terminology and professed faith in Christ, many in the church were uncertain about whether to embrace them as brethren or reject them as heretics.

Major struggles between early gnosticism and the gospel dominated the second century. That is why some of the most important figures who stand out in that era of church history were *apologists* (defenders of the true faith). They were men who responded to the urgent necessity of distinguishing authentic Christianity from all the cultish flavors of gnosticism. The best-known apologists of the second century included Ignatius of Antioch, Irenaeus, Justin Martyr, and Tertullian. Their main focus was a defense of the incarnation (the truth that God literally became a man)—because that was one of the main doctrines the gnostics always attacked.

In fact, most of the major doctrinal controversies in the first two centuries of church history stemmed directly from the struggle between the gnostics and the Christian apologists. The efforts of gnostics to blend into the church and subvert the truth under the cover of church membership quickly became a far greater danger and a more immediate threat to the long-term health and viability of the church than all the persecutions that were ever carried out by Roman emperors.

Just as the Judaizers' doctrine obscured the gospel by burying it under Jewish tradition, gnosticism altered every distinctive of Christian truth by overlaying it with pagan ideology. Like the Judaizers, the gnostics denied justification by faith and thereby shifted the focus of the gospel. The message they proclaimed instead was all about what people need to do to gain *enlightenment* (the gnostic substitute for salvation)—rather than the truth of what Christ did to save helpless sinners from divine judgment. Since gnosticism attacked truth at the very foundations, every variety of this error needed to be answered and strongly opposed. And this was no easy task.

One example of how gnostics tried to subvert the doctrine of the incarnation involved one of the very earliest gnostic sects, led by a false teacher named Cerinthus. He taught that Jesus (the human person) was actually indwelt by a divine spirit-being known as "the Christ." Cerinthus therefore insisted that Jesus' deity was an illusion. According to this flavor of gnosticism, Jesus' divine nature was something extraneous to Him—an attribute that belonged to a divine spirit who possessed Him—and not anything essential to His own true nature. In other words, Jesus and "the Christ" were supposedly two distinct beings who simply shared the same body. That doctrine confused many people in the early church, and the apostle John therefore refuted it thoroughly in his epistles. He wrote, for instance, "Who is a liar but he who denies that Jesus is the Christ?" (1 John 2:22).

Another dominant variety of gnosticism (known as *Docetism)* taught that all the manifestations of Jesus' human nature—including His physical body (and hence His crucifixion and resurrection)—were only illusions. God could not *really* have come to earth in the true material form of authentic human flesh, the Docetists said, because matter itself is evil. The apostle John replied to that error and all others like it when he wrote, "By this you know the Spirit of God: Every spirit that confesses that Jesus Christ has come in the flesh is of God, and every spirit that does not confess that Jesus Christ has come in the flesh is not of God. And this is the spirit of the Antichrist, which you have heard was coming, and is now already in the world" (1 John 4:2–3).

> BECAUSE GNOSTICISM CONSTANTLY MUTATED AND METAMORPHOSED AND SPAWNED NEW ERRORS, GNOSTIC THOUGHT WAS LIKE A PERSISTENT VIRUS ATTACKING BIBLICAL CHRISTIANITY FOR MANY CENTURIES. AS A MATTER OF FACT, GNOSTICISM WAS NEVER TOTALLY AND THOROUGHLY EXTERMINATED. SOME OF THE MOST ANCIENT EXPRESSIONS OF GNOSTIC ERROR ARE EXPERIENCING A POWERFUL COMEBACK IN THE CURRENT GENERATION.

Gnosticism (and every error of a similar magnitude) is exactly what John had in mind in 2 John 10–11, where he gave clear instructions about how to respond to a pseudo-Christian teacher who denies the core truths of Christian doctrine: "Do not receive him into your house nor greet him; for he who greets him shares in his evil deeds." John evidently applied that principle in his own practice too. Irenaeus (who was born shortly after John died and was personally acquainted with people who had sat under John's teaching) records that John once refused to enter a public bathhouse in Ephesus when he learned Cerinthus was inside. So much did John love the truth and hate falsehood that he refused any kind of fellowship (or even casual association) with the peddlers of gnostic notions.

Because gnosticism constantly mutated and metamorphosed and spawned new errors, gnostic thought was like a persistent virus attacking biblical Christianity for many centuries. As a matter of fact, gnosticism was never totally and thoroughly exterminated. Some of the most ancient expressions of gnostic error are experiencing a powerful comeback in the current generation.

You may have noticed quite a lot of publicity lately about early pseudo-Christian documents such as *The Gospel of Thomas* and *The Gospel of Judas*. In 2006 even *National Geographic* released a television special heralding *The Gospel of Judas* as if it were a monumental new discovery hitherto unknown to Bible scholars. Actually, the "gospels" of Thomas and Judas are both well-documented gnostic works. They are pure fiction masquerading as history—full of demonstrably false claims and fanciful mythology. Scholars of every kind (Christian and secular scholars alike) all agree that although these works are authentic relics of early gnostic teaching, they cannot possibly be what the *gnostics* claimed they were. Like virtually all other gnostic writings, they are anonymous frauds, full of gnostic lies.

Furthermore, these books do not really contain any newly uncovered or long-forgotten truths. The existence of these works and many others like them has always been well-known to scholars. *The Gospel of Judas*, for example, was first mentioned at the end of the second century by Irenaeus, who connected it with an especially evil cult of gnostics who had made heroes of Cain, Esau, the men of Sodom, Korah, and all the other villains of Scripture.[4] They produced *The Gospel of Judas* in order to portray Judas as a hero. The work turns the biblical account of Jesus' life and ministry on its head, borrowing truth from Scripture here and there—but then poisoning it with out-and-out lies. That is the kind of satanic truth twisting that gnostics have always been best known for.

In a very similar way, the popular best-selling novel and motion picture *The Da Vinci Code* is based on a handful of revived gnostic myths blended with more recent conspiracy theories and held together with some rather inventive gnostic-style historical revision-ism. The book is sold as fiction, but author Dan Brown often claims the story is based on historical facts. The premise that "facts" are involved has proved sufficient to create the illusion in some people's minds that the entire Da Vinci conspiracy is not fiction at all, but some deep, secret, long-guarded knowledge that is finally being revealed. That sort of attack on biblical Christianity is classically gnostic.

## A CAUTION FOR THE PRESENT TIME

What was happening in Jude's day is still happening today. The enemy's strategy in the Truth War hasn't changed. Therefore Jude's admonition applies to us as much as it applied to the original recip-ients of the epistle. False teachers still assault the church with quasi-Christian ideas. Heretics also still arise from within the church itself, and they still demand recognition and tolerance from Christians, even while they are laboring hard to undermine the very foundations of true faith. They are even repeating all the same lies. Their teach-ing must be opposed and clearly refuted with the plain truth of God's Word. The apostle Paul said something similar, but in even stronger terms: "[their] mouths must be stopped" (Titus 1:11).

Now, as we have stressed already, neither Paul nor any other New Testament writer ever sanctions violence, physical force, or carnal weaponry in the Truth War. On the contrary, such things are emphat-ically and repeatedly condemned (Matthew 26:52; 2 Corinthians

10:3–4). Titus 1:11 is by no means an exception to that principle. Paul is in no way suggesting that heretics' mouths must be stopped by physical force. He is very clear about how Titus was to silence the "insubordinate . . . idle talkers and deceivers" (v. 10): Titus needed to confront and refute their lies thoroughly with the clear proclamation of the truth. There is a negative aspect to that: "Rebuke them sharply, that they may be sound in the faith" (v. 13). And there is a positive duty as well: "As for you, speak the things which are proper for sound doctrine" (2:1).

Even though it is clear from the context that Paul is not advocating the use of any kind of brute violence, his statement about stopping the mouths of false teachers has both a tone of authority and a settled certainty to it that make it sound less-than-politically-correct to postmodern ears. This is not a message well suited for our age.

But then again, Scripture has always been contrary to worldly culture. We need to allow Scripture to rebuke and correct the spirit of our age, and never vice versa. Unfortunately, the visible church today is filled with people who have decided that biblical discernment, doctrinal boundaries, and the authority of divinely revealed truth are worn-out relics of a bygone era. They are weary of the battle for truth, and (in effect) they have already unilaterally ceased resistance. As we've noted from the start, Christians today often actually seem more distressed about believers who think the Truth War is still worth fighting than about the dangers of false doctrine. Their complaint has become a familiar refrain: "Why don't you just lighten up? Why don't you ease off the campaign to refute doctrines you disagree with? Why must you constantly critique what other Christians are teaching? After all, we all believe in the same Jesus."

But Scripture clearly and repeatedly warns us that not everyone who claims to believe in Jesus really does. Jesus Himself said *many* would claim to know Him who actually do not (Matthew 7:22–23). Satan and his ministers have always masqueraded as ministers of righteousness (2 Corinthians 11:15). We are not ignorant of his devices (2 Corinthians 2:11). After all, this has been his strategy from the very start.

So it is the very height of folly (and disobedience) for Christians in the current generation to decide all of a sudden that in the name of "love" we ought to sweep aside every aberrant idea about the gospel and unconditionally embrace everyone who claims to be a Christian. To do that would be to concede the whole battle for truth to the enemy.

We *must* continue the fight.

# 5

## HERESY'S SUBTLETY:
## WHY WE MUST REMAIN VIGILANT

*Certain men have crept in unnoticed.*

—Jude 4

Jude's command "to contend earnestly for the faith" is not merely being neglected in the contemporary church; it is often greeted with outright scorn. These days anyone who calls for biblical discernment or speaks out plainly against a popular perversion of sound doctrine is as likely as the false teachers themselves to incur the disapproval of other Christians. That may even be an understatement. Saboteurs and truth vandals often seem to have an easier time doing their work than the conscientious believer who sincerely tries to exercise biblical discernment.

Practically anyone today can advocate the most outlandish ideas or innovations and still be invited to join the evangelical conversation. But let someone seriously question whether an idea that is gaining currency in the evangelical mainstream is really biblically sound, and the person raising the concern is likely to be shouted down by others as a "heresy hunter" or dismissed out of hand as a pesky whistle-blower. That kind of backlash has occurred with such predictable regularity that clear voices of true biblical discernment have nearly become extinct. Contemporary evangelicals have almost completely abandoned the noble practice of the Bereans, who were commended for carefully scrutinizing even the apostle Paul's teaching. They "searched the Scriptures daily to find out whether these things were so" (Acts 17:11).

> THE MORE AGGRESSIVELY SOMETHING IS MARKETED TO CHRISTIANS AS THE LATEST, GREATEST NOVELTY, THE LESS LIKELY MOST EVANGELICALS ARE TO EXAMINE IT CRITICALLY. AFTER ALL, WHO WANTS TO BE CONSTANTLY DERIDED AS A GATEKEEPER FOR ORTHODOXY IN A POSTMODERN CULTURE? DEFENDING THE FAITH IS A ROLE VERY FEW SEEM TO WANT ANYMORE.

But in our generation it sometimes seems as if the more aggressively something is marketed to Christians as the latest, greatest novelty, the less likely most evangelicals are to examine it critically. After all, who wants to be constantly derided as a gatekeeper for orthodoxy in a postmodern culture? Defending the faith is a role very few seem to want anymore.

In England, where the reigning monarch is titular head of the Anglican Church, one of the important subsidiary titles that goes with the crown is "Defender of the Faith." (The common abbreviation appears on all British coins as FD, for *fidei defensor.*) In all candor, almost none of England's monarchs have really deserved such a label or taken the duty very seriously. In fact, the formal title dates back to the time of Henry VIII, a man for whom the title was ludicrous—because his lifestyle was notoriously sinful, memorable mostly for his shoddy treatment of several successive wives.[1]

Prince Charles, current heir apparent, announced in 1994 that he would prefer to tweak the title so as not to elevate Christianity over Islam, Hinduism, or Wicca: "I personally would rather see it as Defender of Faith, not *the* Faith," he said.[2] In a verbal cascade of perfect postmodern eloquence, the prince went on to say that he views himself as a defender "of the divine in existence, the pattern of the divine which is, I think, in all of us but which, because we are human beings, can be expressed in so many different ways."

Prince Charles's discomfort with the kingly title is an exact parallel to what has happened in the evangelical movement. After years of neglecting to defend the faith, many evangelicals now simply refuse the duty. They have become uncomfortable with the whole idea of militancy in defense of the truth. They have in effect embraced the postmodern axiom that dialogue is morally superior to debate, a conversation is inherently more edifying than a controversy, and fellowship is always better than a fight.

As we have seen repeatedly, Scripture clearly says otherwise. If we want to be faithful, we are *required* to become warriors in defense of truth. If the apostles and their immediate heirs had not earnestly fought for the faith, the church might have been overwhelmed by the errors of the Judaizers and the gnostics. The work done by the apostles in the first century and the apologists of the second century was heroic. Their valiant defense of the faith and their crystallization of so much doctrine—often at the cost of their very lives—illustrates why the Truth War is serious. We must be likewise willing to pay a price to fight for truth in our generation.

The early church's battles with error in their midst also exemplify why we must remain vigilant and not be lulled into a sense of false security. Every time the church wins a significant battle in the Truth War, another major assault breaks out somewhere, usually on a completely different front. The pattern is seen over and over again in church history. There has never been a truce in the Truth War. The enemy is relentless.

The Judaizers and the gnostics were by no means the last major incursions into the church by the enemy in his long war against truth. Other serious errors were also being incubated inside the church, even during those early centuries while gnosticism was gaining and losing adherents. Many of the "new" errors were spin-offs and imitations of various gnostic heresies about the incarnation of Christ. Because so much confusion and misunderstanding were sown by gnostic teaching, the question of how to understand Jesus' deity together with His humanity became a fertile ground for doctrinal disputes. By the end of the third century, several serious disagreements had already broken out within the church over the deity of Christ and the nature of the triune Godhead. These were not the same old debates between apostolic Christians and gnostics. A whole new wave of heresy developed within a segment of the church that had previously remained faithful to the apostles' teaching.

Truth never changes with the times, but heresy *always* does. In fact, heresy's sublety is seen most clearly in the ever-shifting tides of change. The church is threatened by some grave error until a defense is finally mounted, and the threat is defeated. But then the polar opposite of that error springs up somewhere with a totally different, but equally grave, threat. Then the trend shifts back to a variation of the first error. And thus it has been throughout the history of the church. No error can ever comfortably be counted as dead and gone, because the same old errors keep springing up in new dress.

## SABELLIANISM

One of the first and most troublesome false doctrines to grow out of the disputes over the person of Christ began in Rome under the influence of one of the leading teachers in the church there—a man named Sabellius. From its inception in the mid-third century, Sabellianism spread very quickly to churches all around the Mediterranean region.

Sabellius stressed the oneness of the Godhead to the extent of denying any meaningful distinctions between the members of the Trinity. He did not question the essential deity of Father, Son, or Holy Spirit. But he pointed to passages like Deuteronomy 6:4 ("Hear, O Israel: The LORD our God, the LORD is one!") and insisted that the unity of the Godhead rules out any possibility of three distinct persons. Instead, Sabellius claimed, the three names all belong to one divine person, who simply manifests Himself at different times as different characters.

Sabellius's system is sometimes referred to as *modalism*, because he was essentially claiming that God has three different "modes" of expression. Sabellians believed God transforms Himself from one of these manifestations to another consecutively, as if changing costumes. So in Sabellius's system, the Father and the Son (or the Son and the Holy Spirit) could never actually exist simultaneously as distinguishable yet coeternal divine persons.

That view, of course, entails a denial of the true nature of God as He is revealed in the New Testament. It contradicts the opening statement of John's gospel, for example: "In the beginning was the Word, and the Word was *with God,* and *the Word was God*" (John 1:1, emphasis added). It mixes up the person and work of Christ with that of the Father and the Holy Spirit. Of course, even a simple statement like the familiar gospel summary of John 3:16 ("God so loved the world that He gave His only begotten Son") makes no good sense in the Sabellian scheme of things. Sabellianism therefore seriously clouded the doctrine of the atonement, and it likewise undermined practically every other major doctrine of the Christian faith. What the Sabellians had devised was nothing less than an alternative christ and a fundamentally different version of Christianity. Their system wasn't really Christian at all.

Obviously, consistent Sabellianism would have required a complete overhaul of apostolic doctrine, changing the essential character of the faith once for all delivered to the saints. That fact stirred a number of key church leaders to rise up in opposition. The most important and most effective adversary of Sabellianism was Tertullian (who as we noted earlier was also a skilled apologist against gnosticism). Tertullian demonstrated from the New Testament that Sabellianism is seriously at odds with what God has revealed. Most of Tertullian's works were rediscovered during the Renaissance era, and they endure today as fine examples of the early church fathers' best biblical scholarship. Tertullian made a careful, systematic, scriptural case to show that the triune nature of the Godhead is one of the central doctrines of authentic apostolic Christianity—and that those who deny it have in effect rejected the faith delivered once for all to the saints. The work done by Tertullian and others was so definitive that Sabellianism has been universally rejected as a serious heresy by every major branch of Christendom since the end of the third century.[3]

## THE ARIANS

But hard on the heels of Sabellianism came an even more significant threat to the very essence of gospel truth. A new heresy known as Arianism was introduced (also by a popular teacher within the church) at the start of the fourth century. Arianism was a frontal assault on the deity of Christ. This deadly false doctrine quickly became one of the most blatant yet most aggressive of all the heresies that have ever threatened the Christian faith. The Arians flatly denied that Jesus is eternal God incarnate. They also fought obstinately for recognition as authentic Christians. So the conflict over Arianism literally became a fierce battle for the identity of the true church—and ultimately a war for the survival of Christianity itself.

Arius, the man most responsible for fabricating this belief system, began his career as a bright young presbyter and assistant to the bishop of Alexandria (a major city on the coast of North Africa). Arius had studied theology in Antioch and was ordained in Alexandria in 311 AD. He quickly gained a reputation as someone who was serious and articulate, with a keen mind and striking good looks. He came on the scene disguised as an angel of light, and he soon gained a loyal following.

Arius was wary of Sabellian influences but lacked the maturity to make wise and careful distinctions. His answer to Sabellianism was if anything worse than the original error. He claimed that the Father and the Son are two separate beings with completely different natures. So when Arius heard his bishop teaching that God the Father and God the Son share the same divine nature and substance (i.e., they are equal in their deity and eternality), Arius accused the bishop of teaching a subtle form of Sabellianism. Arius would not budge from that charge no matter how carefully the bishop explained his position.

In fact, Arius's response was to run headlong to the opposite extreme from Sabellianism. He simply denied the deity of Christ altogether and declared that Christ is a created being. "Before the Son was begotten, he was not," was Arius's way of expressing his view. When it became clear that Arius would not recant or rethink his position, he was excommunicated by his bishop.

But Arius already had a number of influential friends in positions of leadership in various churches scattered all around the empire. Even in Alexandria he had a large number of followers who continued to support him. Far from ending Arius's campaign, his excommunication only fueled it.

Arius devised crafty ways to popularize and spread his teaching. For example, he reduced his views to short lines of simple doggerel. He published the stanzas in a book known as *Thalia* (named for the muse of comedy and pastoral poetry in Greek mythology). Each of Arius's verses hammered the same consistent theme, but always in slightly different expressions: the Son is not eternal; He cannot perfectly comprehend the Father; He did not exist until God began creation; there was a time when the Father was alone; and so on. Virtually every line contained a similar denial of Jesus' deity or eternality. The words were simple and straightforward, and the meaning was bold and plain. Arius then set those lyrics to catchy tunes, and his songs quickly became the popular music of the time. Arian ideas were thus disseminated by sailors and travelers throughout the empire. In a very short time, Arius's blasphemous ditties even began to replace the hymnody of the church.

IN ARIUS'S SYSTEM, JESUS WAS NEARLY GOD BUT NOT QUITE. CAREFUL NUANCING OF ARIUS'S SYSTEM ALLOWED HIM TO MASK THE SERIOUSNESS OF HIS ERROR WITH ORTHODOX-SOUNDING WORDS, AND HE BECAME VERY SKILLED AT IT.

Arius acknowledged, by the way, that Jesus was something more than a mere man; but he insisted that He was something less than fully God—an archangel. He thus downgraded Christ's full deity to a kind of quasi perfection. So he still spoke of the "divinity" of Christ, affirmed Christ as "Lord," and acknowledged that Christ is a worthy object of worship. In Arius's system, Jesus was nearly God but not quite. Careful nuancing of Arius's system allowed him to mask the seriousness of his error with orthodox-sounding words, and he became very skilled at it. For example, Arius answered the charge that he was a heretic by insisting that he could honestly affirm, without reservation, every word of the Apostles' Creed. Although the Apostles' Creed implicitly affirms the deity of Christ by referring to the Savior as "Jesus Christ, [God's] only Son, our Lord," the idea of lordship was no problem for Arius. He affirmed "lordship," just not deity. He even affirmed that Jesus was God's "only-begotten Son." Arius simply redefined that expression in a way that divested Christ of both deity and eternality.

In fact, Arius turned the language of the creed on its head. The very idea of "sonship," he said, proves that Christ derived His being from the Father. Jesus could not possibly be both eternal and a "son." Furthermore, according to Arius, the expression "only-*begotten* Son" proves that Christ had a beginning point somewhere in time.

So Arius could wholeheartedly affirm the words of the Apostles' Creed, but not the intended meaning. Lots of Christians in that era were completely stymied by Arius's claim, unsure of what to do with someone who affirmed the basic expressions of Christian belief but interpreted the words differently. The Truth War has often hinged on precisely those kinds of fine distinctions.

# WHY ARIANISM TOOK HOLD SO EASILY

Unfortunately, a mood of ease and comfort had lulled many Christians in that generation into a state of blithe passivity about doctrine. Emperor Constantine had only recently converted to Christianity and issued the Edict of Milan (313), formally outlawing every form of persecution against the church throughout the vast empire. Constantine had also vanquished his last remaining military foe, so Rome virtually ceased from warfare after several long years of strife. Material prosperity, together with a spirit of tranquility and tolerance, swept across the whole empire. It was generally supposed that the peace and reunification of the empire were tokens of God's favor and blessing prompted directly by the emperor's conversion to Christianity. For the first time ever, an atmosphere of goodwill toward the church prevailed—even in secular Roman society. Throughout the Roman world, the church began to gain converts (not to mention cultural influence) at an unprecedented rate.

Naturally, no one was eager to incite a conflict over doctrine within the church at the very moment when it seemed the long-embattled people of God could finally enjoy peace.

Throughout most of the fourth century, therefore—during a time when people were coming into the church in massive numbers—there was almost no clear and solid consensus within the organized church on the question of what to do about Arianism. As a matter of fact, over the course of that century, those who steadfastly opposed Arian doctrine gradually became a distinct minority within the church. The few outspoken opponents of Arianism were often accused by less-discerning Christians of being harsh, overly meticulous, unduly critical, and maliciously divisive. Sound familiar? People seemed to wish the whole conflict could simply be set aside—as if it didn't matter all that much whether Jesus is truly and fully God or just nearly so.

If you only glanced at a time line of key events during that era, you might assume the Arian controversy was settled once and for all in 325, when the Council of Nicea ruled decisively against Arius's views. That famous council met at the behest of the emperor himself. Some three hundred bishops from all over the Roman Empire convened at Nicea, not far from the alternative capital the emperor was building for himself at Constantinople.

Their agenda included a short list of important issues to be discussed and settled, but the list was headed by the conflict over Arius's teaching.

The council dealt Arianism a severe blow. They handed down one of the most important and far-reaching decisions of any church council in history, unequivocally affirming the deity of Christ while anathematizing the central ideas of Arianism. Their rejection of Arianism has been echoed by the collective consensus of every major stream of Christianity since the fifth century.

But the Nicene Council's decision against Arius actually came near the beginning of the long conflict over Arianism in the church. After the Nicene Council ruled against him, Arius, disappointed but undeterred, simply continued to teach his beliefs anyway. He had powerful friends, some who were bishops in important cities throughout the empire, who continued to give him a platform, moral support, and financial backing. Although his excommunication and the ruling of Nicea against him were serious embarrassments and meant the loss of his official status as a teacher within the church, in the long run, Arius actually gained visibility, sympathy, and influence when he was forced into the role of an underdog.

> ALTHOUGH HIS EXCOMMUNICATION AND THE RULING OF NICEA AGAINST HIM WERE SERIOUS EMBARRASSMENTS AND MEANT THE LOSS OF HIS OFFICIAL STATUS AS A TEACHER WITHIN THE CHURCH, IN THE LONG RUN, ARIUS ACTUALLY GAINED VISIBILITY, SYMPATHY, AND INFLUENCE WHEN HE WAS FORCED INTO THE ROLE OF AN UNDERDOG.

That is because the politics of the dispute were on Arius's side. The emperor's main goal in convening the council in the first place was only to settle a debate in the church. Constantine really didn't seem to have strong personal convictions about the issue. He apparently did not really care one way or the other which side won the debate. He just wanted to end the conflict. Constantine himself was a novice who had not yet even received baptism. He apparently considered the whole argument a case of useless theological hairsplitting. He was weary of the conflict, and he even opened the council with an impassioned speech pleading for unity. He said he regarded discord in the church as more painful and more fearful than any war. He also expressed disappointment that while the Roman Empire was finally enjoying peace, the church was at war within itself. He urged delegates to put away the causes of strife.

The famous historian Eusebius was present at the council and wrote an account of the proceedings. His version is the most complete eyewitness report we have today. Eusebius's account is certainly not slanted in favor of the winners, because the historian took a somewhat neutral position on the conflict. While the council was in session, Eusebius actually led a behind-the-scenes effort to achieve a compromise between Arius and his opponents.

According to Eusebius, a young deacon named Athanasius was also present, serving as secretary to the bishop of Alexandria. (Bear in mind, this bishop was the same one whom Arius originally accused of Sabellianism—and he was also the one who then excommunicated Arius.) A few years later, when the bishop of Alexandria died, Athanasius became his successor. Athanasius subsequently became Arius's most devoted foe and the one man who did more than anyone else on earth to defend the deity of Christ against the original onslaught of Arian heresy. But during the Nicene Council, he was a young man of limited influence. He remained more or less a silent observer, watching and learning.

In the end, the conflict between the parties at Nicea turned on a single word—or more precisely, just one small letter. The orthodox bishops proposed a statement affirming that Christ and the Father are "of the same substance"—or *homoousion* in Greek. The Arians offered a compromise: they would affirm a statement declaring Christ and His Father *homoiousion*, or "of like substance." The difference between the two words is so small as to be almost imperceptible. It boiled down to one iota (the Greek letter corresponding to an "i") in the middle of the word. But the whole doctrine of Christ's deity hinged on that letter.

During the discussion, some excerpts were read from Arius's sermons and letters. His actual denials of Christ's deity were not as carefully toned down as the expressions of Arianism that had previously been presented to the council. When the bishops finally heard in blunt terms what Arius was actually teaching, the council overwhelmingly affirmed the famous Nicene Creed.

We believe in one God, the Father Almighty, maker of all things visible and invisible; and in one Lord Jesus Christ, the Son of God, the only-begotten of his Father, of the substance of the Father, God of God, Light of Light, very God of very God, begotten not made, being of one substance [homoousios] with the Father. By whom all things were made, both which is in heaven and in earth. Who for us men and for our salvation came down [from heaven] and was incarnate and was made man. He suffered and the third day he rose again, ascended into heaven. And he shall come again to judge both the living and the dead. And we believe in the Holy Spirit.

The following anathema was added to the creed, targeting some of the very expressions Arius had been using:

But those who say: "There was a time when he was not"; and "He was not before he was made"; and "He was made out of nothing"; or "He is of another substance" or "essence"; or "The Son of God is created" or "changeable" or "alterable"—they are condemned by the holy catholic and apostolic Church.[4]

# THE RISE OF ARIANISM
# AFTER ITS INITIAL DEFEAT

The fact that the council finally passed such a strong resolution against Arius was remarkable. Several of the bishops at Nicea apparently remained sympathetic to Arius's views. Many others (led by Eusebius) continued trying to hammer out a compromise that would accommodate both parties and restore Arius to his teaching position. Constantine, who had had no doctrinal agenda in the first place, revealed through his subsequent behavior that his concerns remained almost completely pragmatic.

Nonetheless, Arius's adversaries clearly understood the real magnitude of the issues, and they were determined. It was wise of them to let Arius's own words, taken mostly from his published works, provide the strongest evidence against his view. The council's decision, though sudden, surprising, and in the view of some observers, premature, was the right decision, secured by God's providence for the preservation of Christ's true church. Both the clear teaching of Scripture and the practically unanimous affirmation of every subsequent generation of believers gives testimony to that fact.

Arius was a wily false teacher. Although the council's condemnation of his views did not persuade him to change his mind, it did seem to motivate him to redouble his efforts. With behind-the-scenes support of several influential church leaders, Arius staged an unrelenting campaign to plead for formal reinstatement to his ecclesiastical office. More important, the unfavorable ruling of the council provoked Arius to alter his strategy in a significant way. Without actually modifying his views, he worked hard to refine his language to make himself sound as orthodox as possible. He insisted that he had been misunderstood and misrepresented. He continued to profess his adherence to all the major creeds and apostolic doctrinal formulae. He even occasionally claimed that he had no major disagreement with the Nicene Council's position. The actual difference between them was very slight, he insisted.

Of course, the Arian heresy was no insignificant matter at all. The difference between Christ as God and a false christ who is merely a created being has enormous significance in every aspect of theology. But Arius continued to defend his view, protest his excommunication, and fan the flames of controversy. Over the course of time, he won much sympathy while managing to portray his adversaries as uncharitable obstructionists. He succeeded in turning the politics of the dispute in his favor.

For one thing, the emperor himself grew wearier than ever of the argument and subsequently tried to use his power to persuade Arius's critics to find a way to compromise and reinstate the heretic. Within two years after Nicea, Constantine apparently concluded that the hard-line position taken by the council was a mistake because it had not really settled the issue. He declared amnesty for the Arian leaders and employed his enormous political clout against faithful bishops to try to enforce the amnesty. He became frustrated when Athanasius refused to compromise with the Arians, and at one point he forced Athanasius into exile. Gradually, Constantine grew increasingly contemptuous of Arianism's adversaries. When the emperor was finally baptized, it was an Arian bishop who performed the ritual.

As Arius grew more aggressive, what little opposition remained against his teaching gradually fell silent. Within a decade *after* Nicea, popular opinion had clearly shifted toward sympathy for Arius, if not for his doctrine. Over time, the campaign to receive him back into the church gained overwhelming popular support. Meanwhile, public opinion against Arius's adversaries became extremely severe.

Even when Arius died suddenly, eleven years after Nicea, popular sympathy for his doctrine continued to spread like leaven for several decades after that. At one point it seemed the whole church might become Arian. In fact, much of the visible church in the fourth century (including a large number of bishops) did ultimately fall prey to Arianism in one way or another. (Even the bishop of Rome signed an Arian creed.) Many who never formally affirmed the heresy were nonetheless perfectly willing to make peace with those who did. Jerome, who lived and ministered when Arianism was at the peak of its popularity, recounted afterward that the whole world awoke with a groan, "astonished to find itself Arian."[5] The voice in the church who continued to oppose Arianism most loudly was Athanasius. He steadfastly refused, against intense political and ecclesiastical pressure, to settle the dispute by compromise. He would not consent to the reinstatement

> MANY WHO NEVER FORMALLY AFFIRMED THE HERESY WERE NONETHELESS PERFECTLY WILLING TO MAKE PEACE WITH THOSE WHO DID. JEROME, WHO LIVED AND MINISTERED WHEN ARIANISM WAS AT THE PEAK OF ITS POPULARITY, RECOUNTED AFTERWARD, SAID THAT THE WHOLE WORLD AWOKE WITH A GROAN, "ASTONISHED TO FIND ITSELF ARIAN."

of Arius. He continued to write and preach about the deity of Christ.

When someone suggested to Athanasius that the whole world was against his unyielding, uncompromising stance in the controversy, he replied, "Then I am against the world." To this day, the slogan *"Athanasius contra mundum"* ("Athanasius against the world") is the epitaph usually associated with his name. He patiently and thoroughly refuted the Arian heresy point by point with Scripture. He remained firm no matter what the cost to him personally. In fact, over the course of his life, Athanasius was ultimately forced into exile no less than five times by a succession of emperors with strong Arian sympathies. He died before seeing the full fruits of his labors, but he is remembered today as one of the most courageous truth warriors the church has ever produced.

## Arianism's Final Demise

Even the sudden death of Arius did not instantly resolve the Arian crisis. But perhaps it did mark the beginning of the end. Arianism simply could not withstand biblical scrutiny in the long run. Without Arius's personal charisma, ability to shade word meanings, and skill at cleverly obscuring the seriousness of the error, Arianism's real character became all too obvious. The influence of this heresy soon began to decline and finally all but disappeared from mainstream Christianity. The persistence and biblical commitment of Athanasius and a handful of others finally paid off.

A letter from Athanasius to a fellow bishop records how Arius met his end in Constantinople in 336. Arius had appealed directly to Constantine for formal reinstatement to the church. By then, Constantine's eagerness to see Arius reinstated was well-known, and he agreed to a personal meeting with the heretic. Constantine listened to Arius swear that his faith was orthodox. The emperor then gave Arius a somewhat equivocal blessing: "If your faith is orthodox, you have sworn well. But if your faith is impious and yet you have sworn, let God from heaven judge you."[6]

Although Constantine's authority was civil and not ecclesiastical, the relationship between church and state under a Christian ruler was not an issue the church had dealt with before Constantine's time. Whether the emperor should have any kind of authority in church issues or not was a point that had not yet been adequately considered by most in the church. Because of the emperor's political clout, however, most bishops automatically deferred to his wishes as a matter of policy. His words of blessing upon Arius may have been regarded by most bishops as a binding order to reinstate the heretic.

Arius certainly took it that way. He left his meeting with the emperor and went straight to the church to attempt to partake of Communion. There he was refused permission by the godly bishop of Constantinople.

Some of Arius's friends who were still members in good standing in the church immediately wrote a strong protest to the bishop. As far as they were concerned, the emperor's pronouncement was a formal and legal sanction that the bishop was obliged to honor. They announced that a large group of them intended to accompany Arius to the church on the following day to receive Communion together.

Athanasius records that the bishop of Constantinople prayed, "If Arius is to be joined to the Church tomorrow, let me depart, and do not destroy the pious with the impious. But if you will take pity and spare the church . . . remove Arius, so that heresy may not come in with him, and impiety not be regarded as piety."

According to Athanasius, Arius evidently emboldened by his audience with the emperor and his friends' subsequent support, spent the afternoon making speeches and boasting of his impending triumph, until "compelled by a call of nature," he quickly excused himself. Stricken by a sudden and violent attack of cholera, Arius died that very day.

Again, Arianism did not instantly die with him. The error continued to trouble the church for at least a generation after that. But finally, owing to the convincing biblical defense made by Athanasius, the poisonous effects of Arian doctrine itself, and the rise of younger, more faithful men like Jerome to positions of influence in the church, the tide began to turn. Within a hundred years, Arianism had all but died out.

Although Arianism persists even today in quasi-Christian groups like the Jehovah's Witnesses, Mormonism, and a few lesser cults,[7] the demise of Arianism as a dominant force in church history is a testimony to the power of one man's faithful diligence in the Truth War.[8] God uses faithful warriors for the truth as His instruments to preserve the gospel for each succeeding generation. Only the unfaithful have no interest in being useful to the Lord in that way.

My salvation and yours depends on a true understanding of Christ and who He is. A false christ is a damning deception (1 John 4:15; 5:1, 5, 10–12, 20; 2 John 7–11). The doctrine of Christ is no mere academic or secondary truth. This whole episode is a prime lesson about how much is at stake in the Truth War. It is also a classic example of how false teachers use subtlety to advance their cause.

## WHY WE MUST KEEP OUR GUARD UP

The Arian conflict also exemplifies what kind of spiritual chaos false teachers can cause when the church becomes weary of conflict and decides to cease fighting for a season.

One of the main lessons of Jude's epistle is that Christians must never cease fighting. We cannot pretend error is no longer worth battling in our generation. We should not imagine that the enemy has finally shifted into retreat mode. The war against the truth goes on continuously, unrelentingly, on multiple fronts—and it always has.

Jude's epistle has a very broad sweep. That fact stands out starkly because the epistle is so short. Jude takes a condensed, fish-eye view of all history, starting from the beginning of time. He shows that the Truth War has been a perpetual reality ever since sin first entered the universe. The long struggle between truth and falsehood is one of the central themes of all history. It has been a long, protracted, uninterrupted state of siege—and we are still in the thick of the battle.

> JUDE TAKES A CONDENSED, FISH-EYE VIEW OF ALL HISTORY, STARTING FROM THE BEGINNING OF TIME. HE SHOWS THAT THE TRUTH WAR HAS BEEN A PERPETUAL REALITY EVER SINCE SIN FIRST ENTERED THE UNIVERSE. THE LONG STRUGGLE BETWEEN TRUTH AND FALSEHOOD IS ONE OF THE CENTRAL THEMES OF ALL HISTORY.

Jude mentions, for example, the fall of Satan and the angels who followed him (v. 6). He refers to Adam by name (v. 14). He speaks of the error of Cain (v. 11). He alludes to the preaching of Enoch, and hence the apostasy of that generation (v. 14–15) He recounts the immorality of Sodom and Gomorrah (v. 7), the false teaching of Balaam (v. 11), and the rebellion of Korah (v. 11). The spiritual war as he describes it covers the whole course of human history.

The big-picture perspective is deliberately designed to help us understand the sweeping saga of what God is doing. What Jude lays out in a few words is a CliffsNotes perspective on the long war against truth. The point is that we are still embroiled in that conflict today, and we cannot afford to lay down our arms. There is a good and valid reason that the church on earth has always been known as "the church militant." Our generation has by no means been granted an exemption from the necessary conflict. As a matter of fact, Christianity in our time is besieged with spiritual pretenders, and their lies are as subtle and as dangerous as ever. Some of them are even the same old lies simply recycled for a new generation.

Sabellianism, for instance, has made a strong comeback. The hallmark of "Oneness Pentecostalism" is a denial of the Trinity and a view of the Godhead that is indistinguishable from ancient Sabellianism. Yet many—perhaps *most*—in the evangelical movement today are perfectly willing to ignore the lessons of Scripture and history, set aside the whole disagreement as something entirely nonessential, and embrace contemporary Sabellianism as a legitimate expression of authentic Christian faith. For at least a decade now, evangelical best-seller lists have included a steady stream of works by authors and musicians who deny the doctrine of the Trinity. They hold to a distinctive version of *modalism.* That is the official position of "Oneness Pentecostals" and the United Pentecostal Church International. As these groups and their popular spokespersons have found increasing acceptance in the evangelical mainstream, modalism is suddenly being accepted as if it were a valid evangelical option.

In that regard, our era mirrors exactly what was happening in Athanasius's time. Multitudes have blithely declared all conflict and strife over doctrine in the church a thing of the past—as if all the serious threats to the truth had already been vanquished and the church could now ignore the threat of ungodly false teachers who creep in unnoticed.

The reality is quite different. The false church is growing. Waves of apostasy are rolling higher and higher and higher as we move ever closer to the coming of the Lord Jesus Christ. Remember that in 2 Thessalonians 2:3, Paul indicates that the final cataclysmic earthly judgment (the day of the Lord) will be preceded by "*the falling away*"—an era of apostasy, and a time of "unrighteous deception" (v. 10, emphasis added) more widespread and more spiritually devastating than anything the world has ever seen.

The ages-old war against truth is simply setting the stage for that final, desperate uprising. All of history has been one long, steady march to that goal. It is now closer than it has ever been.

# 6

## THE EVIL OF FALSE TEACHING: HOW ERROR TURNS GRACE INTO LICENTIOUSNESS

*Certain men have crept in unnoticed, who long ago were marked out for this condemnation, ungodly men, who turn the grace of our God into lewdness.*

—Jude 4

hy is it so vital to fight for the truth? Because truth is the only thing that can liberate people from the bondage of sin and give them eternal life (John 8:32; 14:6). That is precisely what Paul meant when he said the gospel is the power of God unto salvation (Romans 1:16; 1 Corinthians 1:18).

Truth (the simple truth of the gospel, to be specific) is necessary for salvation. "For 'whoever calls on the name of the LORD shall be saved.' [But how] shall they call on Him in whom they have not believed? And how shall they believe in Him of whom they have not heard? And how shall they hear without a preacher?" (Romans 10:13–14). Scripture is clear about this: there is no hope of salvation apart from hearing and believing the truth about Christ (cf. 1 Corinthians 1:21).

That is why nothing is more destructive than false religion. Mere ignorance is devastating enough: "My people are destroyed for lack of knowledge" (Hosea 4:6). But gospel-corrupting apostasy is the most sinister of all evils. It not only conceals the very core of all truth from those who most desperately need it, but it also breeds more and more iniquity.

> APOSTATE FALSE TEACHERS WHO REMAIN IN THE CHURCH AND UNDERMINE TRUE FAITH ARE OFTEN EXTREMELY SUBTLE, BUT THEY ARE NEVER HARMLESS. HERESY ALWAYS BREEDS MORE EVIL, AND THE CLOSER ANY LIE COMES TO THE HEART OF THE GOSPEL, THE MORE DIABOLICAL IS THE FRUIT IT BEARS.

As a matter of fact, apostate religion is dynamic in the same way gospel truth is—but it produces exactly the opposite results. It intensifies sin's bondage, multiplies sin's pollutions, and magnifies sin's consequences. In every way imaginable, false religion makes the calamity of sin worse than ever.

In other words, teaching gospel-corrupting error as if it were biblical truth is no insignificant sin. Apostasy is always portrayed in Scripture as a deadly danger. Apostate false teachers who remain in the church and undermine true faith are often extremely subtle, but they are never harmless. Heresy always breeds more evil, and the closer any lie comes to the heart of the gospel, the more diabolical is the fruit it bears.

Furthermore, the evil borne by false doctrine is no incidental or unintentional side effect. The actual goal—and the inevitable result—of all false doctrine is to "turn the grace of our God into lewdness" (Jude 4). That is also the true aim and ambition of every apostate. According to Jude, in the mix of the evil motives behind every heresy, you will always discover an appetite for evil things.

The driving passion of all false teachers is their lust (vv. 18–19). It may be a craving for carnal pleasure (v. 7), greed for money and material things (v. 11), or a rebellious hankering after power (v. 11). Many times it is all of the above. Look closely at any false teacher and you will see corruption caused by lust—manifest not only in the love of money and power but also in an inability to control the flesh.

Peter said exactly the same thing. Scoffers are driven by "their own lusts" (2 Peter 3:3). In fact, Peter says that one of the primary objectives of every apostate teacher is to lure people back into the bondage of immorality after they have been exposed to the liberating truth of the gospel: "When they speak great swelling words of emptiness, they allure through the lusts of the flesh, through lewdness, the ones who have actually escaped from those who live in error. While they promise them liberty, they themselves are slaves of corruption" (2:18–19).

The many striking parallels between 2 Peter and Jude indicate that both epistles were most likely written to deal with the same outbreak of apostasy. Although neither epistle can be definitively dated, it appears 2 Peter was written before Jude, because as pointed out in chapter 3, Peter was prophesying that false teachers would come, and Jude was warning that they were already there. Like Jude, Peter warned that heretics would originate within the church: "There will be false teachers among you, who will secretly bring in destructive heresies, even denying the Lord who bought them, and bring on themselves swift destruction. And many will follow their destructive ways, because of whom the way of truth will be blasphemed" (2:1–2).

And don't forget that the apostles Paul and John frequently gave similar warnings about the imminent danger of apostates within the visible church (Acts 20:28–31; 2 Timothy 3:1–9; 1 John 2:18–19). So did Jesus (Matthew 7:15; 24:23–25). It is surely significant that the Holy Spirit gave us so many reminders to remain constantly on guard. False teachers abound, and they are playing a devious charade that is a serious and perpetual threat to unwary Christians in every age and every place.

But don't imagine for a moment that God is fooled or His plans are really thwarted by the subtleties of lying, false teachers. In fact, consider the implications of all the various biblical warnings and prophecies declaring that false teachers will arise from the church. In Jesus' words, "Take heed; see, I have told you all things beforehand" (Mark 13:23). These are not merely warnings designed to make us fearful; they are also prophecies that prove God knows what He is doing. He has a plan for the false teachers too. He will accomplish all His good pleasure despite their best efforts. And because Christ Himself is building His church, the gates of hell will not prevail against it. The powers of darkness cannot win the Truth War.

Jude hints at this in verse 4 when he refers to the false teachers as "certain men . . . who long ago were marked out for this condemnation." That phrase is an implicit affirmation of God's sovereignty over the efforts of the false teachers. Try as they might, they cannot overthrow or even slightly derail the eternal purposes of God. In fact, His eternal plan included their ultimate condemnation! Jude simply states this truth without any further explanation or argument, but because so many people find the topic of God's sovereignty so difficult—*especially* when we consider God's sovereignty with respect to evildoers—it is worth some effort to try to gain a better understanding of the biblical perspective on a dilemma all of us find troublesome from time to time: Is God really sovereign over evil? If so, why hasn't He already put a stop to it?

Those are some of the hardest questions in all theology. Let's try to simplify them as much as possible.

## FALSE TEACHERS CANNOT
## THWART GOD'S SOVEREIGNTY

God is absolutely sovereign, even over false teachers. That is the main truth Jude wants to emphasize when he declares that the damnation of false teachers has been planned and prepared by God already. Their judgment was "marked out" long ago. The Greek word Jude employs is *prographo*—literally, "written out in advance." Their condemnation is preprogrammed and prerecorded in the eternal decrees of God.

Jude's statement clearly suggests, first of all, that God's ultimate judgment against the false teachers is unavoidable. Their apostasy marks them as men who are past any hope of redemption (Philippians 3:18–19; Hebrews 6:4–6; 10:26–27; 2 Peter 2:20; cf. Matthew 12:31–32; 1 John 5:16). Thus he takes a very hard line against them. There is no point in trying to persuade them, appeal to them, or rescue them from their own heresy. We *do* seek to rescue their victims from a similar fate, of course (Jude 22–23), but the false teachers themselves are people who have already seen the truth and rejected it. They are deadly, children of destruction, sons of wrath marked out for judgment.

The text also plainly means that God Himself decreed their destruction as part of His original plan. Their end was predetermined "long ago." ("Ages ago" might capture more of the true sense of the Greek expression. It is very similar to the language of 2 Kings 19:25, where God says to Hezekiah, "Did you not hear *long ago* how I [ordained judgment], *from ancient times* that I formed it? Now I have brought it to pass" [emphasis added].) In other words, the verdict concerning these apostates is not something God decided just recently. It was decreed before time began, in eternity past. It is still in effect even now—with full, infallible, divine authority.

This, of course, is an unqualified affirmation of the absolute sovereignty of God. Every tiny detail of His eternal plan will be fulfilled to absolute perfection. His grand design has always included both the false teachers and their inevitable destruction. So their evil work never disrupts any component of His plan or derails even one aspect of His good intentions. On the contrary, long ago, in God's own perfect wisdom and eternal purpose, the apostates themselves were an integral part of the original plan— and even their final doom was forever settled by God's eternal decree.

Jude is declaring the same thing Peter affirms in 1 Peter 2. These men were "appointed" by God to doom and thus ordained to judgment (v. 8). "For a long time their judgment has not been idle, and their destruction does not slumber" (2 Peter 2:3). In other words, the condemnation of these false teachers has always been operating. Their ultimate destruction is an absolute certainty, ordained from the beginning in the immutable plan of God.

> SCRIPTURE PUTS NO LIMITS ON GOD'S SOVEREIGNTY. HE EXERCISES SOVEREIGN CONTROL EVEN OVER FALSE TEACHERS AND EVERYTHING THEY DO. HE SETS THE LIMITS OF THEIR APOSTASY AND CIRCUMSCRIBES THE BOUNDARIES OF THEIR INFLUENCE. LIKE SATAN IN THE TEMPTATION OF JOB, THEY CAN DO NOTHING MORE THAN WHAT GOD SOVEREIGNLY PERMITS.

Do not misunderstand the implications of this. Scripture puts no limits on God's sovereignty. He exercises sovereign control even over false teachers and everything they do. He sets the limits of their apostasy and circumscribes the boundaries of their influence. Like Satan in the temptation of Job, they can do nothing more than what God sovereignly permits.

That does not mean, however, that God is the agent or the direct cause of any evil. We are not to imagine that God actively makes wicked people diabolical in the same sense that He sovereignly conforms true believers to the image of Christ. "Let no one say when he is tempted, 'I am tempted by God'; for God cannot be tempted by evil, nor does He Himself tempt anyone. But each one is tempted when he is drawn away by his own desires and enticed" (James 1:13–14).

God's sovereignty in no way makes Him responsible for the evil that corrupts the hearts of apostates. The fact that He has already decreed their condemnation in no way absolves them of their own guilt. Their willful renunciation of the truth is a sin for which they and they alone are entirely responsible. God does not compel them or entice them to sin. Scripture is absolutely clear about that. Guilty sinners will not be able to plead in the judgment that they are somehow "victims" of God's sovereignty, or that God is in any way to blame for their transgressions. God does not make anyone sin.

Nevertheless, God often exercises His sovereignty over the minds and wills of sinners for judicial purposes in a way that actually seals their doom and hastens their condemnation. For example, the apostle John, paraphrasing Isaiah 29:10, wrote, "He has blinded their eyes and hardened their hearts, lest they should see with their eyes, lest they should understand with their hearts and turn, so that I should heal them" (John 12:40).

Even that does not suggest that God ever coerces anyone to do evil. Consider these three main ways Scripture says God brings His sovereign influence to bear on the sinner's will: He turns stubborn hearts to stone. God sometimes hardens the hearts of evildoers (Romans 9:18). He does this the same way the sun hardens a lump of clay; not by sovereignly injecting an alien evil motive into an otherwise pure heart. In a classic sermon on Romans 9 and the hardening of Pharaoh's heart, Jonathan Edwards said this:

> When God is here spoken of as hardening some of the children of men, it is not to be understood that God by any positive efficiency hardens any man's heart. There is no positive act in God, as though he put forth any power to harden the heart. To suppose any such thing would be to make God the immediate author of sin. God is said to harden men in two ways: by withholding the powerful influences of his Spirit, without which their hearts will remain hardened, and grow harder and harder; in this sense he hardens them, as he leaves them to hardness. And again, by ordering those things in his providence which, through the abuse of their corruption, become the occasion of their hardening.[1]

God doesn't need to infuse evil intentions into a false teacher's heart to seal that person's apostasy and thus fulfill the divine decree. God simply withdraws the light of His truth, the influence of His Spirit, and the mercy of His grace—and the evildoer's own evil motives are sufficient to guarantee his own doom. He confounds unbelievers' vision. God also sometimes withholds or obscures the truth from those who hate truth anyway. In effect, He "blinds" them (John 9:39; 2 Thessalonians 2:11–12).

Of course, bright light can be as blinding as utter darkness. "The light shines in the darkness, and the darkness did not comprehend it" (John 1:5). When God sovereignly blinds someone who already loves darkness more than light (John 3:19), it certainly doesn't mean God Himself is operating in the realm of darkness or that there is any darkness in Him (1 Timothy 6:16).

He employs evil agents for His own good purposes. Sometimes the Lord will engage Satan or other "second causes" to provoke actions that stem from evil motives in the heart of a sinner (compare, for example, 2 Samuel 24:1 and 1 Chronicles 21:1; see also Ezekiel 14:7–9). But again, every evil motive behind every sinful act stems from the fallen creature, never from God.

Of course, God's own motives, purposes, and actions are emphatically pure and holy all the time (Genesis 50:20). He accomplishes good in and through *all* things (Romans 8:28)—and that includes all the evil done by all the powers of darkness. So while God may properly be said to "foreordain," "predetermine," or "decree" the actions of evildoers (2 Samuel 12:11; 16:10; Acts 2:23; 4:27–28), He does not *approve* the evil in the act. "God is light and in Him is no darkness at all" (1 John 1:5). The will to sin always stems from the sinner's own heart, not from God. He is never the author or efficient cause of evil.

## UNDERSTANDING GOD'S SOVEREIGNTY AND THE FACT OF EVIL

Whenever we consider God's sovereignty and the reality of evil alongside each other, it poses some difficult doctrinal and philosophical dilemmas. We might get sidetracked discussing those questions for a long time. But it is not necessary to trace and untangle every thread in the tapestry to see the big picture. Jude makes the main idea stand out as boldly as possible when he says the false teachers are marked out for condemnation. Here, in simple terms, is the whole point of the matter as Scripture lays it out for us: God will ultimately overthrow every wicked deed and every malicious intention of every evildoer. In the meantime, He is free to use every evil deed done by fallen creatures to bring about ultimate good. In fact, He does so without fail. But in no case does God ever do evil so that good may come.

Before leaving the subject, let me stress that two common errors must be avoided in our thinking about God's sovereignty as it relates to evil. One, of course, is this notion (sometimes advocated by certain hyper-Calvinists) that God actively and directly causes evildoers to be evil. As we have already seen, that idea violates several

> THE PICTURE OF DIVINE SOVEREIGNTY IN SCRIPTURE IS THAT GOD POSITIVELY ORDAINS WHATSOEVER COMES TO PASS. HE ALWAYS ACTS WITH A PURPOSE. EVEN THE WICKED UNWITTINGLY DO HIS BIDDING, AND THEY THUS FULFILL HIS SOVEREIGN PURPOSE IN THE END.

emphatic statements of Scripture that God is never the source or the direct agent of evil. "[He is] not a God who takes pleasure in wickedness, nor shall evil dwell with [Him]" (Psalm 5:4).

But an opposite error lies at the other end of the spectrum. We are not to think God's command over evil and evildoers is limited to a kind of passive, prescient foreknowledge in which He reluctantly and grudgingly gives His consent to something He knows evildoers are going to do anyway.

Rather, the picture of divine sovereignty in Scripture is that God positively ordains whatsoever comes to pass. He always acts with a purpose. Even the wicked unwittingly do His bidding, and they thus fulfill His sovereign purpose in the end. Here are God's own words:

For I am God, and there is no other;

I am God, and there is none like Me,

Declaring the end from the beginning,

And from ancient times things that are not yet done,

Saying, "My counsel shall stand,

And I will do all My pleasure,"

Calling a bird of prey from the east,

The man who executes My counsel, from a far country.

Indeed I have spoken it;

I will also bring it to pass.

I have purposed it;

I will also do it. (Isaiah 46:9–11)

Or to borrow Paul's words, God "works all things according to the counsel of His will" (Ephesians 1:11).

This is admittedly a difficult subject, but it is also profoundly important. And the main ideas we need to keep in mind turn out to be fairly simple: The biblical picture of God's sovereignty is that *He works in and through all that happens.* Rather than merely trying to circumvent evil or rearrange His plan to accomplish good in spite of evil, He harnesses the deeds of the wicked to accomplish His good and perfect ends. He also guarantees the ultimate destruction of evil itself. Meanwhile, nothing thwarts any aspect of His plan. Even the most stubborn actions of the worst sinners turn out to be no actual impediment to the divine purpose. He simply employs them as tools to accomplish His will.

That, after all, is precisely what Scripture says happened at the cross—which was the worst atrocity ever carried out by the collective forces of evil. But in the hands of a sovereign God, it was also the greatest good ever accomplished on behalf of sinners (Acts 2:23–24; 4:27–28).

## GOD'S ZERO-TOLERANCE POLICY FOR APOSTATES

Someone might be tempted to think that if God is sovereign and can always overrule sinners' evil intentions, the threat posed by apostasy and false teaching cannot really be critical. If everything currently happening is in complete accord with the eternal plan and decree of God, God Himself could not really be displeased with false teachers.

Of course, Scripture says otherwise. God's wrath against sin is real and terrifying.

> God is a just judge,
> And God is angry with the wicked every day.
> If he does not turn back,
> He will sharpen His sword;
> He bends His bow and makes it ready. (Psalm 7:11–12)

> Who can stand before His indignation?
> And who can endure the fierceness of His anger?
> His fury is poured out like fire,
> And the rocks are thrown down by Him. (Nahum 1:6)

God's anger against false prophets and heretics is particularly fierce. The condemnation of apostates was a common theme in the Old Testament prophetic writings. Jeremiah 5:13–14, for example, quotes this message from the Lord:

> "And the prophets become wind,
> For the word is not in them.
> Thus shall it be done to them."

Therefore thus says the LORD God of hosts:

> "Because you speak this word,
> Behold, I will make My words in your mouth fire,
> And this people wood,
> And it shall devour them."

Notice that both the false prophets and the people who departed from God's Word to follow their lying words are all devoured by God's judgment.

Hosea 9:7–9 levels this condemnation at false prophets:

The days of punishment have come;
The days of recompense have come.
Israel knows!
The prophet is a fool,
The spiritual man is insane,
Because of the greatness of your iniquity and great enmity.
The watchman of Ephraim is with my God;
But the prophet is a fowler's snare in all his ways—
Enmity in the house of his God.
They are deeply corrupted,
As in the days of Gibeah.
He will remember their iniquity;
He will punish their sins.

Various Old Testament prophecies were full of similar condemnations, all announcing, as Jude does, that the doom of the apostates was sure and certain.

Why all the repeated warnings and pronouncements of doom against people who had turned away from God? If their judgment was really sure, if God had already turned His face away, if there was no more grace that might save them, the apostates clearly were not going to turn from their error anyway.

I am convinced these warnings are primarily a message to those still under the influence of the truth. It is a deterrent, first of all, for people who might be sitting on the fence. Apostasy is nothing to trifle with. If you willfully abandon the truth after the Holy Spirit has graciously opened your eyes, there is no coming back. (Again, I believe that is the whole message of the difficult warning passages in Hebrews, especially 6:4–6; 10:26–29; and 12:15–17.) "If the salt loses its flavor, how shall it be seasoned? It is then good for nothing but to be thrown out and trampled under-foot by men" (Matthew 5:13).

But the multiple warnings are also a reminder to all the faithful about the seriousness of the Truth War. Jude is urging us to rise up and contend earnestly for the faith against apostates and their false teaching. Remember: he is dealing with gospel-corrupters and Christ-deniers, not merely people with whom we might disagree on peripheral issues. These are heretics who have abandoned the faith once delivered to the saints, and now they are trying to get others in the church to follow them in that error. We are not to allow such false teachers to remain unmolested inside the church, calling themselves Christians, spreading their evil doctrines. We don't need to be hesitant about engaging them in conflict or refuting their lying words, especially for the sake of those they are seducing. We don't need to waste a lot of angst wondering if we are alienating them—because they have already deliberately rejected the truth, and they have already been ordained to condemnation.

That is, when we attack the lies of an utter apostate with the truth, we are doing the work of God. There is no need to pull punches. Handling false doctrine with kid gloves is never a good tactic. There is no value in toning down the truth with ambiguities or withholding the hard parts. Do what Jude did: sound a clear signal. Those who are being deceived can be rescued only by the gospel. The more clearly we proclaim the message and the more starkly we set it in opposition to the error, the better.

Jude is issuing a deliberately shrill call to battle. The threat he observed was both imminent and serious. His words about these men being destined for damnation are not mere childish triumphalism. That pronouncement, preceded by Jude's militant call to contend earnestly for the faith, is meant to shock us out of lethargy. The danger these apostates posed was of far greater concern to Jude in this instance than the niceties of polite discourse.

# A TIME TO BE TOUGH;
# A TIME TO BE TENDER

Remember, Jude is writing about apostates and gospel corrupters. He is not suggesting that every trivial flaw in someone's thinking about nonessential or difficult doctrines is an occasion to bring out the heavy weapons. He is certainly not exhorting us to get militant every time there is a disagreement in the church. Sometimes, even close friends and true brothers in Christ disagree sharply. In such cases, if reconciliation proves impossible, parting company amicably is preferable to a fight (Acts 15:37–41). As the Old Testament sage reminds us, there is "a time to keep silence, and a time to speak; a time to love, and a time to hate; a time of war, and a time of peace" (Ecclesiastes 3:7–8).

I touched on this point briefly in chapter 2 and again at the end of chapter 3. But the caveat is worth stating again here with emphasis: honest disagreements between true brethren should never escalate into mortal combat (Psalm 133:1; John 13:35; 1 Corinthians 1:10; Ephesians 4:3–6). Jude's call to battle applies when there is a serious threat to "the faith which was once for all delivered to the saints"—the kind of false teaching that undermines the foundations of the gospel. The error Jude has in mind does not stem from some slight misunderstanding about a difficult text. He is talking about heresy that is ultimately rooted in willful unbelief—a denial of "the only Lord God and our Lord Jesus Christ" (Jude 4). He has in mind an error that corrupts the essential character of the gospel. He is talking about *damnable* error. He stresses that fact when he says the purveyors of such heresies are destined for condemnation. Now, bear in mind that such errors are often subtle and hard to spot. The only way to develop the discernment necessary for detecting such subtle error and correctly assessing its danger is by applying oneself conscientiously to the

> THE ERROR JUDE HAS IN MIND DOES NOT STEM FROM SOME SLIGHT MISUNDERSTANDING ABOUT A DIFFICULT TEXT. HE IS TALKING ABOUT HERESY THAT IS ULTIMATELY ROOTED IN WILLFUL UNBELIEF—A DENIAL OF "THE ONLY LORD GOD AND OUR LORD JESUS CHRIST" (JUDE 4). HE HAS IN MIND AN ERROR THAT CORRUPTS THE ESSENTIAL CHARACTER OF THE GOSPEL. HE IS TALKING ABOUT *DAMNABLE* ERROR. HE STRESSES THAT FACT WHEN HE SAYS THE PURVEYORS OF SUCH HERESIES ARE DESTINED FOR CONDEMNATION.

task of rightly dividing the Word of God (2 Timothy 2:15). That skill must be perfected over time through faithful diligence.

Furthermore, as I have stressed from the start, apostates are usually clandestine about their unbelief. The mere fact that someone professes to be a brother in Christ and insists that he is only making negligible and perfectly benign doctrinal distinctions does not make it so. In fact, that is exactly what Jude is describing: false teachers who deliberately try to remain unnoticed—who *pretend* loyalty to Christ, but whose doctrine contradicts that profession. It can be quite difficult to see past someone's phony profession of faith and assess the true gravity of his error. That is one of the main reasons harsh judgments are not to be made lightly. "Do not judge according to appearance, but *judge with righteous judgment*" (John 7:24, emphasis added).

But that verse (often erroneously cited as an argument for withholding all judgments completely) is actually the opposite: a *command* to judge righteously. We can't set aside all judgment just because discernment is difficult. Willful gullibility is disobedience to God's Word. "Do not believe every spirit, but test the spirits, whether they are of God; because many false prophets have gone out into the world" (1 John 4:1).

Still, overzealousness is clearly a danger we need to guard against carefully. There are indeed some full-time critics operating today, always looking for a fight, taking fleshly delight in controversy merely for controversy's sake, and making judgments that may be too harsh or too hasty. Don't fall into the trap of assuming that the most censorious and nitpicking opinions are automatically the most "discerning" ones. Watch out for the person who shows no caution or restraint about making severe judgments and yet claims to be a "discernment" expert. True discernment is gained by applying our hearts and minds to biblical wisdom, not by fostering a critical spirit.

As a matter of fact, Scripture says that those who are merely pugnacious or quarrelsome are unfit for spiritual leadership (1 Timothy 3:3). When Paul laid out the qualifications for church leaders, he was emphatic about this. "A servant of the Lord must not quarrel but be gentle to all, able to teach, patient, in humility correcting those who are in opposition, if God perhaps will grant them repentance, so that they may know the truth" (2 Timothy 2:24–25). That is the spirit we must cultivate. Contending earnestly for the faith does not require us to become brawlers. Let's acknowledge that as plainly as possible and never lose sight of it.

But by far the greater danger facing the church today is utter apathy toward the truth and indifference about false teaching. Frankly, we are not very good these days at guarding the truth. We tend not to see truth the way Scripture presents it—as a sacred treasure committed to our trust (1 Timothy 6:20–21). I think that is why evangelicals on the whole don't take seriously the duty to expose and refute false teachers. Too many have decided it is easier and seems so much "nicer" to pretend that every doctrinal deviation is ultimately insignificant. That kind of thinking has given Christians a dangerous sense of false comfort and security.

## HOW TO SPOT AN APOSTATE

Jude seems to suggest that the church in his day had been lulled into a similar state of deadly apathy, and the false teachers were having a heyday because of it. Perhaps that is why his warning sounds so shrill.

In fact, the sharpness of the warning is suited to the danger posed by the purveyors of heresy. As we shall shortly observe, their ungodliness had multiple dimensions.

*Ungodly* is one of the key words in Jude's epistle. In verse 15 alone, he uses the word four times. (The Lord is coming, he says, "to execute judgment on all, to convict all who are *ungodly* among them of all their *ungodly* deeds which they have committed in an *ungodly* way, and of all the harsh things which *ungodly* sinners have spoken against Him" [emphasis added].) In verse 4 he uses the word as a general description of the apostates themselves. This is their chief characteristic: they were ungodly. They were without God. They were godless in their thoughts, their affections, and their doctrine. They claimed to belong to God, to represent God, and to speak for God. But of all the lies they told, that was probably the most glaringly untrue. They were actually ungodly—without any real love or obedience in their hearts toward the true God.

Jude then points out three major ways the ungodliness of the false teachers was manifest:

Their character. First, Jude candidly refers to the false teachers as "ungodly men" (v. 4). That is his assessment of their character. They had no integrity, were not men of principle, and were utterly lacking in all the fruits of true godliness. They were without any actual reverence for God and evidenced no true love for Him. They were barren of any authentic holiness. Aside from their phony profession of faith in Christ, they had no vital connection to Him whatsoever. They certainly did not reflect any degree of Christlikeness in their character. They simply played at religion.

Their conduct. Second, these "ungodly men . . . turn[ed] the grace of our God into lewdness" (v. 4). That means they presumptuously regarded God's kindness to sinners as a license for immoral conduct. They talked a lot about "grace" and promised "liberty," but they themselves were slaves of corruption (2 Peter 2:19). All their stress on freedom in Christ was actually a backhanded assault on God's grace. "Grace" to them was nothing more than a phony justification for lust-driven behavior.

Jude 18 echoes the same charge, again using the key word *ungodly* as a description of the false teachers' character: they "walk according to their own ungodly lusts."

Get the picture here: these were seriously ungodly men, and they were in the church. They were teaching and influencing people with nice-sounding words about grace and freedom in Christ, while in reality they were driven by their own unbridled lust and evil desires. Nevertheless, they gained a following in the church.

We must not be naive. Evil apostates like that are still in the church today. Their ungodliness is not always instantly evident. Some try to hide it under religious robes, divert attention from it by affecting kindliness or congeniality, or mask it with some other superficial kind of piety. They work hard to keep up the spiritual facade, but their true character is ungodly, and they cannot ultimately suppress the inevitable fruit of that. "The works of the flesh are *evident,* which are: adultery, fornication, uncleanness, lewdness, idolatry, sorcery, hatred, contentions, jealousies, outbursts of wrath, selfish ambitions, dissensions, heresies, envy, murders, drunkenness, revelries, and the like" (Galatians 5:19–21, emphasis added).

The ungodliness of an apostate system will occasionally become gross, widespread, and scandalous. A network of pedophile priests, for example—carefully camouflaged under a methodical cover-up that has been orchestrated by the church hierarchy—is a pretty clear sign of a system shot through with apostasy. No amount of clerical garb can mask the evil in that.

But the fruits of apostasy and ungodliness are not necessarily that obvious. Apostates are not unique to any single denomination or theological system. They are by no means limited to cults and fringe groups. On the contrary, they often deliberately conceal themselves within the heart of the evangelical mainstream. Some teach in evangelical seminaries and Bible colleges. Some pastor churches. They publish Christian-themed weblogs. They write books that are sold in evangelical bookstores.

How is their ungodly character manifest? In worldly lifestyles and unwholesome preoccupations. In private behavior that contradicts the carefully crafted public image. In sensual talk and carnal conduct. In the kind of hypocrisy that practices religion merely for the praise of men but cares not about pleasing God (Matthew 6:1–8).

Proof that ungodliness is rampant in evangelical circles is evident in megachurches that purposely cater to the preferences of the ungodly—furnishing entertainment and amusements in place of authentic worship and Bible teaching. More proof is found in a popular doctrinal system that deliberately removes the lordship of Christ from the gospel proclamation to give a theological justification for "carnal Christians"—people who profess to believe in Christ but live ungodly lives.

Still more proof is seen in the erosion of evangelicals' commitment to clear biblical moral standards. As the Emerging movement gains strength, more and more voices within are suggesting that evangelicals should back away from confronting Western culture over moral evils like abortion and homosexuality. Tony Campolo, for example, explained to a reporter why he wrote his book *Speaking My Mind:* "My purpose in writing the book was to communicate loud and clear that I felt that evangelical Christianity had been hijacked. When did it become anti-feminist? When did evangelical Christianity become anti-gay? When did it become supportive of capital punishment? Pro-war? When did it become so negative towards other religious groups?"[2]

Brian McLaren says he is not sure "what we should think about homosexuality." He called for a five-year moratorium on making any pronouncements about whether homosexuality is a sin or not. "In five years, if we have clarity, we'll speak" he said. "If not, we'll set another five years for ongoing reflection."[3]

The recent wave of popular books written by leading figures in the Emerging Church movement has unleashed an unprecedented flood of vulgarity and worldliness onto Christian booksellers' shelves. Obscenity is one of the main trademarks of the Emerging style. Most authors in the movement make extravagant use of filthy language, sexual innuendo, and uncritical references to the most lowbrow elements of postmodern culture, often indicating inappropriate approval for ungodly aspects of secular culture. In the popular book *Blue Like Jazz*, for example, Donald Miller writes of his experience in one of the best-known Emerging churches in the Pacific Northwest, referring to the pastor as "Mark, the Cussing Pastor":

> Even though Mark said cusswords, he was telling a lot of people about Jesus, and he was being socially active, and he seemed to love a lot of people the church was neglecting, like liberals and fruit nuts. About the time I was praying that God would help me find a church, I got a call from Mark the Cussing Pastor, and he said he had a close friend who was moving to Portland to start a church and that I should join him.

Rick and I got together over coffee, and I thought he was hilarious. He was big, a football player out of Chico State. At the time we both chewed tobacco, so we had that in common. He could do a great Tony Soprano voice, sort of a mafia thing. He would do this routine where he pretended to be a Mafia boss who was planting a church. He said a few cusswords but not as bad as Mark.[4]

A secular writer doing an article on the Emerging Church movement and postmodern Christianity summed up the character of the movement this way: "What makes a postmodern ministry so easy to embrace is that it doesn't demonize youth culture—Marilyn Manson, 'South Park,' or gangsta rap, for example—like traditional fundamentalists. Postmodern congregants aren't challenged to reject the outside world."[5]

I've noticed the same thing. Whole churches have deliberately immersed themselves in "the culture"—by which they actually mean "whatever the world loves at the moment." Thus we now have a new breed of trendy churches whose preachers can rattle off references to every popular icon, every trifling meme, every tasteless fashion, and every vapid trend that captures the fickle fancy of the postmodern, secular mind. Worldly preachers seem to go out of their way to put their carnal expertise on display—even in their sermons. In the name of "connecting with the culture" they boast of having see all the latest programs on MTV; memorized every episode of South Park; learned the lyrics to countless tracks of gangsta rap and heavy metal music; or watched who-knows-how-many R-rated movies. They seem to know every fad top to bottom, back to front, and inside out. They've adopted both the style and the language of the world—including lavish use of language that used to be deemed inappropriate in polite society, much less in the pulpit. The want to fit right in with the world, and they seem to be making themselves quite comfortable there.

Let's face it. Scripture speaks quite plainly against such a mentality (James 4:4). Many of the worlds' favorite fads are toxic, and the are becoming increasingly so as our society descends further into the death-spiral described in Romans 1. It's like a radioactive toxicity, so while those who immerse themselves in it might not notice its effects instantly, they nevertheless cannot escape the inevitable, soul-destroying contamination. And woe to those who become comfortable with sinful fads of secular society. The final verse of Romans 1 expressly condemns those "who, knowing the righteous judgment of God, that those who practice such things are deserving of death, not only do the same but also approve of those who practice them."

Disturbing evidence of this kind of ungodliness is becoming more prevalent across the spectrum of the visible church these days. In fact, it gets even worse. An Anglican committee commissioned to study the morality of extramarital sex suggested that the church should drop its opposition to cohabitation between unwed adults and regard the practice as "a new path from the single state to the married one."[6]

> APOSTATES FACE AN INTERESTING DILEMMA. THEY FREQUENTLY BECOME SO LOST TO HONOR, SO LACKING IN DECENCY, SO INDIFFERENT TO DISGRACE THAT THEY OFTEN DON'T CARE WHO SEES THEIR SIN, ESPECIALLY IN THEIR OWN INNER CIRCLE. THEY WEAR IT ARROGANTLY LIKE A BADGE OF HONOR. IN JUDE'S WORDS, THEY BECOME LIKE "RAGING WAVES OF THE SEA, FOAMING UP THEIR OWN SHAME."

Apostates face an interesting dilemma. They frequently become so lost to honor, so lacking in decency, so indifferent to disgrace that they often don't care who sees their sin, especially in their own inner circle. They wear it arrogantly like a badge of honor. In Jude's words, they become like "raging waves of the sea, foaming up their own shame" (v. 13).

On the other hand, they have to do something to hide their ungodliness from the people they are tying to dupe. Their words might be more carefully guarded in public venues, and they often maintain a whole different public persona. As we have learned from far too many televangelist scandals, accomplished media figures tend to be very good at this sort of hypocrisy.

The other common approach for masking ungodliness is the one Jude hints at in verse 4: they proclaim a message that transforms the idea of grace into license for sin. Thus they try to give a spiritual-sounding justification for their ungodliness.

This brings up a third major characteristic of every ungodly apostate:

*Their creed.* Apostates "deny the only Lord God and our Lord Jesus Christ." Jude is obviously not suggesting this is something they do with bold and straightforward candor, or else they could not be in the church "unnoticed." Sadly, that is probably less true today than it was in the early church. Nowadays people literally do deny Christ in some denominations and even remain bishops.

But while the false teachers in Jude's day were perhaps a little more subtle about their apostasy, in some way or another, they denied Christ's lordship. They would not live obediently under the sovereign lordship of Christ. They refused His headship over His church.

This is true of all apostates. At the heart of their apostasy is rebellion against Christ's lordship. Even if they confess with their lips, they deny with their lives. They may call Jesus, "Lord, Lord," but they do not do what He says (Luke 6:46). In the words of Paul to Titus, "They profess to know God, but in works they deny Him, being abominable, disobedient, and disqualified for every good work" (Titus 1:16). Their apostasy eventually poisons all their doctrine. They twist and pervert and reinvent teachings of Christ. They adjust the gospel to suit their own tastes. When you get to the core of where they are, they simply want to be kings of their own domain.

That brings us full circle back to the issue of character. Apostate false teachers are not humble. They are not broken. They are not submissive. They are not meek. They are blatant, proud sovereigns of their own religious empires. And while they like to use Christ's name for their advantage, they do not really know, obey, or love the truth—written or Incarnate.

Nevertheless, God alone is truly sovereign. His eternal purposes are not the least bit threatened by the efforts of false teachers. His truth *will* triumph in the end. And tragic consequence for the false teachers and all who follow them is sure and certain condemnation. As Jude says, they already have a long-standing appointment to that end.

Of course, that doesn't alter or diminish our duty to oppose them and contend earnestly for the faith here and now. In the chapter to come, we'll examine some of the difficulties of that duty.

# 7

## The Assault on Divine Authority: Christ's Lordship Denied

*Certain men have crept in unnoticed, who . . .*
*deny the only Lord God and our Lord Jesus Christ.*

—Jude 4

Contending for the faith has never been easy work. But as we have been seeing, the postmodern shift has made the challenge more difficult than ever.

The mood that currently prevails in the evangelical movement doesn't help. Contemporary evangelicalism seems bent on shaping itself into the most stylish, trendy movement in the history of the church. Old certainties are often met with automatic suspicion just because they have been affirmed by generation after generation of evangelicals. These days it is fashionable to question everything. And most evangelicals frankly don't care all that much about their spiritual heritage in the first place. They don't have a very strong commitment to understanding Scripture precisely or defending its vital doctrines against the encroachment of subtle errors. They just want something new and fresh. Above all, they are desperate to stay in step with the world.

Multitudes of "enlightened" evangelicals have therefore wholeheartedly embraced those cardinal postmodern virtues—broad-mindedness and diversity—while deliberately setting aside critical biblical values, such as discernment and fidelity to the truth.

How many well-known evangelical leaders do we see squander wonderful opportunities to make the truth clear and plain when they are handed a microphone by the secular media? They often balk or simply give the wrong answer when put on the spot by questions about whether Christ is really the only way to heaven. Apparently, some evangelicals are prepared to let the dogmas of political correctness trump any article of faith. It seems many have already imbibed the full array of postmodern values without even realizing it.

That attitude is especially dominant in the elite echelons of the evangelical academic world, and it filters down from there. Long-held biblical and evangelical convictions are easily discounted, but trendy scholars can't wait to endorse the latest new perspective. Novel ideas about doctrine are never supposed to be repudiated with any degree of force; that is considered seriously uncouth. Read the reviews in almost any theological journal, and you will notice this. Anyone who comments on the latest opinions sweeping the evangelical world is expected to spend a significant amount of time and energy pointing out strengths and saying positive things. Perhaps no one is more generous or more reckless than contemporary evangelicals when it comes to handing out indiscriminate affirmation.

It is hard to imagine anything more at odds with the biblical command to contend earnestly for the faith. Evangelicals need to stop and think very seriously about how our movement got where it is today and where it is headed from here.

# How Did Evangelicalism Morph into Such a Mess?

For the past two decades or more, the evangelical movement has been pounded with an unrelenting barrage of outlandish ideas, philosophies, and programs. Never in the history of the church has so much innovation met with so little critical thinking.

Giving a thoughtful biblical response becomes harder and harder all the time. Merely sorting through all the evangelical trends and recognizing which of these novelties really represent dangerous threats to the health and harmony of the church is challenging enough. Effectively answering the huge smorgasbord of accompanying errors poses an even greater dilemma. New errors sometimes seem to multiply faster than the previous ones can be answered.

To be an effective warrior in the battle for truth today, several old-fashioned, Christlike virtues are absolutely essential: biblical discernment, wisdom, fortitude, determination, endurance, skill in handling Scripture, strong convictions, the ability to speak candidly without waffling, and a willingness to enter into conflict.

Let's be honest: those are not qualities the contemporary evangelical movement has cultivated. In fact, the exact opposite is true. Consider the values and motives that prompt postmodern evangelicals to do the things they do. The larger evangelical movement today is obsessed with opinion polls, brand identity, market research, merchandizing schemes, innovative strategies, and numerical growth. Evangelicals are also preoccupied with matters such as their image before the general public and before the academic world, their clout in the political arena, their portrayal by the media, and similar shallow, self-centered matters.

Maintaining a positive image has become a priority over guarding the truth.

*The PR–driven church.* Somewhere along the line, evangelicals bought the lie that the Great Commission is a marketing mandate. The leading strategists for church growth today are therefore all pollsters and public relations managers. In the words of Rick Warren, "If you want to advertise your church to the unchurched, you must learn to think and speak like they do."[1] An endless parade of self-styled church-growth specialists has been repeating that same mantra for several decades, and multitudes of Christians and church leaders now accept the idea uncritically. Both their message to the world and the means by which they communicate that message have been carefully tailored by consumer relations experts to appeal to worldly minds.

Many church leaders have radically changed the way they look at the gospel. Rather than seeing it as a message from God that Christians are called to proclaim as Christ's ambassadors (without tampering with it or changing it in any way), they now treat it like a commodity to be sold at market. Rather than plainly *preaching* God's Word in a way that unleashes the power and truth of it, they try desperately to *package* the message to make it subtler and more appealing to the world.

*Runaway pragmatism and trivial pursuit.* The most compelling question in the minds and on the lips of many pastors today is not

> MANY CHURCH LEADERS HAVE RADICALLY CHANGED THE WAY THEY LOOK AT THE GOSPEL. RATHER THAN SEEING IT AS A MESSAGE FROM GOD THAT CHRISTIANS ARE CALLED TO PROCLAIM AS CHRIST'S AMBASSADORS (WITHOUT TAMPERING WITH IT OR CHANGING IT IN ANY WAY), THEY NOW TREAT IT LIKE A COMMODITY TO BE SOLD AT MARKET.

"What's true?" but rather "What works?" Evangelicals these days care less about *theology* than they do about *methodology*. Truth has taken a backseat to more pragmatic concerns. When a person is trying hard to customize one's message to meet the "felt needs" of one's audience, earnestly contending for the faith is out of the question.

That is precisely why for many years now, evangelical leaders have systematically embraced and fostered almost every worldly, shallow, and frivolous idea that comes into the church. A pathological devotion to superficiality has practically become the chief hallmark of the movement. Evangelicals are obsessed with pop culture, and they ape it fanatically. Contemporary church leaders are so busy trying to stay current with the latest fads that they rarely give much sober thought to weightier scriptural matters.

In the typical evangelical church, even Sunday services are often devoted to the trivial pursuit of worldly things. After all, churches are competing for attention in a media-driven world. So the church vainly tries to put on a bigger, flashier spectacle than the world.

*Evangelical fad surfing.* Contemporary evangelicals have therefore become very much like "children, tossed to and fro and carried about with every wind of doctrine" (Ephesians 4:14). They follow whatever is the latest popular trend. They buy whatever is the current best seller. They line up to see any celebrity who speaks spiritual-sounding language. They watch eagerly for the next Hollywood movie with any "spiritual" theme or religious imagery that they can latch on to. And they discuss these fads and fashions endlessly, as if every cultural icon that captures evangelicals' attention had profound and serious spiritual significance.

Evangelical churchgoers desperately want their churches to stay on the leading edge of whatever is currently in vogue in the evangelical community. For a while, any church that wanted to be in fashion had to sponsor seminars on how to pray the prayer of Jabez. But woe to the church that was still doing Jabez when *The*

*Purpose-Driven Life* took center stage. By then, any church that wanted to retain its standing and credibility in the evangelical movement had better be doing "Forty Days of Purpose." And if your church didn't get through the "Forty Days" in time to host group studies or preach a series of sermons about *The Da Vinci Code* before the Hollywood movie version came out, then your church was considered badly out of touch with what really matters.

It is too late now if you missed any of those trends. To use the language of the movement, they are all *so* five minutes ago. If your church is not already experimenting with Emerging-style worship, candles, postmodern liturgy, and the like (or—better yet—anticipating the next major trend), then you are clearly not in a very stylish church.

Of course, I'm not suggesting that all those trends are equally bad. Some of them are not necessarily bad at all. For example, there can be great benefit in teaching a congregation how to respond to something like *The Da Vinci Code.* But contemporary evangelicals have been conditioned to anticipate and follow *every* fad with an almost mindless herd mentality. They sometimes seem to move from fad to fad with an uninhibited and undiscerning eagerness that does leave them exposed to things that may well be spiritually lethal. In fact, the question of whether the latest trend is dangerous or not is not a welcome question in most evangelical circles anymore. Whatever happens to be popular at the moment is what drives the whole evangelical agenda.

That mentality is precisely what Paul warned against in Ephesians 4:14. It has left evangelical Christians dangerously exposed to trickery, deceitfulness, and unsound doctrine. It has also left them completely unequipped to practice any degree of true biblical discernment.

The sad truth is that the larger part of the evangelical movement is already so badly compromised that sound doctrine has almost become a nonissue.

The mad pursuit of nondoctrinal "relevancy." Even at the very heart of the evangelical mainstream, where you might expect to find some commitment to biblical doctrine and at least a measure of concern about defending the faith, what you find instead is a movement utterly dominated by people whose first concern is to try to keep in step with the times in order to be "relevant."

*Sound doctrine?* Too arcane for the average churchgoer. *Biblical exposition?* That alienates the "unchurched." *Clear preaching on sin and redemption?* Let's be careful not to subvert the self-esteem of hurting people. *The Great Commission?* Our most effective strategy has been making the church service into a massive Super Bowl party. *Serious discipleship?* Sure. There's a great series of group studies based on *I Love Lucy* episodes. Let's work our way through that. *Worship where God is recognized as high and lifted up?* Get real. We need to reach people on the level where they are.

Evangelicals and their leaders have doggedly pursued that same course for several decades now—in spite of *many* clear biblical instructions that warn us not to be so childish (in addition to Ephesians 4:14, see also 1 Corinthians 14:20; 2 Timothy 4:3–4; Hebrews 5:12–14).

What's the heart of the problem? It boils down to this: Much of the evangelical movement has forgotten who is Lord over the church. They have either abandoned or downright rejected their true Head and given His rightful place to evangelical pollsters and church-growth gurus.

## USURPING THE CHURCH'S TRUE HEAD

Jude's initial description of apostates in the early church culminates in this statement: "[They] deny the only Lord God and our

Lord Jesus Christ" (Jude 4). Of all the many doctrinal flaws in their system that Jude might have called attention to, this is the one that heads his list and sums up all the others. The false teachers' absolute rejection of Christ's authority was the root and the real motive for their apostasy in the first place. They resented the lordship of Christ and disowned Him as their true Master because they had rebellious hearts and wanted the authority for themselves.

Jude stresses that the major reasons for their rebellion are immorality, greed, and lust. These sins are characteristic of virtually all false teachers. (They "turn the grace of our God into lewdness" [v. 4]; they have "given themselves over to sexual immorality" [v. 7]; they "defile the flesh" [v. 8]; and they "run greedily in the error of Balaam for profit" [v. 11].) Again, this is a reminder that the root cause of false doctrine is nearly always immorality or sinful lust rather than ignorance or misunderstanding. The person who wants to indulge his or her own evil desires and self-will must reject Christ's authority.

> THE FALSE TEACHERS' ABSOLUTE REJECTION OF CHRIST'S AUTHORITY WAS THE ROOT AND THE REAL MOTIVE FOR THEIR APOSTASY IN THE FIRST PLACE. THEY RESENTED THE LORDSHIP OF CHRIST AND DISOWNED HIM AS THEIR TRUE MASTER BECAUSE THEY HAD REBELLIOUS HEARTS AND WANTED THE AUTHORITY FOR THEMSELVES.

However, to mask their evil motives, most false teachers also deliberately keep their rebellion against Christ's authority covert—usually under the disguise of some sort of religiosity. As we have seen from the start, the false teachers Jude was dealing with could not have penetrated the church secretly unless they had somehow kept their utter contempt for Christ's lordship clandestine. They no doubt *professed* to know God and recognize the lordship of Christ, but *in their works* they denied Him (Titus 1:16).

Even today most false teachers operate that way. They give lip service to Christ but have no true love for Him. They *call* Him "Lord, Lord," but they don't do what He commands (Luke 6:46). They disguise themselves with the appearance of spirituality, artificial piety, and cordiality. But look closely at any apostate, and you will see someone who despises divine authority.

It is no wonder, then, that evangelicalism's recent flirtations with apostasy have always involved some kind of effort to oust Christ from His rightful place as Lord over the church. Most of these involve indirect or subtle assaults on Christ's lordship, but every one of them may nonetheless be used to mask a heart that seeks to turn God's grace into lewdness while utterly denying the only Lord God and our Lord Jesus Christ (Jude 4).

"Seeker-sensitive" methodologies. As churches have tailored their Sunday services to suit the tastes of "seekers," for example, there is less and less emphasis on edifying the saints and more and more stress on entertaining unbelievers. Drama, music, comedy, and even forms of vaudeville have often replaced preaching in the order of service. That strips Christ of His headship over the church by removing His Word from its rightful place and thereby silencing His rule in the life of His people. In effect, it surrenders the headship of the church to unchurched seekers.

Furthermore, any time a preacher squelches or softens a hard truth of Scripture to make the message more palatable, that preacher has suppressed Christ's true message and thereby usurped His rightful authority as Lord over the church.

No-lordship theology. In previous books, I have critiqued a popular system of theology that argues that every reference to the lordship of Christ should be omitted from the gospel message.[2] According to this view, surrender to Christ's lordship is an optional matter, relevant only after someone has been a Christian for some time. The gospel is therefore reduced to an invitation to believe in Jesus as Savior, while carefully omitting any reference to His authority as Lord. Gone from the message are Christ's call to discipleship, all His hard demands about cross-bearing and self-denial (Matthew 16:24; Mark 10:21; et al.), and His admonition to count the cost of following Him (Luke 14:26–33). The no-lordship "gospel" meticulously avoids calling sinners to repentance too.

No-lordship doctrine rose to popularity in the mid-twentieth century and was almost unchallenged as the dominant system of theology in American evangelicalism for several decades. The no-lordship message has filled the church with people lacking spiritual fruit and absent every other vital evidence of living faith—who nonetheless are convinced they are authentic Christians.

In fact, according to no-lordship doctrine, someone who lives an utterly debauched lifestyle should nevertheless be embraced as a true Christian if he or she ever once professed faith in Christ. These so-called "carnal Christians" are regularly given strong reassurances that their salvation is secure no matter how long or how egregiously they rebel against Christ's authority. Of course, that completely eliminates the meaningful exercise of church discipline. It also effectively unseats Christ from His rightful place of authority over the church.

In fact, it is hard to think of a more direct or more deliberate way to attack the rightful lordship of Christ over His church.

Accommodations to political correctness. Evangelicals willing to bend biblical truth to make Christianity seem more politically correct are in effect denying Christ as the true Head of the church. For example, Scripture expressly forbids women to teach men or have authority over them in the church (1 Timothy 2:12). Many evangelicals have chosen to ignore that principle or tried desperately to explain it away. Some even go so far as to write it off as an uninspired, misogynistic expression of the apostle Paul's personal opinion.

> CHRIST'S HEADSHIP IN THE CHURCH IS LIKEWISE BEING CHALLENGED BY THOSE IN THE EMERGING CHURCH MOVEMENT WHO HAVE SUGGESTED THAT SCRIPTURE IS SIMPLY NOT CLEAR ENOUGH TO ALLOW US TO PREACH ITS TRUTH WITH ANY DEGREE OF CLARITY, CERTAINTY, OR CONVICTION.

Thus we have seen an influx of women into pastoral and teaching roles, even in evangelical circles. Many evangelical seminaries are now aggressively recruiting women for pastoral training programs. Numerous once-conservative evangelical churches are ordaining women as elders, encouraging them to teach adult classes filled with men, and even appointing them to pastoral and preaching roles.

Such feminism has gnostic roots. It is an opinion that was universally rejected by mainstream Christianity until the current generation, when it was proposed mainly as a politically correct way to respond to the secular feminists' charge that Christianity is too male dominated and therefore outmoded. The rapid acceptance of "evangelical" feminism is a measure of how many in the church are determined at all costs to bend Scripture to make it fit worldly opinion.

The same kind of mentality drives Bible translators who have revamped the language of Scripture itself to make gender references as nonspecific as possible, in an effort to make the Bible seem "inclusive" enough to satisfy postmodern standards.

## POSTMODERNISM'S ANGST ABOUT CERTAINTY.

Christ's headship in the church is likewise being challenged by those in the Emerging Church movement who have suggested that Scripture is simply not clear enough to allow us to preach its truth with any degree of clarity, certainty, or conviction. Most would never come right out and deny that the Bible is the Word of God, but they accomplish exactly the same thing when they insist that no one has any right to say for sure what the Bible means.

Brian McLaren epitomizes this mentality in the introduction to his book *A New Kind of Christian*:

> I drive my car and listen to the Christian radio station, something my wife always tells me I should stop doing ("because it only gets you upset"). There I hear preacher after preacher be so absolutely sure of his bombproof answers and his foolproof biblical interpretations. . . . And the more sure he seems, the less I find myself wanting to be a Christian, because on this side of the microphone, antennas, and speaker, life isn't that simple, answers aren't that clear, and nothing is that sure.[3]

Thus "evangelical" postmodernism has transformed doubt, uncertainty, and qualms about practically every teaching of Scripture into high virtue. Strong convictions plainly stated are invariably labeled "arrogance" by those who favor postmodern dialogue.

Now, obviously, we cannot righteously be dogmatic about every peripheral belief or matter of personal preference. Virtually no one believes *every* opinion is worth fighting about. Scripture draws the line with ample clarity: we're commanded to defend the faith once delivered to the saints; but we're forbidden to pick fights with one another over secondary issues (Romans 14:1).

Some are now suggesting, however, that humility requires everyone to refrain from treating *any* truth as incontrovertible. Instead, we are supposed to put *everything* back on the table and "admit that our past and current formulations may have been limited or distorted."[4]

This approach has been referred to by some as "a hermeneutic of humility"—as if it is inherently too prideful for any preacher to think he knows what God said about anything. Of course, such a denial of all certainty has nothing to do with true humility. It is actually an arrogant form of unbelief, rooted in an impudent refusal to acknowledge that God has been sufficiently clear in His self-revelation to His creatures. It is actually a blasphemous form of arrogance, and when it governs even how someone handles the Word of God, it becomes yet another expression of evil rebellion against Christ's authority.

Christ has spoken in the Bible, and He holds us responsible to understand, interpret, obey, and teach what He said—as opposed to deconstructing everything the Bible says. Notice that Christ repeatedly rebuked the Pharisees for twisting Scripture, disobeying it, setting it aside with their traditions, and generally ignoring its plain meaning. Not once did He ever excuse the Pharisees' hypocrisy and false religion by apologizing for any lack of clarity in the Old Testament.

Jesus held not only the Pharisees but also the common people responsible for knowing and understanding the Scriptures. "Have you not read . . . ?" was a common rebuke to those who challenged His teaching but did not know or understand the Scriptures as they should have (Matthew 12:3, 5; 19:4; 22:31; Mark 12:26). He addressed the disciples on the road to Emmaus as "foolish ones, and slow of heart to believe" because of their ignorance about the Old Testament's messianic promises (Luke 24:25). The problem lay not in any lack of clarity on Scripture's part but in their own sluggish faith.

The apostle Paul, whose writings are most under debate by scholars today, wrote virtually all his epistles for the common man, not for scholars and intellectuals. Those addressed to churches were written to predominantly *Gentile* churches, whose understanding of the Old Testament was limited. He nevertheless expected them to understand what he wrote (Ephesians 3:3–5), and he held them responsible for heeding his instruction (1 Timothy 3:14–15).

Paul and Christ both consistently made the case that it is every Christian's duty to study and interpret Scripture rightly (2 Timothy 2:15). "He who has ears to hear, let him hear!" (Matthew 11:15; 13:9, 16; Mark 4:9).

Even the book of Revelation, arguably one of the most difficult sections of Scripture to interpret, isn't too hard for a typical lay reader to understand sufficiently and profit from. Hence it begins with this blessing: "Blessed is he who reads and those who hear the words of this prophecy, and keep those things which are written in it; for the time is near" (Revelation 1:3).

Protestant Christianity has always affirmed the *perspicuity* of Scripture. That means we believe God has spoken distinctly in His Word. Not everything in the Bible is equally clear, of course (2 Peter 3:16). But God's Word is plain enough for the average reader to know and understand everything necessary for a saving knowledge of Christ. Scripture is also sufficiently clear to enable us to obey the Great Commission, which expressly requires us to teach others "all things" that Christ has commanded (Matthew 28:18–20).

Two thousand years of accumulated Christian scholarship has been basically consistent on all the major issues: The Bible is the authoritative Word of God, containing every spiritual truth essential to God's glory, our salvation, faith, and eternal life. Scripture tells us that all humanity fell in Adam, and our sin is a perfect bondage from which we cannot extricate ourselves. Jesus is God incarnate, having taken on human flesh to pay the price of sin and redeem believing men and women from sin's bondage. Salvation is by grace through faith, and not a result of any works we do. Christ is the only Savior for the whole world, and apart from faith in Him, there is no hope of redemption for any sinner. So the gospel message needs to be carried to the uttermost parts of the earth. True Christians have always been in full agreement on all those vital points of biblical truth.

As a matter of fact, the postmodernized notion that everything should be perpetually up for discussion and nothing is ever really sure or settled is a plain and simple denial of both the perspicuity of Scripture and the unanimous testimony of the people of God throughout redemptive history. In one sense, the contemporary denial of the Bible's clarity represents a regression to medieval thinking, when the papal hierarchy insisted that the Bible is too unclear for laypeople to interpret it for themselves. (This belief led to much fierce persecution against those who worked to translate the Bible into common languages.)

In another sense, however, the postmodern denial of Scripture's clarity is even worse than the darkness of medieval religious superstition, because postmodernism in effect says *no one* can reliably understand what the Bible means. Postmodernism leaves people permanently in the dark about practically everything.

That, too, is a denial of Christ's lordship over the church. How could He exercise headship over His church if His own people could never truly know what He meant by what He said? Jesus Himself settled the question of whether His truth is sufficiently clear in John 10:27–28, when He said, "My sheep hear My voice, and I know them, and they follow Me. And I give them eternal life, and they shall never perish; neither shall anyone snatch them out of My hand."

*Other theological fads and novelties.* Dozens of other challenges to Christ's headship over the church are currently percolating in the wider evangelical movement. Some impugn Christ's lordship by their faulty doctrine. *Open theism,* for example, suggests that God doesn't know the future infallibly. That diminishes the truth of divine sovereignty and thereby undermines the whole basis of Christ's lordship.

Others would formally affirm Christ's sovereignty and spiritual headship over the church, but they resist His rule in practice. To cite just one instance of how this is done, many churches have set various forms of human psychology, self-help therapy, and the idea of "recovery" in place of the Bible's teaching about sin and sanctification. Christ's headship over the church is thus subjugated to professional therapists. His design for sanctification, however, is by means of the Word of God (John 15:3; 17:17). So wherever the work of God's Word is being replaced with twelve-step programs and other substitutes, Christ's headship over the church is being denied in practice.

Popular entrepreneurial styles of church leadership (where the pastor casts himself in the role of a corporate CEO rather than being a faithful shepherd to Christ's flock) likewise undermine the headship of Christ over the church. Such enterprises may be labeled churches, but often they are merely the products of human ingenuity and carnal energy. They are works of "wood, hay, straw" in the words of 1 Corinthians 3:12, good for nothing eternal but destined to be burned up at the judgment seat of Christ. He is building the true church (Matthew 16:18), and He alone is its true Head (Ephesians 5:23). His rule is mediated not through the cleverness and industry of entrepreneurial leaders, but solely and only by His revealed truth as it is rightly preached, explained, applied, and upheld.

Sadly, almost everywhere we look in the contemporary evangelical movement, Christ's headship over the church is being challenged, rejected, ignored, overruled, or otherwise disputed. A right understanding of the church begins with this recognition: Christ is the one true Head of the church, and whatever interferes with His headship has the seeds of apostasy in it. Conversely, every form of apostasy is an implicit denial of "the only Lord God and our Lord Jesus Christ" (Jude 4) and is therefore a form of rebellion against the church's one true Head.

## WHAT DOES *Head* MEAN?

What is included in the biblical idea of headship? It is a much-disputed idea these days, thanks to evangelical feminism. For the past two decades or so, people seeking an egalitarian understanding of the New Testament have had to grapple with the clear meaning of Ephesians 5:23: "The husband is head of the wife, as also Christ is head of the church." They have sought creative ways to strip the concepts of leadership and authority from the notion of headship.

If the husband's role as head in a marriage relationship involves any degree of authority over the wife, the feminist and egalitarian approach to gender relationships is biblically untenable. Evangelical feminists have therefore long insisted that the word "head" in Ephesians 5:23 means nothing more than "source." They suggest that it means the husband is to be a loving protector to the wife, but it does not grant him any particular leadership responsibility over her. Marriage is an absolutely equal partnership, they say, with neither husband nor wife having any kind of authority over the other.

But the headship of Christ is so linked to the headship of the husband in Ephesians 5, that if the husband's role is divested of authority, Christ's authority over the church is likewise diminished. As a matter of fact, in 1 Corinthians 11:3, Paul even links the idea of headship to the relationship of authority and submission between the Father and the Son within the Trinity: "I want you to know that the head of every man is Christ, the head of woman is man, and the head of Christ is God." So in the same way Christ voluntarily submitted Himself to His Father's will (John 6:38), wives are commanded to submit themselves to their husbands, and the church is to submit to Christ (Ephesians 5:24).

The notion that headship involves no idea of leadership or authority is entirely without linguistic support. The Greek word translated "head" in Ephesians 5 is *kephale.* In 1985 Wayne Grudem began an exhaustive study of that word and its usage in ancient Greek literature. He examined 2,336 occurrences of the word, beginning with Homer in the eighth century BC and ranging to the church fathers in the fourth century. He found that whenever the word is used of a person (as opposed to the cranial appendage), it always speaks of someone in a position of authority. Nowhere in any extant Greek literature does the word ever mean "source" without any notion of authority.[5]

> CHRIST IS THE ONE TRUE HEAD OF THE CHURCH, AND WHATEVER INTERFERES WITH HIS HEADSHIP HAS THE SEEDS OF APOSTASY IN IT. CONVERSELY, EVERY FORM OF APOSTASY IS AN IMPLICIT DENIAL OF "THE ONLY LORD GOD AND OUR LORD JESUS CHRIST" (JUDE 4) AND IS THEREFORE A FORM OF REBELLION AGAINST THE CHURCH'S ONE TRUE HEAD.

That is how Scripture uses the word too. Jesus' role as Head of the church is inseparable from His position as Lord over all (Philippians 2:9–11). Paul told the Ephesians: "He raised Him from the dead and seated Him at His right hand in the heavenly places, far above all principality and power and might and dominion, and every name that is named, not only in this age but also in that which is to come. And He put all things under His feet, and gave Him to be head over all things to the church" (Ephesians 1:20–22). So Christ is given to the church *as* "head over all things." Or, as a different version renders verse 22, "God placed all things under his feet and appointed him to be head over everything for the church" (NIV). It is for the church's sake that Christ is Lord of all, and it is in that very capacity that He has been given to the church as its true and sovereign Head. To interpret headship in a way that eliminates the idea of authority is to empty the idea of its true significance.

## WHO MADE CHRIST HEAD?

Ephesians 1 also makes it clear that Christ's headship over the church is at the very heart of His Father's eternal purpose. God the Father planned and orchestrated the entire plan of redemption as a way of exalting His Son as Lord of all creation. In fact, everything God is doing in the universe ultimately pivots on His plan to make Christ Lord over all and give Him as Lord to be the church's loving Head. As Paul describes it, God's electing purpose, all the work of salvation, the resurrection of Christ, the glorification of His physical body, and His final exaltation to the right hand of God all culminate in this objective: that all things would be put under His feet, and that in His capacity as Lord of all, He would be Head of the church and the church would be His body and bride.

Notice the multiple ways Paul underscores Christ's authority as supreme and sovereign Lord over all. He says that God has "seated Him at His right hand in the heavenly places, far above all principality and power and might and dominion, and every name that is named" (Ephesians 1:20–21). That authority applies "not only in this age but also in that which is to come" (v. 21). It is absolute supremacy in every sense. Not only are all things put under Christ's feet (v. 22), but He also "fills all in all" (v. 23).

So the church's Head is ordained to be the consummate authority in all the universe by God the Father Himself. This is the ultimate expression of the Father's eternal love for His only begotten Son. He did not give an archangel like Michael or Gabriel to be head of the church. He didn't establish an earthly priesthood to mediate the headship of the church either. But by God the Father's own decree, Christ alone is Head of the church, and all others must fall on their knees before Him.

Colossians 1:18 settles every question about the relationship of Christ's authority as Lord to His headship over the church. There Paul says, "He is the head of the body, the church, who is the beginning, the firstborn from the dead, that in all things He may have the preeminence." First place belongs to Him. Nowhere should that be truer and more clearly evident than in the church, where His people openly submit to Him as Lord. Christ is the *only* proper and legitimate Head of the church. No king, no pope, and no politician has any right to usurp the title or pretend to occupy the office.

That also means earthly church leaders are undershepherds who are to serve the Great Shepherd. No one has the prerogative to fabricate his own doctrine, devise his own self-serving agenda, or invent his own novel idea of what the church should be. Christ alone is the church's true Head, and only those who recognize His authority and bow to it unconditionally have any true right to serve as undershepherds to His flock. All the rest are ravenous wolves.

In his commentary on Colossians 2:19, John Calvin perfectly

summed up the point of all this: "Should anyone call us anywhere else than to Christ, though in other respects he were big with heaven and earth, he is empty and full of wind: let us, therefore, without concern, bid him farewell. The constitution of the body will be in a right state, if simply the Head, which furnishes the several members with everything that they have, is allowed, without any hindrance, to have the pre-eminence."[6]

Apostates and false teachers actually think they are their own masters. Rarely do they admit it, but that is their true perspective. They prove it when they tamper with or attempt to tone down the gospel to make it more acceptable to unbelievers (1 Corinthians 1:22–25). They show it by seeking the approval of men rather than God (Galatians 1:10). They declare it by trying to reinvent the church so that it will be more pleasing to the world (John 15:18–19). All those trends effectively overrule the authority of Scripture in the church—and in that sense, they "deny the only Lord God and our Lord Jesus Christ" (Jude 4).

That is no exaggeration. The fact that all those approaches to ministry reflect the dominant philosophy among today's evangelicals is no reason to discount the evil in that way of thinking. On the contrary, it is an urgent reason to be deeply concerned about the future of the evangelical movement, and it ought to serve as a reminder that we had better get back to fighting the war for truth.

The way to begin is by giving Christ His due position of pre-eminence in the church once more.

# 8

## How to Survive in an Age of Apostasy: Learning from the Lessons of History

*But I want to remind you, though you once knew this . . .*
—Jude 5

Why do so many evangelicals act as if false teachers in the church could never be a serious problem in *this* generation? Vast numbers seem convinced that they are "rich, have become wealthy, and have need of nothing—and do not know that [they] are wretched, miserable, poor, blind, and naked" (Revelation 3:17).

In reality, the church today is quite possibly *more* susceptible to false teachers, doctrinal saboteurs, and spiritual terrorism than any other generation in church history. Biblical ignorance within the church may well be deeper and more widespread than at any other time since the Protestant Reformation. If you doubt that, compare the typical sermon of today with a randomly chosen published sermon from any leading evangelical preacher prior to 1850. Also compare today's Christian literature with almost anything published by evangelical publishing houses a hundred years or more ago.

Bible teaching, even in the best of venues today, has been deliberately dumbed-down, made as broad and as shallow as possible, oversimplified, adapted to the lowest common denominator—and then tailored to appeal to people with short attention spans. Sermons are almost always brief, simplistic, overlaid with as many references to pop culture as possible, and laden with anecdotes and illustrations. (Jokes and funny stories drawn from personal experience are favored over cross-references and analogies borrowed from Scripture itself.) Typical sermon topics are heavily weighted in favor of man-centered issues (such as personal relationships, successful living, self-esteem, how-to lists, and so on)—to the exclusion of the many Christ-exalting doctrinal themes of Scripture.

In other words, what most contemporary preachers do is virtually the opposite of what Paul was describing when he said he sought "to declare . . . the whole counsel of God" (Acts 20:27). Not only that, but here's how Paul explained his own approach to *gospel* ministry, even among unchurched pagans in the most debauched Roman culture:

> I, brethren, when I came to you, did not come with excellence of speech or of wisdom declaring to you the testimony of God. For I determined not to know anything among you except Jesus Christ and Him crucified. I was with you in weakness, in fear, and in much trembling. And my speech and my preaching were not with persuasive words of human wisdom, but in demonstration of the Spirit and of power, that your faith should not be in the wisdom of men but in the power of God. (1 Corinthians 2:1–5)

Notice that Paul deliberately refused to customize his message or adjust his delivery to suit the Corinthians' philosophical bent or their cultural tastes. When he says later in the epistle, "To the Jews I became as a Jew . . . to those who are without law, as without law

. . . to the weak I became as weak, that I might win the weak. I have become all things to all men, that I might by all means save some" (1 Corinthians 9:20-22), he was describing how he made himself a servant to all (v. 19) and the fellow of those whom he was trying to reach. In other words, he avoided making *himself* a stumbling block. He was *not* saying he adapted the gospel message (which he plainly said *is* a stumbling block—1:23). He did not adopt methods to suit the tastes of a worldly culture.

Paul had no thought of catering to a particular generation's preferences, and he used no gimmicks as attention-getters. Whatever antonym you can think of for the word *showmanship* would probably be a good description of Paul's style of public ministry. He wanted to make it clear to everyone (including the Corinthian converts themselves) that lives and hearts are renewed by means of the Word of God and nothing else. That way they would begin to understand and appreciate the power of the gospel message.

> THE CHURCH TODAY IS QUITE POSSIBLY *MORE* SUSCEPTIBLE TO FALSE TEACHERS, DOCTRINAL SABOTEURS, AND SPIRITUAL TERRORISM THAN ANY OTHER GENERATION IN CHURCH HISTORY. BIBLICAL IGNORANCE WITHIN THE CHURCH MAY WELL BE DEEPER AND MORE WIDESPREAD THAN AT ANY OTHER TIME SINCE THE PROTESTANT REFORMATION.

By contrast, today's church-growth experts seem to have *no* confidence in Scripture's power. They are convinced the gospel needs to be "contextualized," streamlined, and revamped anew for every generation. Forty years of that approach has left evangelicals grossly untaught, wholly unprepared to defend the truth, and almost entirely unaware of how much is at stake. The evangelical movement itself has become a monstrosity, its vast size and visibility belying its almost total spiritual failure. One thing is certain: the cumbersome movement that most people today would label "evangelical" is populated with large numbers of people who are on the wrong side in the Truth War.

We are right back in the same situation the church was in a hundred years ago, when modernists were busily reinventing the Christian faith. Far from being a strong voice and a powerful force for the cause of truth, the evangelical movement itself has become the main battleground.

Moreover, the postmodernists who are beginning to dominate the evangelical movement are employing exactly the same strategies, pleading for precisely the same kinds of doctrinal modifications, and even using some of the very same arguments modernists used when they took over the mainline denominations a century ago.

To cite one rather serious and significant doctrinal example, the principle of substitutionary atonement (always a favorite target of modernists) has recently been under heavy assault again at the hands of those who insist that evangelicals need to adapt their message to accommodate *post*modern sensibilities. Scripture is clear: Christ suffered on the cross as a substitute for sinners (Isaiah 53:4–10), taking the full brunt of the punishment we deserved (2 Corinthians 5:21; Hebrews 9:27–28; 1 Peter 3:18). His death was a *propitiation*, or a satisfaction of divine wrath against sin on believers' behalf (Romans 3:25; Hebrews 2:17; 1 John 2:2; 4:10). But that view has been forcefully attacked in recent years by people who insist it makes God seem harsh and barbaric. They are in effect advocating the elimination of the offense of the cross because it is too uncouth for their tastes. One influential author referred to the principle of substitutionary atonement as "twisted," "morally dubious," and "a form of cosmic child abuse."[1] Others in the Emerging Church movement have said similar things. Brian McLaren, for example, has repeatedly voiced misgivings about whether it is appropriate for Christians to describe the atonement as a penal substitution. At one point, the hero in one of McLaren's quasi-fictional books says the notion of Christ being punished for others' sins "just sounds like one more injustice in the cosmic equation. It sounds like divine child abuse. You know?"[2]

Various Emerging Church books and weblogs have repeatedly advocated the dismantling and wholesale reimagining of some of the very same doctrines earlier evangelicals have fiercely defended for generations against modernists and theological liberals—including the inerrancy and authority of Scripture, the doctrine of original sin, and the exclusivity of Christ. Almost any biblical doctrine and evangelical distinctive you can name has at one point or another been maligned by this or that celebrity in the Emerging Church movement.

What lesson does history teach us about movements like this? I was surprised to find the unambiguous answer to that question spelled out recently in an op-ed piece in the *Los Angeles Times*:

> Embraced by the leadership of all the mainline Protestant denominations, as well as large segments of American Catholicism, liberal Christianity has been hailed by its boosters for 40 years as the future of the Christian church.
>
> Instead, as all but a few diehards now admit, all the mainline churches and movements within churches that have blurred doctrine and softened moral precepts are demographically declining and, in the case of the Episcopal Church, disintegrating.[3]

The article recounted how during denominational meetings in the summer of 2006, Episcopalians refused to heed a plea from the worldwide Anglican communion that they repent of their decision to appoint an admitted, practicing homosexual as bishop. Refusing to reconsider that decision, the Episcopalians further elected as their presiding bishop a woman who has openly blessed same-sex unions, embraced the most radically feminist theological agenda, and led public prayers in which she referred to Christ as "our Mother Jesus."[4]

Practically the same week, the Presbyterian Church (USA) approved alternative designations for the persons of the Trinity—setting aside Father, Son, and Holy Spirit in favor of "Mother, Child, and Womb" or "Rock, Redeemer, and Friend."[5]

Those denominations—and all others who ever embraced modernism (or theological liberalism)—are declining to the point of utter irrelevance. Today there are about half as many Episcopalians in America as there were less than fifty years ago. In 1965, there were 3.4 Episcopalians; now, there are 2.3 million.[6] That denomination is on a trajectory to lose its entire constituency and (fittingly) declare bankruptcy before the end of the decade. It could not happen soon enough. And just a week before voting to rename the Trinity, the general

> I AM CONVINCED THAT THE GREATEST DANGER FACING CHRISTIANS TODAY HAS INFILTRATED THE CHURCH ALREADY. COUNTLESS FALSE TEACHERS ALREADY HAVE PROMINENT PLATFORMS IN THE EVANGELICAL MOVEMENT; EVANGELICALS THEMSELVES ARE LOATH TO PRACTICE DISCERNMENT OR QUESTION OR CHALLENGE ANYTHING TAUGHT WITHIN THEIR MOVEMENT; AND MANY LEADING EVANGELICALS HAVE CONCLUDED NO DOCTRINE OR POINT OF THEOLOGY IS WORTH EARNESTLY CONTENDING FOR.

assembly of the Presbyterian Church (USA) announced layoffs for seventy-five of their employees and budget cuts totaling more than nine million dollars.[7] To one degree or another, every denomination that welcomed modernists has seen precisely the same effect. Modernism has failed demonstrably—in spectacular ways.

But the war against truth has not abated one bit. Just when evangelicals ought to be celebrating the triumph of the biblical doctrines and evangelical principles they have long fought for against modernist influences, large segments of evangelicalism are instead adopting the rubric of *post*modernism—and thus unwittingly resurrecting the very same dangerous kinds of doctrinal compromise our spiritual ancestors stood against when they opposed modernism.

I wrote at length about the close parallels between early modernism and the "seeker-sensitive" philosophy of ministry in 1993.[8] I compared the slippery slope of evangelical pragmatism to the infamous "Down Grade" of late nineteenth-century modernism. I recounted how the early warnings of Charles Spurgeon went largely unheeded by the evangelicals of his day, to the detriment of the church's testimony and influence. Fourteen years after my book on that subject was published, I wouldn't change a word of what I wrote then. There is still an eery similarity between the course taken by the mainstream denominational churches of my great grandfather's era and the rapid downhill shortcut the evangelical movement is blindly pursuing today. If anything, the situation today looks worse by several degrees of magnitude than it was just a scant decade and a half ago, because indifference over doctrinal decline is now much more widespread and much more deeply engrained.

I am convinced that the greatest danger facing Christians today has infiltrated the church already. Countless false teachers already have prominent platforms in the evangelical movement; evangelicals themselves are loath to practice discernment or question or challenge anything taught within their movement; and many leading evangelicals have concluded no doctrine or point of theology is worth earnestly contending for. The evangelicalism *movement* as we speak of it today is already doomed. It stands roughly where the mainstream denominations were in the early part of the twentieth century when those denominations began formally excommunicating conservative voices of dissent from their midst—and sounder evangelicals began actively separating from those denominations en masse.

Unfortunately, the evangelical movement is amorphous, and that is one of the key factors that has allowed it to become such a monstrosity. There is no "membership," no mechanism for excommunication, no clear process for dealing with false teachers. Anyone can declare himself "evangelical" and make himself a teacher—and who's to say otherwise? Churches today are often planted by individuals who are neither doctrinally nor personally qualified for church leadership. This is frequently done with no oversight by any group of elders and no accountability to a senior body. Megachurches have been built by men with strong entrepreneurial skills and weak exegetical skills. As they have reproduced themselves, the evangelical movement has been flooded with ministers who are grossly unprepared for ministry and deliberately undiscerning when it comes to doctrine. Evangelicalism is now dominated by leaders who regard big numbers as proof of success and divine blessing and who are convinced that careful doctrinal teaching is actually the enemy of church growth. No wonder theological chaos now reigns in the evangelical movement.

When the movement as a whole remained committed to core biblical distinctives, it was not easy for false teachers to usurp that kind of influence. But the very doctrines that once defined the evangelical position are currently being challenged by people within the movement. The evangelical consensus is gradually being dismantled, all boundaries are being systematically erased, and everything is suddenly up for grabs.

It is time for the faithful remnant to redraw clear lines and step up our energies in the Truth War—contending *earnestly* for the faith. In light of all the biblical commands to fight a good warfare, it is both naive and disobedient for Christians in this postmodern generation to shirk that duty.

I see a close analogy in the political situation that dominates the secular Western world today. The West loves openness, tolerance, freedom, and acceptance. That is understandable on a certain level, of course. There is a true sense in which all those values have an important place in every civilized society.

But abandon *moral* values, throw a few lawless terrorists into the mix, and the situation changes. Terrorists don't yield to any law. They hide by simply mixing into a free society, pretending to be other than they really are, taking advantage of society's openness in order to gain access to places where they can attack the very foundations of the society that grants them such freedom.

Western society, by and large, does not have the will or the inclination to construct boundaries for its own self-defense. Years after the terror war supposedly got serious, America's borders are still basically open to all comers. Much of European society still opposes the idea of any military response to the terrorist threat. Postmodern values and political correctness rule out profiling, monitoring the conversations of suspicious people, targeting illegal residents, and other means that would help identify who the terrorists are. Analysts in the media perform all sorts of intellectual gymnastics to avoid saying that the roots of terrorism have anything to do with a particular culture or religion. "Who are we to sit in judgment on another culture or say that their values or way of life need to change?"

The evangelical movement has been similarly naive. Spiritual terrorists are plotting the destruction of the church. Scripture expressly warns us about this. Yet evangelicals in recent decades have done very little to restrain apostates or expose them. False teachers are not stopped at the border anymore. The rankest apostates now have almost complete freedom in the evangelical movement. Unhindered, they have infiltrated evangelical churches, denominations, and Christian colleges and seminaries. They write weblogs, they give interviews on Christian radio stations, and they write books explicitly targeting evangelical readers.

Scripture expressly warns believers not to be so blithe about the threat of spiritual terrorism. Christians are not supposed to be gullible. We are not to turn a blind eye to the danger. We are not to have fellowship with the unfruitful works of darkness but rather expose them (Ephesians 5:11). We simply cannot be all-embracing without allowing false teachers to infiltrate and be destructive. And that danger is both real and imminent. Jude has given us a wake-up call and a summons to battle.

What should be our response? What should be our reaction? Jude himself tells us:

> But you, beloved, remember the words which were spoken before by the apostles of our Lord Jesus Christ: how they told you that there would be mockers in the last time who would walk according to their own ungodly lusts. These are sensual persons, who cause divisions, not having the Spirit.
>
> But you, beloved, building yourselves up on your most holy faith, praying in the Holy Spirit, keep yourselves in the love of God, looking for the mercy of our Lord Jesus Christ unto eternal life. And on some have compassion, making a distinction; but others save with fear, pulling them out of the fire, hating even the garment defiled by the flesh. (Jude 17–23)

# Remember

Notice, first of all, that Jude urges his readers to *remember what was prophesied*. After all, the apostles said false teachers would come. Jude's words are virtually an exact quotation from 2 Peter 3:3. That, clearly, is the prophecy he was referring to.

Here's the point: once again Jude is stressing that God is sovereign and has not lost control. He's reminding his readers once more that the influx of false teachers into the church doesn't mean the plan of God has gone awry. God is not surprised by this development; it is what His Word prophesied. Even in the worst of times, we can be certain that nothing is happening that wasn't already foreknown by God. He even *told* us we should expect an influx of apostasy. We were warned about it, and here it is.

Our duty, then, is to respond rightly. Not only should we not be surprised when false teachers appear in the church; we ought to have anticipated and prepared for the reality of it. It is a wake-up call. When an absolutely reliable source tells us terrorists are coming, it then behooves us to find out who they are and expose them before they do their damage.

Today's evangelicals have no excuse for not being vigilant. We have been warned—repeatedly. Jesus commanded us to be on guard against false christs and false prophets. The apostolic era was filled with examples of wolves in sheep's clothing. Church history is strewn with more examples, one after another. Only sinful and willful unbelief can account for the refusal of so many in the church today to heed those warnings.

# Remain

A second way we ought to respond to apostasy is by remaining faithful. We need to build one another up in the faith and maintain our spiritual stability. Above all, stay committed to the truth. Don't waver.

Jude includes four aspects of this principle. First, he says we must seek to remain faithful by "building yourselves up on your most holy faith." He is urging us to edify one another by the Word of God. The phrase "your most holy faith" is a reference to sound doctrine—a right understanding of the truth as it is revealed in Scripture. Build yourself up on that, Jude says. Here's how Peter says it in the parallel passage: "You therefore, beloved, since you knowthis beforehand, beware lest you also fall from your own steadfastness, being led away with the error of the wicked; but grow in the grace and knowledge of our Lord and Savior Jesus Christ" (2 Peter 3:17–18). Be strengthened. Become mature. This is a call to the spiritual discipline of studying the Word.

Second, maintain your spiritual stability and equilibrium by "praying in the Holy Spirit." Commune constantly with the Spirit of God, going before God in the power and the will of the Spirit to demonstrate your dependence on God and to cry out for His protection, His grace, His insight, and His power. The faithful life is kept

> JESUS COMMANDED US TO BE ON GUARD AGAINST FALSE CHRISTS AND FALSE PROPHETS. THE APOSTOLIC ERA WAS FILLED WITH EXAMPLES OF WOLVES IN SHEEP'S CLOTHING. CHURCH HISTORY IS STREWN WITH MORE EXAMPLES, ONE AFTER ANOTHER. ONLY SINFUL AND WILLFUL UNBELIEF CAN ACCOUNT FOR THE REFUSAL OF SO MANY IN THE CHURCH TODAY TO HEED THOSE WARNINGS.

steady through means of the spiritual disciplines of study and prayer.

Third, Jude says, "Keep yourselves in the love of God" (v. 21). That is a way of reminding us to be obedient. Jesus said, "He who has My commandments and keeps them, it is he who loves Me. And he who loves Me will be loved by My Father, and I will love him and manifest Myself to him" (John 14:21). "Abide in My love," He told the disciples. "*If you keep My commandments, you will abide in My love,* just as I have kept My Father's commandments and abide in His love" (John 15:9–10, emphasis added). Jude 21 is simply echoing that commandment. It is a call for obedience.

Finally, Jude says, keep "looking for the mercy of our Lord Jesus Christ unto eternal life." That speaks of an eager expectation of Christ's second coming.

All of those are ways of reminding us to set our minds on heavenly things, not on the things of this world (Colossians 3:2). That is the only way to survive in a time of apostasy. Ultimately, only what is eternal really matters—and that means the truth matters infinitely more than any of the merely earthly things that tend to capture our attention and energies.

# REACH

Jude mentions a way we ought to respond in an age of apostasy: *reach out.* Not only are there deceivers in the church; many have been deceived. As I noted early in this book, our duty in the Truth War is not only to oppose the false teachers but also to rescue those who have been led astray by them.

The language Jude uses is very picturesque: "And have mercy on some, who are doubting; save others, snatching them out of the fire; and on some have mercy with fear, hating even the garment polluted by the flesh" (vv. 22–23 NASB). His words convey the utmost urgency and sobriety, and he uses starkly vivid terminology to reflect exactly what God thinks of apostasy.

Notice that Jude describes three kinds of people who are affected by apostasy. The first group are the *confused*. They are doubters. They have been exposed to false teaching, and it has shaken their confidence in the truth. They aren't committed to the error yet, just doubting. Perhaps they aren't truly committed to the truth yet either. These may well be people who have never fully and savingly believed the gospel. On the other hand, they could be authentic believers—either young or spiritually feeble. Either way, exposure to false teachers has revealed a dangerous weakness in their faith by causing them to doubt.

Have mercy on them, Jude says. Don't write them off because they are weak and wavering. They are confused because they are absolutely open to any and every teacher, and they are utterly devoid of any discernment. They are the most accessible and the most vulnerable. They need truth, but they are being offered (and duped by) almost everything else.

Churches today are filled with people like that. They drift from church to church. They are often more concerned about whether they like the music than they are about whether they are hearing the truth. They are usually absorbed in religion for self-centered reasons. They want a better life. They are "recovering" sinners looking for fellowship. They are therefore susceptible to anyone who promises to meet their "felt needs." They are the first-line victims of false religion.

Don't write them off or reject them. Show them mercy, Jude says.

And, of course, the chief mercy they need is the mercy of the gospel. Once they lay hold of that truth, they will have a foundation for true discernment and the endless cycle of confusion will be halted.

Group two are the *convinced*. They pose a more difficult problem. You have to snatch them out of the fire, Jude says—suggesting, of course, that they are already *in* the fire. He pictures apostasy as a burning, destructive, potentially lethal conflagration. The imagery underscores both the urgency of the need for rescue and the magnitude of the evil in the false teaching.

The fact that these people are *in* the fire suggests that they have bought the lie. They have (to some degree) owned the false doctrine. They are already being singed by hell. They need something more than mere mercy; this is an urgent rescue operation. Jude is urging us to use any means—*every* legitimate means—to pull them from the fire. These circumstances call for aggressive action.

The principle here is important. When you meet someone who is a convinced follower of some false doctrine, don't automatically turn your back on that person. Don't instantly push such people away or shun them. Don't respond with hostility. They might be more deceived than deceiving.

At the same time, you cannot embrace someone as a part of the true fellowship who rejects essential aspects of gospel truth. You don't offer someone who is convinced of a serious falsehood unconditional acceptance as a believer. But Jude is very specific about how we *should* respond to such people: go after them in a very critical rescue operation. Try to snatch them out of the fire.

Again, snatching them from the fire means giving them the truth—but with accents of urgency befitting the serious danger such people are facing. You come with force. You don't toy with such error or invite the purveyors of it to a dispassionate discussion over tea and biscuits. You treat the situation with an urgency and sobriety that is commensurate with the evil of apostasy.

That is exactly how Jesus responded to the Pharisees. He was strongly confrontive, very blunt; His warnings to them were severe; He spoke to them of judgment, devastation, and hell. His warning was analogous to the kind of warning you would give a neighbor if his house caught fire and you knew he was still inside asleep.

PULLING PEOPLE FROM THE FIRES OF APOSTASY REQUIRES US TO GET CLOSE TO THEM. JUDE SUGGESTS THERE IS SEVERE DANGER IN THIS. WE CAN'T ALWAYS TELL THE DIFFERENCE BETWEEN THE MERELY CONVINCED AND THE FULLY COMMITTED. SOME ARE DECEIVED; OTHERS ARE DELIBERATE DECEIVERS.

In 2 Corinthians 10:4–5, Paul describes spiritual warfare as the demolishing of ideological fortresses: "The weapons of our warfare are not carnal but mighty in God for pulling down strongholds, casting down arguments and every high thing that exalts itself against the knowledge of God, bringing every thought into captivity to the obedience of Christ." The language is deliberately militant. But notice that he is not talking about warfare against *people.* He is describing a battle against evil *ideas*—thoughts, arguments, fortresses made of satanic lies. People are basically victims of the ideas, trapped and imprisoned by false doctrines and evil systems of thought. The point of the warfare is to liberate people from those fortresses.

So there is a ministry of mercy to the confused. There's a more urgent and solemn ministry of rescue to the convinced. And then Jude speaks of a third group: the *committed*. Here Jude employs his strongest and most vivid language: "On some have mercy with fear, hating even the garment polluted by the flesh" (v. 23 NASB).

Obviously, pulling people from the fires of apostasy requires us to get close to them. Jude suggests there is severe danger in this. We can't always tell the difference between the merely convinced and the fully committed. Some are deceived; others are deliberate deceivers. Some are disciples of error; others are the propagators, the leaders—the false teachers themselves. Jude suggests that we ought to show even the false teachers themselves a kind of mercy (for sometimes even the deceivers themselves are, to a degree, deceived, and occasionally, by God's grace, even they can be pulled from the fire). So show them mercy, Jude says. But do it with fear, despising the defilement of their evil.

The expression Jude employs is shocking. It is as coarse as any expression in Scripture. Jude uses a Greek word for "garment" that signifies underwear and a word for "polluted" that means "stained in a filthy manner; spotted and stained by bodily functions." He is comparing the defilement of false teaching to soiled underwear.

If you have ever questioned what God's own view of false religion and apostasy is, that is it. One of the most important aspects of Jude's entire message is this theme, which runs through the whole of it: *false teaching is the deadliest and most abhorrent of evils*, because it is always an expression of unbelief, which is the distillation of pure evil.

The *deadliest? Most abhorrent?* What about pornography, abortion, sexual perversion, marital unfaithfulness? Those are all gross sins, of course, and they are eating away at the fabric of our society. It is certainly right for us to be morally repulsed and outraged at such monstrous evils. But heresy that undermines the gospel is a far more serious sin because it places souls in eternal peril under the darkness of the kind of lies that keep people in permanent bondage to their sin.

That is why there is no more serious abomination than heresy. It is the worst and most loathsome kind of spiritual filth. Therefore, Jude says, we should no more risk being defiled by apostasy than we would want to clasp someone's filthy, stained underwear close to ourselves. Scripture employs this same shocking imagery in other places too. Isaiah 64:6, lamenting the apostasy of Israel, says, "But we are all like an unclean thing, and all our righteousnesses [i.e., self-righteousness and false religion] are like filthy rags." In that text, Isaiah uses a Hebrew expression that speaks of soiled menstrual cloths. In Revelation 3:4, Christ says to the church at Sardis, "You have a few names even in Sardis who have not defiled their garments." That has a similar meaning, for He is referring to the defilement of heresy and apostasy.

These passages not only give insight into what God thinks of apostasy; they give us explicit instructions about how to deal with apostates. False doctrine and the wickedness of those who believe it stain the soul. Don't get close enough to be corrupted. Paul said something similar at the end of Romans: "I urge you, brethren, note those who cause divisions and offenses, contrary to the doctrine which you learned, and avoid them" (16:17). You can't build a real friendship with a false teacher. You cannot pretend to accept such a person as a fellow believer. You have to understand that people who buy into apostasy and damnable error are (either wittingly or unwittingly) agents of the kingdom of darkness and enemies of the truth. Don't risk being defiled by their corruption.

Nevertheless, there is a place for showing apostates mercy. It is a fearful mercy, and once again it involves giving them the light of truth. Confront their error with the truth, for that is the only hope of freeing them from the bondage and defilement of their own apostasy. But do it with the utmost care, always mindful of the dangers such an evil poses.

# What, After All, Is Truth?

What is truth? We began this book with that question, and my earnest hope is that the answer is clear by now: Truth is not any individual's opinion or imagination. *Truth is what God decrees.* And He has given us an infallible source of saving truth in His revealed Word.

For the true Christian, this should not be a complex issue. God's Word is what all pastors and church leaders are commanded to proclaim, in season and out of season—when it is well received and even when it is not (2 Timothy 4:2). It is what every Christian is commanded to read, study, meditate on, and divide rightly. It is what we are called and commissioned by Christ to teach and proclaim to the uttermost parts of the earth.

Is there mystery even in the truth God has revealed? Of course. "'For My thoughts are not your thoughts, nor are your ways My ways,' says the LORD" (Isaiah 55:8). In 1 Corinthians 2:16, Paul paraphrased Isaiah 40:13–14: "Who has known the mind of the LORD that he may instruct Him?"

But then Paul immediately added this: "We have the mind of Christ." Christ has graciously given us enough truth and enough understanding to equip us for every good deed—including the work of earnestly contending for the faith against deceivers who try to twist the truth of the gospel. Although we cannot know the mind of God *exhaustively*, we certainly can know it *sufficiently* to be warriors for the cause of truth against the lies of the kingdom of darkness.

And we are *commanded* to participate in that battle. God

Himself sounded the call to battle when His Spirit moved Jude to write his short epistle and it permanently entered the canon of Scripture. This is not a duty any faithful Christian can shirk. Earthly life for the faithful Christian can never be a perpetual state of ease and peace. That's why the New Testament includes so many descriptions of the Christian life as nonstop warfare: Ephesians 6:11-18; 2 Timothy 2:1-4; 2 Timothy 4:7; 2 Corinthians 6:7; 10:3-5; 1 Thessalonians 5:8. I hope by now you understand that those unwilling to join the fight against untruth and false religion are no true friends of Christ.

The handful of vignettes from church history we have examined together in this book are only a brief introduction to how the Truth War has been fought over the past two millennia. I hope what we have examined here will provoke you to pursue the study further on your own. Look at any period of church history and you will discover this significant fact: Whenever the people of God have sought peace with the world or made alliances with false religions, it has meant a period of serious spiritual decline, even to the point where at times the truth seemed almost to be in total eclipse. But whenever Christians have contended earnestly for the faith, the church has grown and the cause of truth has prospered. May it be so in our time.

In other words, the Truth War is a *good* fight (1 Timothy 6:12). So let's wage good warfare (1 Timothy 1:18)—for the honor of Christ and the glory of God.

# Appendix

## Why Discernment Is Out of Fashion

*This I pray, that your love may abound still more and more
in knowledge and all discernment, that you may approve the
things that are excellent, that you may be sincere and
without offense till the day of Christ.*

—Philippians 1:9–10

This appendix is adapted from my 1994 book, *Reckless Faith*,
which is now out of print. It included a chapter about biblical
discernment, and I am excerpting that section here in the hope
that it will encourage and equip Christians who desire to be
faithful soldiers in the Truth War.[1]

Many summers ago I drove across the country to deliver my
son's car to him. He was a recent college graduate, then playing
minor-league baseball in Florida. He needed his car for local trans-
portation. The cross-country trip fit perfectly with some previously
scheduled ministry engagements on my calendar, so Lance Quinn
(my senior associate pastor at the time) and I made the journey by
automobile together.

As we drove through Lance's home state of Arkansas, our route
took us off the main highways and through some beautiful rural
country. We topped one hill, and I noticed near a rustic house a
homemade sign advertising hand-sewn quilts. I had hoped to stop

> OUR GENERATION IS EXPOSED TO MORE RELIGIOUS IDEAS THAN ANY PEOPLE IN HISTORY. RELIGIOUS BROADCASTING AND THE PRINT MEDIA BOMBARD PEOPLE WITH ALL KINDS OF DEVIANT TEACHINGS THAT CLAIM TO BE TRUTH. THE UNDISCERNING PERSON HAS NO MEANS OF DETERMINING WHAT TRUTH IS, AND MANY ARE BAFFLED BY THE VARIETY.

somewhere along the way to buy an anniversary gift for my wife. She likes handmade crafts and had been wanting a quilt, so we decided to stop and look.

We went to the door of the old house and knocked. A friendly woman with a dish towel answered the door. When we told her we were interested in quilts, she swung the door open wide and ushered us in. She showed us into the living room, where she had several quilts on display.

The television in the corner was on, tuned to a religious broadcast. The woman's husband was lounging in a recliner, half watching the program and half reading a religious magazine. Around the room were piles of religious books, religious literature, and religious videotapes. I recognized one or two of the books—resources from solid evangelical publishers.

The woman left the room to get some more quilts to show us, so the man put aside his magazine and greeted us. "I was just catching up on some reading," he said.

"Are you a believer?" I asked.

"A believer in *what*?" he asked, apparently startled that I would ask.

"A believer in Christ," I said. "I noticed your books. Are you a Christian?"

"Well, sure," he said, holding up the magazine he was reading. I recognized it as the publication of a well-known cult. I took a closer look at the stacks of material around the room. There were a few evangelical best sellers, materials from several media ministries, a promotional magazine from a leading evangelical seminary, and even some helpful Bible study aids. But mixed in with all that were stacks of *The Watch Tower* magazines published by the Jehovah's Witnesses, a copy of *Dianetics* (the book by Scientology founder L. Ron Hubbard), a Book of Mormon, Mary Baker Eddy's *Science and Health*, some literature from the Franciscan brothers, and an incredible array of stuff from nearly every conceivable cult and *-ism*. I watched as he jotted down the address of the television preacher who was at that moment offering some free literature.

"You read from quite an assortment of material," I observed. "These all represent different beliefs. Do you accept any one of them?"

"I find there's good in all of it," he said. "I read it all and just look for the good."

While this conversation was going on, the woman had come back with a stack of quilts and was ready to show them to us. The first quilt she laid out was a patchwork of all different sizes, colors, and prints of fabric scraps. I looked at it, trying to see some kind of pattern or design in it, but there was none. The color combinations even seemed to clash. The quilt itself was—well, ugly.

I described for her the kind of quilt I was looking for, and she pulled one out that was exactly what I wanted. Her price seemed reasonable, so I told her I would take it.

As she wrapped up my purchase, I couldn't help looking again at that first quilt she had brought out from the back room. Frankly, it was the *least* attractive of all her quilts. But she was obviously quite proud of it, having labored over it for hours. It was evidently her personal favorite—and undoubtedly a genuine piece of folk art. But I couldn't imagine anyone else being attracted to that particular quilt.

Her quilt, I thought, was a perfect metaphor for her husband's religion. Taking bits and pieces from every conceivable source, he was putting together a patchwork faith. He thought of his religion as a thing of beauty, but in God's eyes it was an abomination.

Too many people are like that—fashioning a patchwork religion, sifting through stacks of religious ideas, looking for good in all of it. Our generation is exposed to more religious ideas than any people in history. Religious broadcasting and the print media bombard people with all kinds of deviant teachings that claim to be truth. The undiscerning person has no means of determining *what* truth is, and many are baffled by the variety.

Meanwhile, evangelicals (once known for a very prudent and biblical approach to doctrine) are fast becoming as doctrinally clueless as the unchurched people they are so keen to please. At least three decades of deliberately downplaying doctrine and discernment in order to attract the unchurched has filled many once-sound churches with people who utterly lack any ability to differentiate the very worst false doctrines from truth. I constantly encounter evangelical church members who are at a loss to answer the most profound errors they hear from cultists, unorthodox media preachers, or other sources of false doctrine.

## THE RISE OF EXTREME TOLERANCE

A closely related second reason for the low level of discernment in the church today is the growing reluctance to take a definitive stand on any issue. This, too, has been one of the central themes of this book. But it deserves to be stressed one more time.

Discernment is frankly not very welcome in a culture like ours. In fact, the postmodern perspective is more than merely hostile to discernment; it is practically the polar opposite. Think about it: pronouncing anything "true" and calling its antithesis "error" is a breach of postmodernism's one last impregnable dogma. That is why to a postmodernist nothing is more uncouth than voicing strong opinions on spiritual, moral, or ethical matters. People are expected to hold their most important convictions with as much slack as possible. Certainty about anything is out of the question, and all who refuse to equivocate on any point of principle or doctrine are therefore automatically labeled too narrow. Zeal for the truth has become politically incorrect. There is actually zero tolerance for biblical discernment in a "tolerant" climate like that.

In the secular realm, postmodernism's extreme tolerance has been foisted on an unsuspecting public by the entertainment media for several decades. A plethora of talk shows on daily television have led the way. Phil Donahue established the format. Jerry Springer took it to ridiculous extremes. And Oprah made it seem somewhat respectable and refined. Shows like these remind viewers daily not to be too opinionated—and they do it by parading in front of their audiences the most bizarre and extreme advocates of every radical "alternative lifestyle" imaginable. We are not supposed to be shocked or notice the overtly self-destructive nature of so many aberrant subcultures. The point is to broaden our minds and raise our level of tolerance. And if you do criticize another person's value system, it cannot be on biblical grounds. Anyone who cites religious beliefs as a reason to reject another person's way of life is automatically viewed with the same contempt that used to be reserved for out-and-out religious heretics. The culture around us has declared war on all biblical standards.

Some Christians unwittingly began following suit several years ago. That has opened the door for a whole generation in the church to embrace postmodern relativism openly and deliberately. They don't want the truth presented with stark black-and-white clarity anymore. They prefer having issues of right and wrong, true and false, good and bad deliberately painted in shades of gray. We have reached a point where the typical churchgoer today assumes that is the proper way of understanding truth. Any degree of certainty has begun to sound offensive to people's postmodernized ears.

A few years ago I did a live radio interview where listeners were invited to phone in. One caller told me, "You seem like a lot nicer person than I thought you were by listening to your sermons." He meant it kindly, and I took it in that spirit. But I was curious to know what he had heard in my preaching that he interpreted as not "nice." (When I preach, I am certainly not angry or acrimonious.) So I asked what he meant.

"I don't know," he said. "In your sermons, you sound so opinionated, so certain of yourself—so dogmatic. But talking to people one on one, you're more conversational. You just sound nicer." Like many people today, he thought of dialogue as "nicer" than a sermon. Someone who is "loving," by that way of thinking, could never be emphatic, critical, or zealous for the truth. That reflects a severely skewed understanding of what authentic love demands. Real love "does not rejoice in iniquity, but rejoices in the truth" (1 Corinthians 13:6).

One young pastor told me he didn't like the authoritarian implications of the word *preaching*. He said he preferred to speak of his pulpit ministry as "sharing" with his people. He didn't last long in ministry, of course. But sadly, his comments probably reflect the prevailing mood in the church today.

D. Martyn Lloyd-Jones noticed the same trend several decades ago. His marvelous book *Preaching and Preachers* began by noting that modern society was becoming uncomfortable with the whole idea of "preaching":

> A new idea has crept in with regard to preaching, and it has taken various forms. A most significant one was that people began to talk about the "address" in the service instead of the sermon. That in itself was indicative of a subtle change. An "address." No longer the sermon, but an "address" or perhaps even a lecture. . . . There was a man in the U.S.A. who published a series of books under the significant title of *Quiet Talks. Quiet Talks on Prayer*; *Quiet Talks on Power*; etc. In other words the very title announces that the man is not going to preach. Preaching, of course, is something carnal lacking in spirituality; what is needed is a chat, a fireside chat, quiet talks, and so on![3]

Lloyd-Jones was simply noticing one of the subtle harbingers of postmodernism's contempt for clarity and authority. A problem that existed in embryonic form in his era is now a full-grown monster.

At the "Emergent Convention" in 2004, a gathering of some eleven hundred leaders in the Emerging Church movement, Doug Pagitt, pastor of Solomon's Porch (an Emergent community in Minneapolis), told the gathering, "Preaching is broken." He suggested that a completely open conversation where all participants are seen as equals is better suited to a postmodern culture. "Why do I get to speak for 30 minutes and you don't?" he asked. "A sermon is often a violent act," he declared. "It's a violence toward the will of the people who have to sit there and take it."[4]

Rudy Carrasco, a Pasadena-based Emergent pastor, agreed that preaching is simply too one-sided, too authoritative, and too rigid for postmodern times. "Every day, every week, there's stuff that pops up in life, and it's not resolved, just crazy and confusing and painful. When people come across with three answers, and they know everything, and they have this iron sheen about them, I'm turned off. Period. I'm just turned off. And I think that's not unique to me."[5]

By contrast, compromise is what drives this pragmatic, postmodern age. In most people's minds, the very word *compromise* is rich with positive connotations. On one level, that is certainly understandable. Obviously, in the realm of social and political discourse, certain kinds of compromise can be helpful, even constructive. Compromise lubricates the political machinery of secular government. The art of compromise is the key to successful negotiations in business. And even in marriage, small compromises are often necessary for a healthy relationship.

But when it comes to biblical issues, moral principles, theological truth, divine revelation, and other spiritual absolutes, compromise is *never* appropriate.

The church, caught up in the spirit of the age, is losing sight of that reality. In recent years, evangelicals have embraced compromise as a tool for church growth, a platform for unity, and even a test of spirituality. Take an uncompromising stance on almost any doctrinal or biblical issue, and a chorus of voices will call you obstinate, unkind, heartless, contentious, or unloving, no matter how ironically you frame your argument.

> EVANGELICALS HAVE EMBRACED COMPROMISE AS A TOOL FOR CHURCH GROWTH, A PLATFORM FOR UNITY, AND EVEN A TEST OF SPIRITUALITY. TAKE AN UNCOMPROMISING STANCE ON ALMOST ANY DOCTRINAL OR BIBLICAL ISSUE, AND A CHORUS OF VOICES WILL CALL YOU OBSTINATE, UNKIND, HEARTLESS, CONTENTIOUS, OR UNLOVING, NO MATTER HOW IRONICALLY YOU FRAME YOUR ARGUMENT.

Did I say "argument"? Many people have the false idea that

Christians should never argue about anything. We're not supposed to engage in polemics. I hear this frequently: "Why don't you just state truth in positive terms and ignore the views you disagree with? Why not steer clear of controversy, forget the negatives, and present everything affirmatively?"

That ethos is why it is no longer permissible to deal with biblical issues in a straightforward and uncompromising fashion. Those who dare to take an unpopular stand, declare truth in a definitive way—or worst of all, express disagreement with someone else's teaching—will inevitably be marked as troublesome. Compromise has become a virtue while devotion to truth has become offensive.

Martyn Lloyd-Jones called the modern distrust of polemics "very loose and very false and very flabby thinking. . . . The attitude of many seems to be, 'We do not want these arguments. Give us the simple message, the simple gospel. Give it to us positively, and do not bother about other views.'"[6] He responded to those sentiments: "It is important that we should realize that if we speak like that we are denying the Scriptures. The Scriptures are full of arguments, full of polemics."[7] He went on:

> Disapproval of polemics in the Christian Church is a very serious matter. But that is the attitude of the age in which we live. The prevailing idea today in many circles is not to bother about these things. As long as we are all Christians, anyhow, somehow, all is well. Do not let us argue about doctrine, let us all be Christians together and talk about the love of God. That is really the whole basis of ecumenicity. Unfortunately, that same attitude is creeping into evangelical circles also, and many say that we must not be too precise about these things. . . . If you hold that view you are criticizing the Apostle Paul, you are saying that he was wrong, and at the same time you are criticizing the Scriptures. The Scriptures argue and debate and dispute; they are full of polemics.[8]

Then Lloyd-Jones added this helpful qualifier:

> Let us be clear about what we mean. This is not argument for the sake of argument; this is not a manifestation of an argumentative spirit; this is not just indulging one's prejudices. The Scriptures do not approve of that, and furthermore the Scriptures are very concerned about the spirit in which one engages in discussion. No man should like argument for the sake of argument. We should always regret the necessity; but though we regret and bemoan it, when we feel that a vital matter is at stake we must engage in argument. We must "earnestly contend for the truth," and we are called upon to do that by the New Testament.[9]

Not every issue is cast in black and white. There are many questions to which Scripture does not explicitly speak. For example, there is no list of holidays and holy days for Christians to observe or avoid celebrating. The issue is explicitly left in the realm of indifferent matters by the apostle Paul: "One person esteems one day above another; another esteems every day alike. Let each be fully convinced in his own mind" (Romans 14:5). Paul says something similar about foods and dietary restrictions (vv. 2–3).

IN TRUTH, FAR MORE ISSUES ARE BLACK AND WHITE THAN MOST PEOPLE REALIZE. MOST OF THE TRUTHS OF GOD'S WORD ARE EXPLICITLY CONTRASTED WITH OPPOSING IDEAS. JAY ADAMS CALLS THIS THE PRINCIPLE OF *antithesis*, AND HE POINTS OUT THAT IT IS FUNDAMENTAL TO GENUINE DISCERNMENT.

But many of the issues being compromised within the evangelical movement today are not questionable. Scripture speaks very clearly against homosexuality, for example. The Christian position on adultery is not at all vague. The question of whether a believer ought to marry an unbeliever is spelled out with perfect clarity. Scripture quite plainly forbids any Christian to take another Christian to court. Selfishness and pride are explicitly identified as sins. These are not gray areas. There is no room for compromise here.

Nevertheless, I constantly hear every one of those issues treated as a gray area—on Christian radio, on Christian television, and in Christian literature. People want all such matters to be negotiable. And too many Christian leaders willingly oblige. They hesitate to speak with authority on matters where Scripture is plain. The lines of distinction between truth and error, wisdom and foolishness, church and world are being systematically obliterated by such means.

In truth, far more issues are black and white than most people realize. Most of the truths of God's Word are explicitly contrasted with opposing ideas. Jay Adams calls this the principle of *antithesis*, and he points out that it is fundamental to genuine discernment:

In the Bible, where antithesis is so important, discernment—the ability to distinguish God's thoughts and God's ways from all others—is essential. Indeed, God says that "the wise in heart will be called discerning" (Proverbs 16:21).

From the Garden of Eden with its two trees (one allowed, one forbidden) to the eternal destiny of the human being in heaven or in hell, the Bible sets forth two, and only two, ways: God's way, and all others. Accordingly, people are said to be saved or lost. They belong to God's people or the world. There was Gerizim, the mount of blessing, and Ebal, the mount of cursing. There is the narrow way and the wide way, leading either to eternal life or to destruction. There are those who are against and those who are with us, those within and those without. There is life and death, truth and falsehood, good and bad, light and darkness, the kingdom of God and the kingdom of Satan, love and hatred, spiritual wisdom and the wisdom of the world. Christ is said to be the way, the truth, and the life, and no one may come to the Father but by Him. His is the only name under the sky by which one may be saved.[10]

Adams points out that such antithetical teaching is found "on nearly every page of the Bible."[11] "People who study the Bible in depth develop antithetical mindsets: They think in terms of contrasts or opposites."[12] He believes that the Old Testament laws distinguishing between clean and unclean animals have a distinct purpose. Regulations governing choices in clothing, health care, and other matters of daily life were not arbitrary, but were meant to cause God's people to think constantly about the difference between God's ways and the world's way—"to develop in God's people an antithetical mentality."[13]

I agree. All truth sets itself against error. Where Scripture speaks, it speaks with authority. It speaks definitively. It speaks decisively. It calls for absolute conviction. It demands that we submit to God and resist the devil (James 4:7). It urges us to discern between the spirit of truth and the spirit of error (1 John 4:6). It commands us to turn away from evil and do good (1 Peter 3:11). It bids us reject the broad way that seems right to the human mind (Proverbs 14:12; 16:25) and follow the narrow way prescribed by God (Matthew 7:13–14). It tells us that our ways are not God's ways nor our thoughts His thoughts (Isaiah 55:8). It orders us to protect the truth and reject lies (Romans 1:25). It declares that no lie is of the truth (1 John 2:21). It guarantees that the righteous shall be blessed and the wicked perish (Psalm 1:1, 6). And it reminds us that "friendship with the world is enmity with God. Whoever therefore wants to be a friend of the world makes himself an enemy of God" (James 4:4).

Discernment demands that where Scripture speaks with clarity, a hard line must be drawn. Christ is against human philosophy, against empty deception, against human tradition, and against the elementary principles of this world (Colossians 2:8). Those things cannot be integrated with true Christian belief; they must be repudiated and steadfastly resisted. Scripture demands that we make a definitive choice: "How long will you falter between two opinions? If the LORD is God, follow Him; but if Baal, follow him" (1 Kings 18:21). "Choose for yourselves this day whom you will serve. . . . But as for me and my house, we will serve the LORD" (Joshua 24:15).

The modern canonization of compromise represents a detour down a dead-end alley. Both Scripture and church history reveal the danger of compromising biblical truth. Those whom God uses are invariably men and women who swim against the tide. They hold strong convictions with great courage and refuse to compromise in the face of incredible opposition. David stubbornly refused to tremble before Goliath; he saw him as an affront to God. While all Israel cowered in fear, David stood alone before the enemy. Daniel, Shadrach, Meshach, and Abednego all courageously refused the easy path of compromise. It surely would have cost them their lives if God had not sovereignly intervened. Yet they never wavered.

Where are the men and women today with the courage to stand alone? The church in our age has abandoned the confrontive stance. Instead of overturning worldly wisdom with revealed truth, many Christians today are obsessed with finding areas of agreement. The goal has become *integration* rather than *confrontation*. As the church absorbs the values of secular culture, it is losing its ability to differentiate between good and evil. What will happen to the church if everyone proceeds down the slippery path of public opinion?

It is interesting to speculate what the church would be like today if Martin Luther had been prone to compromise. The pressure was heavy on him to tone down his teaching, soften his message, and stop poking his finger in the eye of the papacy. Even many of his friends and supporters urged Luther to come to terms with Rome for the sake of harmony in the church. Luther himself prayed earnestly that the effect of his teaching would not just be divisive—but that the truth would triumph. When he nailed his Ninety-five Theses to the church door, the last thing he wanted to do was split the church.

Yet sometimes division is fitting, even healthy. Especially in times like Luther's—and like ours—when the visible church seems full of counterfeit Christians, it is right for the true people of God to declare themselves. There is no room for compromise.

Discernment demands that we hold biblical convictions with the most fervent tenacity. Titus 1:9 says a basic requirement for every elder is that he be the kind of man who "[holds] fast the faithful word as he has been taught, that he may be able, by sound doctrine, both to exhort and convict those who contradict." It is thus mandated by God that we take issue with error. We must refute those who contradict, or we do not fulfill our divine calling.

In other words, truly biblical ministry must hold forth truths that are absolute. We must take an unmovable stance on all issues where the Bible speaks plainly. What if people don't like such dogmatism? It is necessary anyway.

Sound doctrine divides, confronts, separates, judges, convicts, reproves, rebukes, exhorts, and refutes error. None of these things is very highly esteemed in postmodern thought. But the health of the church depends on our holding firmly to the truth, for where strong convictions are not tolerated, discernment cannot survive.

## A REFUSAL TO SHUN THE WORLD

We have already hinted at another factor contributing to the decline of discernment in the contemporary church. It is a preoccupation with image and influence. It stems from the misconception that to win the world to Christ we must first win the world's favor. If we can get the world to like us, they will embrace our Savior. That has long been the philosophy of seeker-sensitive churches. It is also one of the driving assumptions of the Emerging Church movement.

Such a philosophy suggests that Christians should try to make unconverted sinners feel comfortable with the Christian message. The whole point is to make the church a completely nonthreatening place where unbelievers feel they naturally belong—to tantalize non-Christians rather than confront their unbelief; to make friends with the world rather than standing apart. That all sounds very nice, warm, and friendly to people with post-modern sensibilities, but it is not the strategy for evangelism we are given in Scripture. In fact, it is altogether incompatible with sound doctrine. It is a form of compromise with the world. James called it spiritual adultery (James 4:4).

> IF THE TRUTH CANNOT BE FEARLESSLY PROCLAIMED IN THE CHURCH, WHAT PLACE IS THERE FOR TRUTH AT ALL? HOW CAN WE BUILD A GENERATION OF DISCERNING CHRISTIANS IF WE ARE TERROR-STRUCK AT THE THOUGHT THAT NON-CHRISTIANS MIGHT NOT LIKE HEARING THE UNVARNISHED TRUTH?

And look at the effects of this strategy. In the seeker movement, preaching has been replaced with entertainment. In the Emerging Church movement, truth itself has given way to skepticism. In both movements, any preacher who tries to take a stand for truth and make the biblical message clear is likely to be asked to take his seat instead. He is a problem, an embarrassment, an offense to non-Christians.

If the truth cannot be fearlessly proclaimed in the church, what place is there for truth at all? How can we build a generation of discerning Christians if we are terror-struck at the thought that non-Christians might not like hearing the unvarnished truth?

And since when has it been legitimate for the church to woo the world? Didn't the apostle John write, "Do not marvel, my brethren, if the world hates you" (1 John 3:13)? And did not Jesus say, "The world . . . hates Me because I testify of it that its works are evil" (John 7:7)? Biblical Christians have always understood that they must shun the world. Here are our Lord's own words:

> "If the world hates you, you know that it hated Me before it hated you. If you were of the world, the world would love its own. Yet because you are not of the world, but I chose you out of the world, therefore the world hates you. Remember the word that I said to you, 'A servant is not greater than his master.' If they persecuted Me, they will also persecute you. If they kept My word, they will keep yours also. But all these things they will do to you for My name's sake, because they do not know Him who sent Me." (John 15:18–21)

Does that sound like it gives any latitude for an evangelistic strategy that soft-pedals the offense of the cross?

The apostle Paul frankly would have had no patience for such tactics. He never sought to win the world through intellectual acceptance, personal popularity, image, status, reputation, or things of that sort. He wrote, "We have been made as the filth of the world, the offscouring of all things" (1 Corinthians 4:13). Is the contemporary church right to attempt a "more sophisticated" approach? Dare we set ourselves apart from the godly men of the past, all of whom had to fight for the truth?

Charles Spurgeon said:

We want again Luthers, Calvins, Bunyans, Whitefields, men fit to mark eras, whose names breathe terror in our [foes'] ears. We have dire need of such. Whence will they come to us? They are the gifts of Jesus Christ to the Church, and will come in due time. He has power to give us back again a golden age of preachers, a time as fertile of great divines and mighty ministers as was the Puritan age, and when the good old truth is once more preached by men whose lips are touched as with a live coal from off the altar, this shall be the instrument in the hand of the Spirit for bringing about a great and thorough revival of religion in the land.

I do not look for any other means of converting men beyond the simple preaching of the gospel and the opening of men's ears to hear it. The moment the Church of God shall despise the pulpit, God will despise her.[14]

And, we might add, the moment any church sets out to make friends with the world, that church sets itself at enmity with God (James 4:4).

In practical terms, the movement to accommodate the world has diminished Christians' confidence in divinely revealed truth. If we can't trust the preaching of God's Word to convert the lost and build the church, how can we trust the Bible at all—even as a guide for our daily living? People are being misled by the example of some of their church leaders. They are buying into the delusion that faithfulness to the Word of God is optional.

Furthermore, as biblical preaching continues to diminish, ignorance of Scripture grows. That further exacerbates every problem that stems from the decline of discernment, and the cycle of disaster continues.

Christians ought to have learned by now that we cannot avoid being an offense to the world and still remain faithful to the gospel. The gospel is inherently offensive. Christ Himself is offensive to unbelievers. He is an offense to all in error. He is an offense to all who reject the truth. He is "'a stone of stumbling and a rock of offense.' They stumble, being disobedient to the word, to which they also were appointed" (1 Peter 2:8). The message of the cross is also a stumbling block (Galatians 5:11) and "foolishness to those who are perishing, but to us who are being saved it is the power of God" (1 Corinthians 1:18). Paul wrote, "God forbid that I should boast except in the cross of our Lord Jesus Christ, by whom the world has been crucified to me, and I to the world" (Galatians 6:14).

Authentic Christianity has always recognized that truth is unchanging. The word of God is settled forever in heaven (Psalm 119:89). Jesus Christ is the same yesterday, today, and forever (Hebrews 13:8). God Himself does not change (Malachi 3:6). How could we ever view truth as transient, pliable, or adaptable?

This unchanging view of truth is essential for true discernment. When the church loses its commitment to the inflexibility of truth, it loses its will to discern. It forfeits precise theology, precise morals, and precise conduct.

Right thinking and right living therefore demand careful discipline and an unyielding commitment to the truth. Discernment does not survive in an atmosphere of doctrinal confusion. It will not survive where relativism is tolerated. And it cannot survive if we compromise with the world.

# A Failure to Interpret Scripture Carefully

Another basic factor leading to the decline of discernment is a widespread failure to interpret Scripture properly. Hermeneutics—

Bible interpretation—is an exacting science. Good preaching depends on careful hermeneutics. But too much modern preaching ignores the meaning of Scripture altogether. Pulpits are filled with preachers who are unwilling to do the hard work necessary to interpret Scripture properly. They pad their messages with stories, anecdotes, and clever outlines—all of which disguises the weakness or lack of biblical content.

Some have even gone so far as to suggest that a preoccupation with the meaning of Scripture is unhealthy. A book that rose to the top of the Christian best-seller list a few years ago included a warning to readers that they should be wary of preachers whose emphasis is on *explaining* Scripture rather than *applying* it.

> WITHOUT THE TRUE MEANING OF SCRIPTURE, YOU DON'T REALLY HAVE SCRIPTURE AT ALL. THERE IS NO MAGIC IN THE WORDS THEMSELVES THAT GIVES THEM POWER APART FROM THEIR TRUE MEANING. SO PROPER INTERPRETATION IS CRUCIAL—ESPECIALLY FOR THOSE WHO PREACH.

Certainly application is crucial, but careful interpretation must always come first. To attempt to apply the Word without understanding is sheer folly. Remember, we are expressly commanded to be diligent workers, rightly dividing the Word of truth (2 Timothy 2:15). That familiar text is a mandate for working hard to make sure we have the true sense of what the Bible means. In the words of B.B. Warfield, "The sense of Scripture is Scripture."[15] In other words, without the true meaning of Scripture, you don't really have Scripture at all. There is no magic in the words themselves that gives them power apart from their true meaning. So proper interpretation is crucial—especially for those who preach.

I cringe when I hear a novice wrench a verse out of context

and impose on it a meaning that is totally unwarranted—or even contradictory to the intended sense of the text. Unfortunately, the standard has sunk so low today that even well-known Christian leaders can twist Scripture beyond recognition, yet no one seems to notice. One man who pastors a church of several thousand people recently appeared on nationwide television preaching a message on Acts 26:2, Paul's defense before Agrippa. Paul said, "I think myself happy, king Agrippa, because I shall answer for myself this day before thee touching all the things whereof I am accused of the Jews" (KJV). This man pulled out the phrase "I think myself happy" and preached a sermon on the importance of positive thinking in the midst of adversity! But Paul was not telling Agrippa anything about positive thinking; he was saying, "I consider myself fortunate" (NASB) to be able to make a defense. That preacher had corrupted the intent of Paul's inspired words because he was using the verse out of context to teach an unbiblical doctrine.

Another preacher preached a sermon from Mark 2, which tells about some men who brought their paralyzed friend to Jesus and lowered him through the roof of the house so he could be healed. Mark 2:4 says, "They could not come nigh unto him for the press" (KJV). This man took that phrase as his text and waxed eloquent, sermonizing for more than a half hour about how the press—the news media—are still keeping people from Jesus even to this day! But that verse has nothing to do with the news media. "The press" in that verse refers to the dense crowd. The whole sermon was based on an utter corruption of the meaning of the text.

Bible interpretation is a skill that requires diligent work, an understanding of the meaning of the original languages, a working knowledge of grammar and logic, a grasp of the historical settings, competence in theology, and a broad understanding of the whole of Scripture. Those who lack expertise in Greek and Hebrew must be all the more careful, checking commentaries, dictionaries, and other study helps to analyze the text as carefully as possible.

The postmodern canard is that Bible interpretation is a wholly subjective exercise, and there is therefore no single objective, intended meaning to any text. One person's impression is ultimately as good as another's. As a matter of fact, that idea is one of the main reasons many in the Emerging Church movement are ambivalent about preaching. Who is to say a preacher understands Scripture any better than the novice reader?

A similar attitude causes some people to spurn the use of commentaries and similar resources in their Bible study, as if their own uninformed first impression is just as good as careful study using reference tools. It is becoming more and more common all the time to hear people say, "I don't read commentaries and books *about* the Bible. I limit my study to the Bible itself." That may sound very pious, but is it? Isn't it actually presumptuous? Are the written legacies of godly men of no value to us? Can someone who ignores study aids understand the Bible just as well as someone who is familiar with the scholarship of other godly teachers and pastors?

One textbook on hermeneutics answers the question this way:

> Suppose we select a list of words from Isaiah and ask a man who claims he can bypass the godly learning of Christian scholarship if he can out of his own soul or prayer give their meaning or significance: Tyre, Zidon, Chittim, Sihor, Moab, Mahershalahashbas, Calno, Carchemish, Hamath, Aiath, Migron, Michmash, Geba, Anathoth, Laish, Nob, and Gallim. He will find the only light he can get on these words is from a commentary or a Bible dictionary.[16]

Good answer. It reveals the utter folly of thinking that objective study is unnecessary. The person who is not a diligent student cannot be an accurate interpreter of God's Word. Scripture indicates that such a person is not approved by God and should be ashamed of himself (2 Timothy 2:15).

People do not usually buy into false doctrine purposely. They err because of laziness, ineptness, carelessness, or foolishness in handling Scripture. In 2 Timothy 2:17–18, Paul describes the destructive impact of false teachers this way: "Their message will spread like cancer. Hymenaeus and Philetus are of this sort, who have strayed concerning the truth, saying that the resurrection is already past; and they overthrow the faith of some."

The Greek verb translated "strayed" is *astochi*, which literally means "to miss the mark." It suggests that Hymenaeus and Philetus were aiming at the truth; they just missed it. They weren't actually trying to devise error, but being careless and unskilled in handling the truth, they turned to "profane and idle babblings" (v. 16), which led them to conclude that the Resurrection had already taken place. And their error, absurd as it was, had already upset the faith of others. Now it was spreading like cancer. That is precisely why in verse 15 Paul urged Timothy to be a diligent student of the Word of truth.

What Paul was calling for is exactly the opposite of the shoot-from-the-hip ad-libbing that takes place in many contemporary pulpits. You can see this daily on Christian television. It is one of the chief reasons some of the celebrity televangelists come up with so many novel doctrines. I'm convinced many of them improvise their theology as they speak.

That is a dangerous, deadly approach. It invariably perverts the truth, and it subverts people's ability to differentiate between sound doctrine and error. How can we be discerning if we don't even know how to interpret Scripture rightly? We can't establish sound biblical principles for discernment until we understand what Scripture means.

# The Neglect of Church Discipline

Yet another reason discernment is so rare today and apostasy is such a serious problem is the almost universal failure of churches to follow Jesus' instructions in Matthew 18 on how to deal with sinning church members. Sadly, few Christians obey Christ in this crucial area of confronting sin in one another's lives. Jesus addressed this topic:

> "If your brother sins against you, go and tell him his fault between you and him alone. If he hears you, you have gained your brother. But if he will not hear, take with you one or two more, that 'by the mouth of two or three witnesses every word may be established.' And if he refuses to hear them, tell it to the church. But if he refuses even to hear the church, let him be to you like a heathen and a tax collector." (Matthew 18:15–17)

If you see a brother in sin, go to him. Confront him. Try to lift him up, build him up, strengthen him. Urge him to repent. If he refuses to repent, he must ultimately be put out of the church. Paul said not even to eat with such a person (1 Corinthians 5:11). This is not to suggest you should treat him like an enemy, but rather that you love him enough to seek his repentance by whatever means possible. Paul even instructed the Corinthians to "deliver such a one to Satan for the destruction of the flesh, that his spirit may be saved in the day of the Lord Jesus" (v. 5).

The church must hold up a high and holy standard. A very clear line must be drawn between the world and the church. Known and open sin cannot be tolerated. As soon as the church stops dealing with sin seriously, the world mingles with the church and the difference is obliterated. That is why Christians are not supposed to be able to go on sinning unchallenged by one another.

Why do you think the Lord struck Ananias and Sapphira dead in front of the whole congregation? Scripture is clear: it was so the rest would be fearful of sinning (Acts 5:5, 11; 1 Timothy 5:20). This was not a "seeker-sensitive" strategy. In fact, it was the polar opposite of the contemporary push to make the church as comfortable as possible for sinners.

Do not misunderstand. It is a fine goal to make visitors and unchurched people feel welcome in the church. But deliberately trying to give them the impression that the church or the Word of God has no serious objection to their pet sins is quite another matter. Christ Himself was known as a friend of sinners (Matthew 11:19), but He never condoned or minimized anyone's sin. After all, He came to call sinners to repentance (9:13).

One of my main concerns about the "seeker-sensitive" movement has always been that in their zeal to make the church a "comfort zone" for unchurched people, churches often go too far. Many churches have deliberately downplayed the biblical message of God's hatred of sin, and in some cases they have carefully refrained from identifying certain politically volatile sins—such as abortion and homosexuality—as evil.

Some in the Emerging Church movement have taken that same philosophy to even more outrageous extremes. Chris Seay, for example, has founded Emerging congregations in Waco and Houston. He is a third-generation Southern Baptist pastor and has written a much-talked-about book contrasting his approach to ministry with that of his father and grandfather. Seay argues that doctrinal, cultural, and lifestyle boundaries are bad for the church. Specifically, he believes traditional churches have made too much of the sin of homosexuality and have thereby wrongly excluded homosexuals from their fellowship. He says he wants practicing homosexuals to feel right at home in his congregation.[17] He believes his duty as a preacher is to encourage a relationship with God, not to confront people about specific sins—or even wantonly evil lifestyles. Once a person has established a relationship with God, Seay says, God Himself can deal with whatever needs to be changed in the person's life.[18] Seay is apparently convinced that most people simply grow out of their sinful lifestyles as they become more and more involved in the church—even if the church never actually confronts specific sins and calls sinners to repentance.

What are we to conclude when someone living in open sin can sit in a church service and feel comfortable week after week? Is that church proclaiming what it is supposed to proclaim? I can't imagine that a practicing homosexual—or a heterosexual living in deliberate sin, for that matter—would have sat comfortably under Paul's teaching in Ephesus or Corinth.

The primary message of the church should not be, "We're a nice place; you'll like us." Instead, the message should be, "This is a holy place where sin is despised." Wasn't that, after all, the whole point of the Ananias and Sapphira episode?

We can't lower the standard. We can't deliberately accumulate sinning Christians or try to make non-Christians comfortable in the midst of their sin. The church must purge and discipline and sift and purify. First Peter 4:17 says, "It is time for judgment to begin with the household of God" (NASB). And Paul wrote, "Do you not judge those who are within the church?" (1 Corinthians 5:12 NASB). "If we would judge ourselves, we would not be judged" (11:31).

The church that tolerates sin destroys its own holiness and sub-

> THE PRIMARY MESSAGE OF THE CHURCH SHOULD NOT BE, "WE'RE A NICE PLACE; YOU'LL LIKE US." INSTEAD, THE MESSAGE SHOULD BE, "THIS IS A HOLY PLACE WHERE SIN IS DESPISED."

verts the discernment of its own members. There can be no true church at all without clear boundaries. How can you help people draw clear lines in their own *thinking* when you have already said you are not going to draw any lines to regulate *behavior*? If the goal is to make everyone feel all right, tolerance and compromise must rule. Discernment and discrimination are ruled out.

Jay Adams has written:

Lack of discernment and lack of church discipline walk side by side. Not only does the same mentality lead to both lacks, but by rejecting discipline one naturally downplays the very concerns that make him discerning. When churches reacted to the abuse of church discipline that was all too common in the eighteenth and nineteenth centuries by virtually eliminating church discipline, the broken dike cleared the way for the liberal takeover of the church and allowed the ways of the world to flood in.[19]

Adams calls the collapse of church discipline the most obvious reason for the decline of discernment in the church. As he points out, "Discipline, by its very nature, requires discernment."[20]

But in an undiscerning church, discipline is neglected. And where discipline is neglected, discernment declines further and further.

# A LACK OF SPIRITUAL MATURITY

One more factor in the abysmal lack of discernment today is a growing deterioration of the overall level of spiritual maturity in the church. As knowledge of God's truth ebbs, people follow popular views. They seek feelings and experiences. They hunger for miracles, healings, and spectacular wonders. They grope for easy and instant solutions to the routine trials of life. They turn quickly from the plain truth of God's Word to embrace doctrines fit only for the credulous and naive. They chase personal comfort and success. The brand of Christianity prevalent in this generation may be shallower than at any other time in history.

I have absolutely no confidence in contemporary Christian pollsters, starting with their incorrigible unwillingness to make any kind of meaningful distinction between a heathen who makes a religious profession in the name of Christ, and people who truly seem to believe God's Word, love the Lord, and give credible professions of faith. (That is, of course, the very distinction Christ instructed us to make in Matthew 7:15–20.) But since so many supposedly evangelical churches themselves deliberately refuse to differentiate between sheep and goats, sometimes the opinion-poll data is telling anyway.

For example, a survey released by the Barna Research group in February 1994 suggested that half of all people who describe themselves as "born-again" had no clue what John 3:16 refers to. Large percentages of professing Christians were also at a loss to explain terms such as "the Great Commission" or "the gospel." A number defined "gospel" simply as "a style of music."[21]

Clearly, spiritual ignorance and biblical illiteracy are commonplace among professing Christians. That kind of spiritual shallowness is a direct result of shallow teaching. Solid preaching with deep substance and sound doctrine is essential for Christians to grow. But churches today often teach only the barest basics—and sometimes less than that.

Churches are therefore filled with baby Christians—people who are spiritual infants. That is a fitting description, because the characteristic that is most descriptive of an infant is selfishness. Babies are completely self-centered. They scream if they don't get what they want when they want it. All they are aware of are their own needs and desires. They never say thanks for anything. They can't help others; they can't give anything. They can only receive.

> HOW DO WE GROW SPIRITUALLY? BY "SPEAKING THE TRUTH IN LOVE" TO ONE ANOTHER. WE GROW UNDER THE TRUTH. IT IS THE SAME TRUTH BY WHICH WE ARE SANCTIFIED, CONFORMED TO THE IMAGE OF CHRIST, MADE TO BE MATURE SPIRITUALLY (JOHN 17:17, 19). AS WE ABSORB THE TRUTH OF GOD'S WORD, WE GROW UP AND ARE BUILT UP.

And certainly there is nothing wrong with that when it occurs in the natural stage of infancy. But to see a child whose development is arrested so that he never gets beyond that stage of helpless selfishness is a tragedy.

And that is exactly the spiritual state of multitudes in the church today. They are utterly preoccupied with self. They want their own problems solved and their own comfort elevated. Their spiritual development is arrested, and they remain in a perpetual state of selfish helplessness. It is evidence of a tragic abnormality.

Arrested infancy means people do not discern. Just as a baby crawls along the floor, putting anything it finds in its mouth, spiritual babies don't know what is good for them and what isn't. Immaturity and lack of discernment go together; they are virtually the same thing.

The tendency to stall in a state of immaturity also existed in New Testament times. Paul appeals to Christians repeatedly to grow up spiritually. In Ephesians 4:14–15, he writes, "We should no longer be children, tossed to and fro and carried about with every wind of doctrine, by the trickery of men, in the cunning craftiness of deceitful plotting, but, speaking the truth in love, may *grow up* in all things into Him who is the head—Christ"(emphasis added).

How do we grow spiritually? By "speaking the truth in love" to one another. We grow under the truth. It is the same truth by which we are sanctified, conformed to the image of Christ, made to be mature spiritually (John 17:17, 19). As we absorb the truth of God's Word, we grow up and are built up. We might say accurately that the process of spiritual growth is a process of training for discernment.

Hebrews 5:12–6:1 underscores all this:

> For though by this time you ought to be teachers, you need someone to teach you again the first principles of the oracles of God; and you have come to need milk and not solid food. For everyone who partakes only of milk is unskilled in the word of righteousness, for he is a babe. But solid food belongs to those who are of full age, that is, those who by reason of use have their senses exercised to discern both good and evil. Therefore, leaving the discussion of the elementary principles of Christ, let us go on to [maturity].

The writer of Hebrews is telling his readers, "You're babies. You've been around long enough to be teachers, but instead I have to feed you milk. I have to keep giving you elementary things. You can't take solid food. You're not accustomed to the rich things of the Word—and that is tragic."

Notice that in verse 14 he says that discernment and maturity go hand in hand: "Solid food is for the mature, who because of practice have their senses trained to discern good and evil." Knowing and understanding the Word of righteousness—taking in solid food—trains your senses to discern good and evil.

The word "senses" in that verse is not a reference to the feelings, emotions, or other subjective sensory mechanisms. The writer of this epistle is explicitly encouraging his readers to exercise their *minds*. Those who "because of practice have their senses trained to discern" are the wise, the understanding, people who thrive on the solid food of the Word of God. Discernment results from a carefully disciplined mind. It is not a matter of feelings, nor is discernment a mystical gift. Notice from the wisdom literature of the Old Testament how closely discernment is linked with a seasoned, developed, biblically informed mind.

- Psalm 119:66: "Teach me good discernment and knowledge, for I believe in Your commandments" (NASB).
- Proverbs 2:2–5: "Make your ear attentive to wisdom, incline your heart to understanding; for if you cry for discernment, lift your voice for understanding; if you seek her as silver, and search for her as for hidden treasures; then you will discern the fear of the LORD, and discover the knowledge of God" (NASB).
- Proverbs 10:13: "On the lips of the discerning, wisdom is found" (NASB).
- Proverbs 16:21: "The wise in heart will be called understanding" (NASB).

The path to discernment is the way of spiritual maturity. And the only means to spiritual maturity is mastery of the Word of God.

Most people are discerning about things that are important to them. People who regard a healthy diet as crucial watch carefully what they eat. They read the fine print on the package to see how many grams of fat the food has and what percentage of the daily required nutrients it offers. People who work with pesticides or dangerous chemicals must be very discerning. They study the procedures and the precautions very carefully to avoid any potentially lethal exposure. People who make investments in the stock market usually practice discernment. They study the cryptic listings in the newspaper on the stock market and watch the ticker tape. Lawyers are very discerning with contracts. They have to figure out the legal jargon and make sure they understand what they are signing. People who undergo delicate surgery are usually very discerning. They try to find the doctor with the finest skills—or at least verify that he has plenty of experience in whatever procedure he will be doing. I know a lot of people who are very discerning sports enthusiasts. They watch a football game and can assess any offense, any defense, any play. They often feel they are more discerning than whoever is calling the actual plays. They study statistics and averages and take it all very seriously.

Did you realize those are essentially the same skills that are required in spiritual discernment? Careful thought, keen interest, thorough analysis, close observation—together with alertness, attentiveness, thoughtfulness, and above all, a love of truth. All of us have those skills to some degree, and we use them in whatever field of endeavor is important to us. Yet what could be more important than spiritual discernment?

No valid explanation is readily available for why contemporary Christians are so *un*discerning, but their lack of discernment reveals a spiritual apathy that is deadly evil.

Can we as the church regain our ability to be discerning? Only by growing up spiritually. That means confronting the spirit of a relativistic age and diligently applying ourselves to the unfailing Word of God. We cannot gain discernment overnight or through a mystical experience. Discernment will come only as we train our minds to be understanding in the truth of God's Word and learn to apply that truth skillfully to our lives.

# Notes

1. Spurgeon, Charles, The Metropolitan Tabernacle Pulpit, vol. 5 (London: Passmore & Alabaster, 1879), 41.

## INTRODUCTION: WHY TRUTH IS WORTH FIGHTING FOR

1. Andy Crouch, "The Emergent Mystique," *Christianity Today*, November 2004, 37-38, emphasis added.

2. Ibid.

3. Brian McLaren, *A Generous Orthodoxy* (Grand Rapids: Zondervan, 2004), 293.

4. Ibid., 286.

5. John Foxe, "The Fourth Persecution, Under Marcus Aurelius Antoninus, A.D. 162," *Foxe's Book of Martyrs*. Foxe's famous martyrology is a monumental testimony to the honor and courage of reformers who gave their lives for the truth. The accents are powerful and needed in our comfortable, convictionless day.

6. See also John MacArthur, *Hard to Believe* (Nashville: Nelson, 2003).

7. Data from a survey taken after the 9/11 terrorist attacks and released in November 2001 by the Barna Group indicated that two-thirds of adults who attend a conservative, Protestant churches question whether absolute moral truth exists. "How America's Faith Has Change Since 9/11."http://barna.org/FlexPage.aspx?Page-BarnaUpdate&BarnaUpdateID-102

8. John MacArthur, *The MacArthur New Testament Commentary: 2 Peter and Jude* (Chicago: Moody, 2005).

## CHAPTER 1
## CAN TRUTH SURVIVE IN A POSTMODERN SOCIETY?

1. Brian McLaren, *A Generous Orthodoxy* (Grand Rapids: Zondervan, 2004), 293.

2. Ibid., 23.

3. Cited in Greg Warner, "Brian McLaren: The Story We Find Ourselves In," a positive review at Rick Warren's pastors.com Website, http://www.pastors.com/article.asp?ArtID=4150.

4. Stanley J. Grenz and John R. Franke, *Beyond Foundationalism: Shaping Theology in a Postmodern Context* (Louisville: Westminster John Knox, 2001), 3.

5. Ibid., 30.

6. "A hope-filled theology loses its way when it trots after the illusive foundationalist dream, seeking to secure its own certitude by appeal to a supposedly unassailable anthropological foundation" (Ibid., 248).

7. John Armstrong, "How I Changed My Mind: Theological Method," *Viewpoint* (September–October 2003), 1.

8. Ibid.

9. Ibid., 4.

10. Ibid.

11. Ibid.

12. Ibid., 1.

13. Ibid. In a follow-up on this subject at his weblog, Armstrong likens Christians who have "a high level of certitude" to dictators and tyrants. That article is titled "Certitude Can Be Idolatrous," June 30, 2005, http://johnharmstrong.com.

14. Ibid., 4.

15. Martin Luther, *D. Martin Luthers Werke, Kritische Gesamtausgabe. Briefwechsel,* 18 vols. (Weimar: Verlag Hermann Böhlaus Nachfolger, 1930–85), 3:81.

## CHAPTER 2
### SPIRITUAL WARFARE: DUTY, DANGER, AND GUARANTEED TRIUMPH

1. Sir Basil Liddell Hart, *Sherman: Soldier, Realist, American* (New York: Dodd, Mead & Co., 1929), 402.

2. Charles Spurgeon, *The Metropolitan Tabernacle Pulpit*, vol. 25 (London: Passmore & Alabaster, 1879), 265.

3. Brian McLaren, *A Generous Orthodoxy* (Grand Rapids: Zondervan, 2004), 260.

4. Ibid., 264.

5. Ibid., 32.

6. Ibid., 28.

7. Ibid., 191.

8. Ibid., 192.

9. Ibid., 30.

10. Ibid.

11. John MacArthur, *Reckless Faith: When the Church Loses Its Will to Discern* (Wheaton: Crossway, 1994).

12. McLaren, *A Generous Orthodoxy*, 32.

## CHAPTER 3
### CONSTRAINED INTO CONFLICT:
### WHY WE MUST FIGHT FOR THE FAITH

1. In the King James Version of Acts 1:13 and Luke 6:16, the lesser-known apostle Judas (the one also known as Lebbaeus and Thaddaeus) is called "the brother of James," but the operative words ("*the brother*") are in italics in both texts, indicating that they have been added by translators. The original manuscript literally says "Judas of James," which actually suggests that the apostle's *father* (not his brother) was named James. (That is exactly what most translations of Luke 6:16 and Acts 1:13 now say: "Judas the son of James.")

## CHAPTER 4
### CREEPING APOSTASY: HOW FALSE TEACHERS SNEAK IN

1. J. Gresham Machen, *Christianity and Liberalism* (New York: Macmillan), 24.

2. Ibid.

3. Ibid.

4. "Others again declare that Cain derived his being from the Power above, and acknowledge that Esau, Korah, the Sodomites, and all such persons, are related to themselves. On this account, they add, they have been assailed by the Creator, yet no one of them has suffered injury. For Sophia was in the habit of carrying off that which belonged to her from them to herself. They declare that Judas the traitor was thoroughly acquainted with these things, and that he alone, knowing the truth as no others did, accomplished the mystery of the betrayal; by him all things, both earthly and heavenly, were thus thrown into confusion. They produce a fictitious history of this kind, which they style the Gospel of Judas" (Irenaeus, *Against Heresies*, 1:31:1).

## CHAPTER 5
### HERESY'S SUBTLETY: WHY WE MUST REMAIN VIGILANT

1. Ironically, this title was bestowed on the king by Pope Leo X in 1521 while Henry was still loyal to the Roman Catholic Church. Just five years before, Luther had nailed his Ninety-five Theses to the door of the castle church in Wittenberg. Henry earned the title by writing a lengthy denunciation of Luther's theses. Henry later broke with Rome over the pope's refusal to annul Henry's marriage to his first wife, Catherine. Far from being a true defender of the faith, Henry was a political opportunist and an ungodly man. Although his break with Rome enabled the Protestant Reformation to sweep over England, Henry himself was no more a friend to Protestantism than he turned out to be to the pope. It would be hard to think of a major figure in church history who was less deserving of such a title than he. Nonetheless, the title has remained with the British throne ever since.

2. The statement appears on Prince Charles's own Web site, in an

article titled "The Prince's Work: Religion" at http://www.prince-ofwales.gov.uk/about/wrk_religion.html.

3. Sabellianism is also sometimes referred to as *patripassianism* (from the combination of two Latin words meaning "father" and "suffering") because, if Father and Son are merely distinct modes or manifestations of one divine Person, then the Father suffered on the cross. The same view is sometimes labeled *monarchianism*. Sabellian opinions have faded and revived repeatedly throughout church history. Sabellian modalism is essentially the same view held by "Oneness Pentecostals" today, of whom T. D. Jakes is the dominant media figure.

4. Philip Schaff, *The Creeds of Christendom*, 3 vols. (New York: Harper & Row, 1931), 1:29.

5. Philip Schaff and Henry Wace, eds. *The Principal Works of St. Jerome* in *Nicene and Post-Nicene Fathers, Series II* (14 vols.) Jerome's *Dialogue Against the Luciferians*, 19 (Grand Rapids: Eerdmans, 1954), 6:329.

6. The excerpts cited here have been slightly adapted from chapter 13: "Extract from the letter of Athanasius on the death of Arius" in Philip Schaff, *Early Church Fathers: Nicene and Post-Nicene Fathers* (ser. 2, vol. 3). The language has been modernized, but these are otherwise exact quotations from Schaff's translation of Athanasius's letter.

7. Herbert W. Armstrong and the original Worldwide Church of God were likewise Arian in their Christology. Although the main group of Armstrong's followers have abandoned Arianism and formally adopted a more classically Trinitarian view, several offshoots of that group remain fiercely loyal to their founder's Arian opinions.

8. For more detail on the Arian controversy with particular stress on Athanasius's role as a contender for the true faith, see the excellent account of Athanasius by John Piper, *Contending for Our All* (Wheaton: Crossway, 2006), 40–75.

CHAPTER 6

THE EVIL OF FALSE TEACHING: HOW ERROR TURNS GRACE INTO LICENTIOUSNESS

1. Jonathan Edwards, "God's Sovereignty in the Salvation of Men," in *The Works of Jonathan Edwards*, 2 vols. (Edinburgh: The Banner of Truth Trust, 1995 reprint), 2:849–54.

2 Laura Sheahan, "'Evangelical Christianity Has Been Hijacked': An Interview with Tony Campolo," Beliefnet.com Website (July 2004), http:beliefnet.com/story/150/story_15052_1.html.

3. Brian McLaren, "Brian McLaren on the Homosexual Question: Finding a Pastoral Response," January 23, 2006. This was a post made at the "Out of Ur" blog hosted by *Christianity Today*, http://blog.christianitytoday.com/outofur/archives/2006/01/brian_mclaren_o.html.

4. Donald Miller, *Blue Like Jazz* (Nashville: Nelson, 2003), 133–34.

5. Lori Leibovich, "Generation: A Look Inside Fundamentalism's Answer to MTV: The Postmodern Church," *Mother Jones* (July–August 1998), 77.

6. Ruth Gledhill, "Church Told to Rethink Bar on Sex Before Marriage," *Times of London* (March 31, 2003).

CHAPTER 7

THE ASSAULT ON DIVINE AUTHORITY: CHRIST'S LORDSHIP DENIED

1. Rick Warren, *The Purpose-Driven Church* (Grand Rapids: Zondervan, 1995), 189.

2. John MacArthur, *The Gospel According to Jesus* (Grand Rapids: Zondervan, 1988); *The Gospel According to the Apostles* (Nashville: W Publishing Group, 1993); *Hard to Believe* (Nashville: Nelson, 2003).

3. Brian McLaren, *A New Kind of Christian* (San Francisco: Jossey-Bass, 2003), 14.

4. Brian McLaren, *A Generous Orthodoxy* (Grand Rapids: Zondervan, 2004), 30.

5. "We have never been able to find any text in ancient Greek literature that gives support to [the egalitarian] interpretation. Wherever one person is said to be the 'head' of another person (or persons), the person who is called the 'head' is always the one in authority (such as the general of an army, the Roman emperor, Christ, the heads of the tribes of Israel, David as head of the nations, etc.) Specifically, we cannot find any text where person A is called the 'head' of person or persons B, *and is not in a position of authority over that person or persons.* So we find no evidence for your claim that 'head' can mean 'source without authority.'" Wayne Grudem, "An Open Letter to Egalitarians: Six Questions That Have Never Been Answered" (1998, revised 2003), http://www.the-highway.com/Openletter.html.

6. John Calvin, *Calvin's Commentaries*, 22 vols. (Grand Rapids: Baker, n.d.), 21:198.

## Chapter 8

### How to Survive in an Age of Apostasy: Learning from the Lessons of History

1. Steve Chalke, *The Lost Message of Jesus* (Grand Rapids: Zondervan, 2003), 182.

2. Brian McLaren, *The Story We Find Ourselves In* (San Francisco: Jossey-Bass, 2003), 102.

3. Charlotte Allen, "Liberal Christianity Is Paying for Its Sins," *Los Angeles Times*, July 9, 2006.

4. Ibid.

5. Ibid.

6. Ibid.

7. Jerry L Van Marter, "GAC Releases names of those laid off," PresbyterianNewsService,http://www.pcusa.org/pcnews/2006/06245.htm (accessed) December 5, 2006

8. John MacArthur, *Ashamed of the Gospel: When the Church Becomes Like the World* (Wheaton: Crossway, 1993).

## APPENDIX

1. Material in this appendix is adapted from John MacArthur, *Reckless Faith* (Wheaton, IL: Crossway, 1994), 35–66. That book dealt mainly with several matters that were especially timely in the early 1990s, including the hysteria surrounding the "Toronto Blessing" and intense pressure to gain widespread evangelical support for the original "Evangelicals and Catholics Together" document.

2. Cited in Iain Murray, *D. Martyn Lloyd-Jones: The Fight of Faith, 1939–1981* (Edinburgh: Banner of Truth, 1990), 667.

3. D. Martyn Lloyd Jones, *Preaching and Preachers* (Grand Rapids: Zondervan, 1971), 15–16.

4. Tom Allen, "Postmoderns Value Authenticity, Not Authority," *The Baptist Standard*, July 8, 2004.

5. Ibid.

6. D. Martyn Lloyd-Jones, *Romans: An Exposition of Chapters 3.20–4.25: Atonement and Justification* (Grand Rapids: Zondervan, 1970), 113.

7. Ibid.

8. Ibid., 113–14.

9. Ibid., 114.

10. Jay E. Adams, *A Call to Discernment* (Eugene, OR: Harvest House, 1987), 31.

11. Ibid.

12. Ibid., 29.

13. Ibid., 32.

14. Charles H. Spurgeon, *Autobiography, Volume 1: The Early Years* (Edinburgh: Banner of Truth, 1962), v (emphasis added).

15. B.B. Warfield, *Biblical and Theological Studies* (Philadelphia: Presbyterian & Reformed, 1952), 22.

16. Bernard Ramm, *Protestant Biblical Interpretation* (Grand Rapids: Baker, 1970), 17–18.

17. Chris Seay, *Faith of My Fathers* (Grand Rapids: Zondervan, 2005), 133–38.

18. John Hall, "Ecclesia: Purposely Postmodern," *Baptist Standard* (October 8, 2001), 1.

19. Adams, *A Call to Discernment*, 28.

20. Ibid., 27.

21. "What Happens When Christians Use Bad Language" (February 21, 1994, news release from the Barna Research Group, Ltd.).

2. Associated Press, "Presbyterians Vote on Alternatives to Divine Trinity,," June 19, 2006.

3. Ibid.

4. Episcopal News Service, "From Columbus: Text of Presiding Bishop-elect's June 21 homily," June 21, 2006.